The Story of the [...]
- how it all beca[me possible]

Scotia the Brave

A tale of entrepreneurship, inventiveness, opportunism, risk-taking, and battles for supremacy

Gordon Fraser

Scotia the Brave

Copyright © Gordon Fraser

MMXV

All rights reserved. No part of this publication may be reproduced, distributed, or transmitted in any form or by any means, including photocopying, recording, or other electronic or mechanical methods, without the prior written permission of the publisher, except in the case of brief quotations embodied in critical reviews and certain other noncommercial uses permitted by copyright law.

ISBN-13: 978-1502798190

Printed by Createspace, an Amazon company

About the Author

After spending many years working in finance, Gordon Fraser felt it was time to try some new things and he is now well on the way to becoming an accomplished artist and writer.

He lives in the north west of England.

Scotia the Brave

Acknowledgements

In writing this book I have referred to works by many earlier writers and the most important of these are listed in the bibliography.

In addition I would not have able to produce this book without help from other sources and I would especially like to thank the following for their help in providing research material and/or images - Merseyside Maritime Museum, Liverpool University, Sefton Libraries, Gutenberg, Kobo, the U.S. Library of Congress, the U.S. Naval History and Heritage Command, the State Library of Victoria, the Illustrated London News, British Newspaper Archives and New York Times Archives. I am especially grateful to the National Library of Ireland for granting permission to reproduce some splendid photographs of Brunel's *Great Eastern* and to Nova Scotia Archives for permission to reproduce an early Cunard family advertisement.
Most images in this book were produced and published in the 19th century and are now regarded as being in the public domain. Where possible I have identified the source of the image.

The following works have been particularly useful in the provision of research material and images:

Lardner   *The Steam Engine*
Thurston   *A History of the Growth of the Steam Engine*

Any comments or suggestions regarding anything referred to in this book would be appreciated. Please direct your comments to:

scotiathebravebook@gmail.com

Bibliography

Kay Grant *Samuel Cunard*   1967

L T C Holt   *Isambard Kingdom Brunel*   1957

Chandler *Liverpool Shipping*   1960

Maginnis *The Atlantic Ferry*   1893

Fry *North Atlantic Steam Navigation*   1896

Preble *History of Steam Navigation*   1895

Thurston *A History .. of the Steam Engine*   1884

Lewis *Topographical Dictionary of England*   1837

Boyman *Steam Navigation, its rise and progress* 1840

Corry *History of Liverpool*   1810

Baines *History of the Commerce of Liverpool*   1852

Ramsay Muir *A History of Liverpool*   1907

Smith   *Stranger's Guide to Liverpool*   1843

Preface

Cunard's *Scotia* was the world's finest ever paddle steamer and her like will never be seen again. This book tells the story of what shaped the world to make the *Scotia* possible and, in doing so, it covers a lot of ground (and sea!) and many centuries of history. Obviously there are many elements that I have not been able to deal with in great detail. If I had, this book would have ended up as a multi-part encyclopaedia of historical facts - and that wouldn't have been much fun to read! Of course history is not just about facts, it is primarily about people - their hopes and dreams, their successes and failures, their bad things and good things, and their impact on the course of history - or their failure to make any significant impact at all. In fact they were all just the same as us.

I don't think you will find this another boring old history book and it isn't a book just for those who are interested in ships; it is instead an interesting, informative and readable account of periods in history that changed the world and of those whose enterprise, inventiveness and entrepreneurship helped shape the world that we live in today.

Gordon Fraser

1   (Courtesy Liverpool University)

R.M.S. *Scotia*

Table of contents

Introduction		11
Chapter 1	Trouble at the Top	13
2	Birth of a name	15
3	A new life begins	31
4	The Power of Steam	41
5	Steam Navigation	61
6	Developments in Nova Scotia	83
7	Life without Susan	91
8	Race to be first	99
9	Rise of Liverpool	113
10	Paddle Steamer *Liverpool*	167
11	The Age of the Transatlantic Steamer begins	177
12	"I want that Mail Contract"	181
13	The Cunard Line gets up steam	187
14	The *Britannia* casts off	193
15	Isambard Kingdom Brunel - man of iron	207
16	The Atlantic paddlers - competition!	213
17	Cunard puts up a fight	225
18	The Collins Line begins to founder	231
19	The *Great Eastern*	243
20	New situations	265
21	End of an era	279
22	Life on board the *Scotia*	293
23	James Macaulay's trip on the *Scotia*	297
24	The *Scotia's* new life	305
25	The final journey	307
26	Postscript	309

Introduction

2 Samuel Cunard
(CC-BY (engl.wiki)/Treeman PD-US)

Samuel Cunard was born in 1787 and gave his name to the world's best known shipping line - the Cunard Line. From his early days, he seemed destined to be involved with ships and in particular with ships crossing the North Atlantic. But it was the development of practical steam navigation and the possibility of using it for transatlantic travel that made Cunard famous in the Old and the New World. Most steam vessels in the first half of the 19th century were driven by huge paddle wheels, with sail assistance, and this book tells of the heyday of the big paddle liners that crossed the North Atlantic and of some of their successes and of some of their, sometimes tragic, failures. Fortunately, for Samuel Cunard, it was normally a tale of success.

But this book is not just a story about ships. In fact Samuel Cunard, although well versed in all aspects of ships and shipping, was not a sailor or a ship's captain. He was an astute, practical and opportunistic businessman and he displayed many of the positive and go-ahead qualities of the inventors, engineers and industrialists of his time. It was these qualities that made him and so many others successful during the industrial revolution and the rapid expansion of international trade during the 18th and 19th centuries. Although these businessmen and engineers may not have realised it at the time, they were developing business and engineering principles and practices that would continue to be used way into the future with most still being relevant today.

This is not just a book about ships - the underlying themes are engineering excellence and entrepreneurship.

Chapter 1

Trouble at the Top

"I think we should build the new vessel with a screw propeller".
"I think so too".
"So do I, paddle wheels have had their day, they're old-fashioned".
"No, we will build her with paddles".
"But other people are only building their new liners with screw propellers, we will be left behind".
"I know that but I really want this new vessel to be built with paddles.
"I can't understand your view on this at all, we're already using screw propeller ships on the emigrant Atlantic runs."
"I understand that, and fine vessels they are, but this new ship will be even better and I want it to have paddle wheels".
"I've really had enough of this. If you persist with this paddle wheel idea, I'm getting out of this company."
"I'm really sorry to hear that and I hope you decide to stay with us but this new vessel is for our prestige service and she must be built with paddles."

   This dramatised exchange tells the story of "troubles at the top" at the Cunard Line towards the end of the 1850s. The dissenting voice is that of Samuel Cunard, founder of the Cunard Line and main shareholder of the company. He was also the man who usually got his own way and this time would be no different, the new vessel would be built with paddle wheels.

   Many people at the time, inside and outside the company, were amazed by his decision. After all this was nearly the start of the 1860s, screws were in and paddles were definitely out, at least for the big ocean-going vessels. Paddles were still the preferred choice for coastal and river ferries, and tug boats where their great manoeuvrability was a big advantage, but for long journeys on the open sea, other shipping lines didn't want paddles any more. Modern screw propellers could do the job just as well, so why bother with paddle engines that took up more space than screws and which cost twice as much to run. It was no contest really - screws are better.

But Samuel Cunard stuck to his guns and insisted on paddles for the new vessel. The other Cunard Atlantic mail run vessels were propelled by paddle wheels and they were generally reliable and Samuel Cunard thought that, as well as looking more elegant, passengers liked them because their greater beam size was said to give a smoother ride. And, on top of that, the Admiralty were happy with paddle liners on the mail run so why take risks? But not everyone shared his view and some may have noted that Samuel Cunard was getting on in years and perhaps they thought he was getting a bit past it. Whether this is true or not, and it almost certainly isn't, it doesn't really matter now. The fact is that, by making this decision, he gave the world the *Scotia,* the last and finest of the transatlantic paddle liners and the last and biggest of the pure paddle steamers.

But to enable the *Scotia* to make her maiden voyage on 10th May 1862, a lot of things had had to fall into place over many years - for the Cunard family, for the development of the steam engine and steam navigation, and for the development of transatlantic travel. The *Scotia* would never have happened without input from many people who had the vision, the drive and determination to make things work, the ability to spot an opportunity and the willingness to work hard and, where necessary, take a risk.

This is the story of what made the *Scotia* possible.

Chapter 3

Birth of a name

Our story begins in Crefeld, usually now known as Krefeld, a German town near the Dutch border, about 15 miles from Dusseldorf.

The time is the early part of the 17th century and, for many, these are very difficult days. Much of continental Europe is being ravaged by the Thirty Years War, primarily a conflict between Protestants and Catholics, with parts of Germany often ending up as the main battlefield. At the same time many people are having some difficulties with the teachings of the established Christian churches and are moving to the various religious sects that are developing. This only exacerbated the problem and religious persecution is rife. The penalty for not having the same religious belief as others could be, and often was, severe and vicious.

But the people of the small insignificant town of Crefeld kept their heads down and managed to carry on largely unaffected by what was going on around them. The townspeople just wanted to carry on with their day to day lives and were happy to accommodate the differing religious views of their fellow citizens. Gradually word spread that Crefeld was a town of religious tolerance and many people who followed the various religious sects made their way there, hoping to find sanctuary. The settlers came from many parts including France and other parts of Germany but mainly they were Mennonites from Holland.

Mennonites: During the 16th century a number of religious sects developed which rejected Roman Catholicism and Protestantism. One of these groups developed in both the Netherlands and Switzerland and became known as the Swiss Brethren. However they were also known by their nickname of Anabaptists because the sect believed that infants should not be baptized as this was something that should only happen when people were able to make their own confessions of faith. The group also believed in a literal interpretation of the New Testament and had strongly pacifist and other views which were very out of step with the way of life at the time. Despite a good deal of persecution from both the Catholic and Protestant communities, the sect spread rapidly through Germany. The founder of the Netherlands group was Obbe Philips who left his Anabaptist flock in 1540. His position was taken by Menno Simons and, eventually, followers everywhere became known as Mennonites. The early sect members followed a very simple, conservative and hard-working life with a traditional style of dress being the norm for the members.

Today there are groups of Mennonites in various parts of the world, the biggest concentration being in North America where the Amish and Hutterite communities are modern day Mennonites. However within these groups there are many different views about how to follow their faith and many Mennonnite communities have their own methods of worship and follow their own traditions. The Amish and Hutterite, particularly, shun much of the modern world and prefer to live, in many ways, as their ancestors would have done four or five hundred years ago.

Crefeld expanded considerably as more and more settlers arrived but they usually received a good welcome. Many brought skills with them particularly in dyeing and weaving and the town prospered as it became an important centre for textiles.

> Crefeld would continue to develop as a centre for textiles initially in the manufacture of high quality linens but later also becoming a centre of excellence for the manufacture of silk and velvet, a position it holds to this day. This is reflected in the town's motto "Stadt wie Samt und Seide" (City of Velvet and Silk). The town's prosperity today owes much to the part played by those early settlers.

Mennonites did not want to follow the normal methods of worship and preferred to connect with God in their own way. This did not go down well with the established churches and the Mennonites, and followers of the other religious sects, were always at risk of persecution. Although Crefeld was a much safer town for religious sects than many other towns, some of the Mennonite beliefs, such as, the refusal to take oaths or to subscribe to laws which they considered against the teachings of the Lord, always risked conflict arising but on the whole the settlers enjoyed their new life in Crefeld. They could normally practise their religious belief in safety and they were amongst friends. But these were still dangerous times and it wouldn't take much for the situation to change. The problems affecting other areas of Germany could easily spread as far as the town, particularly as Crefeld was not now the insignificant town it used to be. Or it could be something as simple as a firebrand preacher arriving on the scene who could easily turn people against sect followers. People could never fully relax and they were always at risk of their way of life changing in an instant.

Then stories started to circulate around Holland and Germany about a faraway land where they could practise their way of life and follow their religious beliefs with no risk of persecution. That land was the British American colony of Pennsylvania.

In 1644 the Englishman William Penn was born, the son of Admiral William Penn and Margaret Jasper, a Dutch lady. He was a sensitive child, and a little rebellious, who had to endure long periods with his father away at sea. Perhaps because of this he experienced, at a young age, many periods of spiritual enlightenment including a personal sense of communication with God. One of his friends was the Quaker, John Owen, and William gradually came under the spell of Quakerism much to the disgust of his father who eventually sent him to France and later to Ireland, to manage his estate, in the hope that it would reform his son. Unfortunately for William senior it didn't work and William junior returned to his father in London fully committed to the Quaker cause and effectively became one of its ministers. It is now 1669 and fortunate that, on his return to London, William was able to affect a reconciliation with his father whose health was about to decline rapidly. He died in 1670 and William Penn junior suddenly found himself in possession of a fortune of £1,500 a year and a claim on the Crown in the sum of £16,000 which his father had lent to Charles II. Penn was now devoted to the principles of Quakerism and travelled extensively in England, Holland and Germany to promote his belief. Much as he would have liked to do this every day, he had unfortunately to fit this in with his regular periods in prison for preaching the doctrine, including spending nine months in the Tower of London.

```
Quakers: The Quakers, or more correctly The
(Religious) Society of Friends, was founded by
George Fox, the son of a weaver in
Leicestershire, around 1647. Fox had become
disillusioned with the structure and formality
of conventional worship which he saw as a
```

barrier to connecting with God and to attaining personal fulfilment. Although there is no evidence that he intended to set up a new religious body, he soon attracted a band of followers. The views the Friends had, including pacifism, support for women in ministries and their non-appreciation of the accepted churches, were also held by some other individuals and religious sects at the time but the Friends were probably the first group to co-ordinate all of these views into one religious group. As with other groups, however, the Friends were subject to persecution. The established churches and their followers did not like anyone following a different path and vehemently condemned them. Sometimes the Quakers could become excitable and over-eager in their attempts to convert other people and this did not endear them to the community. In 1650, George Fox was taken before a magistrate on charges of failing to attend church and refusal to pay tithes. Fox is alleged to have told the magistrate that he would "tremble before God" and some believe this threat, which was also used on other occasions, is where the Friend's nickname "Quakers" arose. However a more likely explanation is that the name comes from the meetings of the early followers which, for some, could lead to a high degree of excitability. Many of the early followers were quite fanatical about their belief and their antics at churches and other assemblies and their refusal to follow normal rules of society encouraged hostility towards them. In fact they were sometimes seen as being akin to witches and penalties could be severe. From the beginning of Quakerism in 1647 to 1661, 6,000 followers were imprisoned and nearly 500 suffered a violent death. In 1652 when the first Quakers appeared in the American colonies, they were subjected to torture and whipping and many were hanged. Being a Quaker at that time, or being a follower of one of the other minority religious sects, was certainly a dangerous course of action and took a tremendous amount of personal conviction. The term "standing up to be counted" is barely an adequate way to describe the situation.

However things began to change and, as time went by, their passive resistance to aggression and the toning down of their antics helped them to achieve a degree of tolerance and by 1670 they were becoming almost respectable and the term Quaker was no longer seen as an insult.

By the end of the 17th century Fox and his followers had spread the word amongst many countries including North America, Holland, Italy and, particularly, Germany where it achieved a good deal of support. They tended to stand out from other people in their plain clothing and dislike of some forms of entertainment, such as dancing, and anything which seemed to threaten decency. It was a very puritanical way of life but, nevertheless, more and more people followed them.

Today there are many followers throughout the world who all follow the same basic principles as set by George Fox. One of their basic beliefs is that God is within everyone and is part of day to day life. Churches and elaborate ceremonies are not required, neither are priests as everyone is a priest. They do however hold meetings for worship which could last an hour or more. These meetings are held in silence but people may speak briefly if the spirit takes them where their words come from their soul as opposed to coming from their mind. In this way, they speak on behalf of God.

At the beginning of the 19th century, Quakers in Britain developed a reputation as successful entrepreneurs and some companies still known today were established by members of the sect including Cadbury, Huntley & Palmer, Barclays Bank and Lloyds Bank. Whether these companies still follow any of the Quaker principles today is of course debatable.

In 1680 the thoughts of William Penn turned to America. Earlier he had obtained a large proprietary interest in New Jersey where he had drawn up a radical constitution for this new colony which included the principle of religious freedom and, remarkably for the time, recognition of the position of the native Americans and a willingness and desire to live peacefully with them. He tried to establish a degree of equality within the developing community even setting set up a procedure whereby disputes between them and the settlers were decided in a formal way by mixed juries. The young Penn, though, still agonised at the level of religious intolerance that existed in many areas of North America and in much of Europe and he came up with a plan that would achieve religious peace for himself and for others. He asked the Crown for a tract of land between the Delaware and Maryland in settlement of the debt due to his father. In March 1681 this was agreed and Penn became the owner and governor of a piece of land 300 miles wide by 160 miles long. This would become known as Pennsylvania. Some believe that he just wanted to call the land Sylvania but was pressured by the king into adding "Penn" in memory of his father, which was something that Penn really did not want. However there is another suggestion that the name "Pennsylvania" (Penn's Woods) was actually coined by Penn himself as a tribute to his father.

At some stage Penn relinquished his interest in New Jersey and concentrated on his new home, Pennsylvania. Penn had pretty much a free hand in deciding how the colony should be run and set about establishing what he considered were good Quaker conditions for the residents including religious freedom, pacifism and, in particular, good relations with the native Americans. In fact the native Americans were treated better here than in any of the colonies and Penn's policy of fair dealing with them protected the colony from any hostility from them in most of the colony. However around the edges of the colony, it was a different matter with incursions by hostile native Americans causing damage and loss of life. This stretched the Quaker's "pacifism no matter what" ethos to the limit and eventually Penn accepted that the colony's border had to be defended by whatever means. In later years as more settlers arrived, all with different views, the Quaker's influence gradually declined and their preferred ways of dealing with things were not always followed.

Word of this new land reached Holland and Germany and some of the Mennonites in Crefeld got together with some followers of the Quaker sect and discussed the possibility of moving to the New World. This was a big decision for them to make as it would mean, for some, giving up their relatively comfortable, although precarious, way of life in the prospering town of Crefeld, and taking what may be a one-way journey into the unknown. But the main thing they wanted was to be able to connect with God in their own way and this was their only opportunity to do so in safety. Thirteen families decided to take the plunge and they approached the lawyer, Francis Pastorius in Frankfurt, about acting on their behalf to purchase land in Pennsylvania for a settlement.

Pastorius was a well-educated lawyer, an idealistic young man but with a very troubled soul. He despaired at the level of poverty around him and the restrictions on religious freedom but was drawn to the Mennonite sect and gradually took over as leader of the local group. He is also said to have been a follower of Pietism, a movement of the Lutheran church. Tales of the religious haven in Pennsylvania had already reached him and he jumped at the chance to visit the New World to represent the settlers probably taking the view that he would never return.

On 20th August 1683 he reached Philadelphia, at the time a small but expanding town of less than one hundred houses. He met up with William Penn and, on behalf of the settlers, purchased 15,000 acres of land extending to the north west of Philadelphia.

In the summer of 1683, the thirteen Crefeld families plus some of their weaving equipment set out for Rotterdam and boarded the *Concord,* an armed vessel said to have had 26 guns and 40 crew, a vessel we would probably now think of as a galleon, which was waiting for them. After a stopover at Gravesend, near London, to pick up supplies and more passengers the *Concord* set out across the Atlantic heading for Philadelphia.

Amongst the settlers was Thones Kunder, a dyer by trade, who had acquired 500 acres of land in Pennsylvania, his wife and their three children. In total the group numbered 33, all Quakers or Mennonites.

At this time, the vast majority of North America was still unsettled by Europeans and was a wilderness populated by various tribes of native Americans, many of which were very hostile towards settlers and indeed towards other tribes. The settlers would have heard many stories about the New World, some good and some bad, but of course at that time communications were very limited so the settlers could not really have known what lay ahead but they thought that this opportunity to practise their religious belief was well worth the risk.

Any transatlantic journey at that time must have been a great ordeal, especially for the Crefeld passengers who weren't used to the sea. The settlers were however lucky in that the *Concord*, at 500 tons and 130 by 32 feet, was a big ship for her day but nevertheless conditions on board would have been spartan and uncomfortable. It would be a long time before travellers would have the luxury of private cabins and the settlers would have had to find what space they could on the deck or below, sharing the ship with the crew. Food would have been salted meat or dried peas, often flavoured with bugs, and water would soon become rancid so everyone on board would have to drink beer. On top of that there was the real risk of sickness or fever on board plus the danger of the vessel being overwhelmed in a storm. Crossing the Atlantic at that time was certainly not something for the faint hearted. However the settlers' children probably saw it as a big adventure as they roamed the ship and listened to tales of the sailors' exploits, no doubt relishing the opportunity to learn some new, and dubious, words and expressions to add to their vocabularies!

Despite all the dangers, the settlers arrived safely at Philadelphia on 6th October, 74 days after they set out, and William Penn and Francis Pastorius were on hand to welcome them. According to some reports the crossing had been uneventful but Pastorius is reported to have written about the journey in less glowing terms and talked of storms and everyone on board being seasick. Perhaps the practice of Pastorius of writing in Latin has led to some translation problems! But the journey didn't matter now for the settlers; they had made it to their brave New World which they were sure would give them everything they wanted for the rest of their lives.

On 24th October the town of Germantown was laid out for the new arrivals and lots were drawn to decide the allocation of plots of land alongside the single street. But it would be a very difficult start for the settlers. They had arrived at the worst possible time, just before the start of a hard winter, and construction of proper houses was not possible until the spring. The families were however used to hard work and soon got stuck in digging cellars for their new houses which they covered with canvas to provide some shelter from the elements with some of the settlers reportedly making their home in caves. And that is how they would spend their first winter in the New World.

As soon as they could they got busy with their spinning wheels and looms much to the amusement of some of the people of nearby Philadelphia who were taken aback by the sight of these simply dressed folk who spoke a strange language, didn't do much, if anything, by way of entertainment, and seemed to do nothing but work throughout the day. In addition they thought they were very foolhardy and had little chance of surviving the winter with their lack of proper housing. But the settlers were strong people. They had survived religious persecution and a long and dangerous Atlantic crossing; they were not going to give in now. They all survived the winter and, as soon as they could, they got organised on the construction of their wood and stone houses and the final laying out of the town. A town council was organised and Francis Pastorius took over as the town's leader, its first Bailiff.

Thones Kunder now had to set to work building a new life for himself and his family but he was a Mennonite, later to become a Quaker, and the family's religious belief was based around thrift and industry so working hard on the land or as a cloth dyer was not a problem. The other settlers followed the same work ethos and every day they toiled on their spinning wheels and looms, dyed cloth, made shoes or paper, or worked hard in the fields growing flax to make linen. There was always something to do. Gradually Germantown turned into a centre for the production of quality linens, as with Crefeld, and the people of Philadelphia began to see the Germantown settlers in a different light and provided a ready market for the goods the settlers made as did the developing towns of New York and Boston.

Some writers believe that Thones had become a Quaker before he left Crefeld but, in practice, the Mennonite and Quaker beliefs were perhaps not too dissimilar and the conversion probably happened gradually over time rather than as a result of a conscious decision. In any case the Mennonite community in Germantown remained very small with the Quaker inhabitants exerting stronger and stronger influence on the town. However it seems that Thones had definitely become a Quaker by 1688 as it is recorded that he held a meeting for the Society of Friends (Quakers) at his home in that year. This was a ground-breaking meeting held at his house with four other settlers, including Francis Pastorius, to discuss concerns that some followers of Quakerism were supporting slavery and they thought that this was against a basic Bible rule of "Do unto others as you would have them do unto you". A two page condemnation of slavery was drawn up and sent to the Society of Friends, the ruling body of the Quakers. Whether this achieved anything is debatable but effectively these settlers had formed the first anti-slavery movement in the American colonies. It would however be many years before their views were taken note of in the New World.

This is a record of the anti-slavery meeting held at Thones Kunder's house in 1688 (some words reflecting the use of English at the time).

> *This is to ye monthly meeting held at Richard Worrell's.*
>
> *These are the reasons why we are against the traffik of men-body, as followeth. Is there any that would be done or handled at this manner? viz., to be sold or made a slave for all the time of his life? How fearful and faint-hearted are many on sea when they see a strange vessel — being afraid it should be a Turk, and they should be taken, and sold for slaves into Turkey. Now what is this better done, as Turks doe? Yea, rather is it worse for them which say they are Christians, for*

we hear that ye most part of such negers are brought hitherto against their will and consent and that many of them are stolen. Now tho they are black we cannot conceive there is more liberty to have them slaves, as it is to have other white ones. There is a saying that we shall doe to all men like as we will be done ourselves; making no difference of what generation, descent or colour they are. And those who steal or rob men, and those who buy or purchase them, are they not alike? Here is liberty of conscience wch is right and reasonable; here ought to be likewise liberty of ye body, except of evil-doers, wch is an other case. But to bring men hither, or to rob and sell them against their will, we stand against. In Europe there are many oppressed for conscience sake; and here there are those oppossd who are of a black colour. And we who know that men must not commit adultery — some do commit adultery, in others, separating wives from their husbands and giving them to others; and some sell the children of these poor creatures to other men. Ah! doe consider well this thing, you who doe it, if you would be done at this manner? and if it is done according to Christianity? You surpass Holland and Germany in this thing. This makes an ill report in all those countries of Europe, where they hear off, that ye Quakers doe here handel men as they handle there ye cattle. And for that reason some have no mind or inclination to come hither. And who shall maintain this your cause, or pleid for it? Truly we can not do so, except you shall inform us better hereof, viz., that Christians have liberty to practise these things. Pray, what thing in the world can be done worse towards us, than if men should rob or steal us away, and sell us for slaves to strange countries; separating housbands from their wives and children. Being now this is not done in the manner we would be done at therefore we contradict and are against this traffic of men-body. And we who profess that it is not lawful to steal, must, likewise, avoid to purchase such things as are stolen, but rather help to stop this robbing and stealing if possible. And such men ought to be delivered out of ye hands of ye robbers, and set free as well as in Europe. Then is Pennsylvania to have a good report, instead it hath now a bad one for this sake in other countries. Especially whereas ye

Europeans are desirous to know in what manner ye Quakers doe rule in their province — and most of them doe look upon us with an envious eye. But if this is done well, what shall we say is done evil?

If once these slaves (wch they say are so wicked and stubborn men) should joint themselves — fight for their freedom, — and handel their masters and mastrisses as they did handel them before; will these masters and mastrisses take the sword at hand and warr against these poor slaves, licke, we are able to believe, some will not refuse to doe; or have these negers not as much right to fight for their freedom, as you have to keep them slaves?

Now consider well this thing, if it is good or bad? And in case you find it to be good to handel these blacks at that manner, we desire and require you hereby lovingly that you may inform us herein, which at this time never was done, viz., that Christians have such a liberty to do so. To the end we shall be satisfied in this point, and satisfie likewise our good friends and acquaintances in our natif country, to whose it is a terror, or fairful thing that men should be handeld so in Pennsylvania.

This is from our meeting at Germantown, held ye 18 of the 2 month, 1688, to be delivered to the Monthly Meeting at Richard Worrell's.

Garret hendericks
derick up de graeff
Francis daniell Pastorius
Abraham up Den graef   Source: Quaker History

Germantown continued to prosper under the leadership of Francis Pastorius and, by 1690, a total of 44 families had settled there. In 1691 it received its charter of incorporation and Thones Kunder became one of its first burgesses. As the years went by, Thones and his family prospered with his skills in dyeing being put to good use and hard work on his land making it increasingly productive. He became a very important and influential member of the local community.

Pastorius believed that a good education was vital and he was instrumental in setting up the town's school. Not content with setting up the school and teaching at it, he also wrote a study primer for the pupils covering reading, writing and spelling. This is possibly the first school book ever produced in the thirteen American colonies.

Although Thones was doing really well in his new home, he seemed to have one big problem – his name, perhaps even Thones Kunder was an anglicised version. Either by his own volition or because other settlers had difficulty pronouncing his name he seems to have been known by many different family names including Cunrads, Conrad, Cunraeds and it is possible he sometimes used the first name Dennis. Eventually, and for whatever reason, he became known as Thomas Cunard - and the most famous family name in prestige transatlantic shipping was born.

Everything seemed to go well for the Cunard family and luck seemed to be with them on so many occasions. According to Cunard family legend, one day around 1718, whilst working the land, Thomas and his sons found a bag of gold coins. It is just possible that this is true because pirate's were known to operate around the coast and they had to store their ill-gotten gains somewhere but, whether this is true or not, it is certainly the case that Thomas acquired enough money to buy a ship, a small coastal vessel.

And so not just the Cunard name, but now also the Cunard shipping empire had been born.

The family were born entrepreneurs and set about developing their shipping empire, eventually having a fleet of vessels carrying goods to and from the West Indies, England and coastal colonial towns.

Thomas had many years enjoying life in Pennsylvania and had everything he could possibly have hoped for when his adventure started in Rotterdam. By hard work, he and his family were able to enjoy a very pleasant and comfortable life and when he died in 1729, he was able to leave a considerable estate to his family.

The years have passed by and it is now approaching the end of the 18th century. The family businesses are now under the control of Thomas's descendants, Robert and his son Abraham. As with their ancestors they had continued to work hard and had become very wealthy. They seemed to make a success of everything they did and now they really had it all - the big house, the land, the servants, the successful businesses and they had become one of the top families in Philadelphia - definitely the people it was good to know.

But dark clouds were building on the horizon and the good life, that they had all worked so hard for, was not going to last.

Chapter 3

A New Life begins

Around the middle of the 18th century, life in North America started to become increasingly unstable. Territory disputes between Britain and France culminated in war which didn't end until seven years later in 1763. By the second half of the eighteenth century, the immigrant population in the American colonies was around three million, largely from Britain but with increasing numbers from other countries. Managing the colonies was a major job for the British Government. The distance across the Atlantic was just too great and it would take at least three months, and often a lot more, just to send a letter and receive a reply. The journey across the Atlantic in winter could take three months or more, just one way.

The colonists still mainly saw themselves British at this time, loyal to the old country but, with support from France, these views were beginning to change and many colonists started to adopt an independent and stubborn streak. The cost of fighting the French in Canada had drained the British war coffers and Britain imposed taxes on the American colonists to help build up the reserves. Not unreasonable in principle perhaps as Britain was defending them from French rule but it was the imposition of the taxes, without consultation or representation in Britain's Parliament, that touched a nerve, hence the expression "no taxation without representation". Relations between the two communities deteriorated year by year and the colonists increasingly saw themselves as independent communities remote from Britain. Something eventually had to give and, in 1775 it did, with the start of the American Revolution. To what extent hostilities were supported by the people as a whole in the thirteen colonies, is difficult to accurately assess. In any revolution it is usually the views of a vociferous and aggressive minority which hold sway and most people probably just want to go about their daily lives. Certainly there was little support for the revolution from the Quaker community and from successful merchants who relied on British trade. However there was more than enough support for full scale and bitter fighting and this continued until 1783.

Of course in any conflict, backing the wrong side, especially in a very public manner, can risk problems when the conflict is over. There were many loyalists who backed Britain and, bravely or foolishly depending on how you look at it, were prepared to make their views known. Robert Cunard was one of them and, when the revolution was over and Britain ceded the thirteen colonies, he had to face a day of reckoning as old scores were settled. He was convicted of treason, his assets were confiscated, including his businesses and home, and it was made clear to him that he needed to get out of the new "United States of America". He was not the only one told to get out. Around fifty thousand loyalists, possibly more, were expelled to the continuing British colonies, north of New England. The loyalists tended to be people who had made good with the result that, at a stroke, the new Government had managed to get rid of many of its most educated and skilled people but, no doubt, confiscation of their assets helped to soften the blow.

Two thirds of those expelled headed for the British territories of Nova Scotia and New Brunswick where the British Government spent more than a million pounds, a massive fortune in those days, helping to get them settled with offers of food, clothing, land etc. At least someone realised the potential importance of these educated refugees.

A flotilla of twenty ships, carrying expelled refugees, sailed from New York in 1783. The Cunard family was amongst them, taking with them just what they had been able to carry from their old life, plus at least one servant, a West African slave girl. The Quaker community was largely against slavery so it is very likely that any servants employed by the Cunard family were regarded as free persons whatever their history. However the reality is that any slave leaving their employ would have found life very difficult so in practice they would have been tied to their Quaker family. Amongst the passengers was Thomas Murphy, a shipbuilder, who had built vessels for the Cunard fleet. Robert's son, Abraham, was quite taken by Murphy's daughter, Margaret who was described as a tall, spirited girl of twenty five years of age, perhaps quite old in those days to be without a husband, but Abraham had plans to change that.

The refugees landed at the mouth of the Saint John River in New Brunswick where British officials were on hand to look after them. Robert Cunard was given a tract of land near Saint John while Thomas Murphy, who had managed to bring many slaves and field hands with him, could afford to be more adventurous and chose a large tract of uncleared land in Rawdon in Nova Scotia. Abraham decided to go it alone and set out for Halifax, the chief seaport on the rocky Atlantic shore of Nova Scotia.

Much of Nova Scotia at the time was a wilderness area with Halifax, which was founded around 1749, its only significant town. For maritime use though, the town had two big advantages over many coastal towns on the North American eastern seaboard - it had a big sea-lake, over ten square miles, and it was usually open to shipping all year round. On the other hand it was remote with a sparsely populated hinterland and it couldn't really take advantage of its physical advantages. So it stayed a small and pretty insignificant town, that is until the

American Revolution happened. Almost overnight, Halifax changed into a major British naval and military base.

Abraham was a skilled carpenter who knew all about ships and this soon got him a foreman's job in a Royal Engineer's timber yard. He was offered a choice of land and chose a ten acre strip running uphill from the waterfront. It was a good choice as Halifax's expansion and increasing prosperity caused the value of the land to rocket. He built a house on top of the hill and, when everything was finished, he made his way to Thomas Murphy's house in Rawdon where he married Margaret.

Some top-ranking military people were now based in Halifax and, with the arrival of increasing numbers of rich merchants, an upper-class social structure was developing. Abraham was from a very well connected society in the American colonies so, together with Margaret, it was no problem for him to become part of the developing top society in Halifax. It was a very different life to that which Abraham had had in Philadelphia but it was developing nicely.

The expansion of Halifax as a defence centre and a distribution point for trade goods between Britain and the West Indies enabled many of the entrepreneurial loyalists to grow rich but Abraham was not one of them although he was certainly not poor. He stuck to his job at the timber yard and rose to a position of some importance. In his spare time he dabbled in property, buying land and building some houses with much of the carpentry carried out by himself.

Abraham and Margaret had nine children, two girls and seven boys. Mary was their first child followed, on 21st November 1787, by Samuel, who would always be known as Sam, then came William, Susan, Edward, Joseph, John, Thomas and Henry.

Sam was an outgoing, inquisitive child who, from an early age, acquired two great loves, ships and making money. From his house on top of the hill he would watch the many sailing ships pass by and once a month, from April to November, he would see the Royal Navy brigs arrive with the mail. The vessels ran from Falmouth to New York with a stopover at Halifax with mail for British North America. Everyone, including Sam, turned out to see the mail being ceremoniously carried, under Royal Navy protection, from the ship to the Post Office.

Sam liked to spend time at the wharves and he would be enthralled as the sailors, sometimes hopelessly drunk, would recount the tales of the sea and ships. But there were many sailors who never made it as far as Halifax. The Nova Scotia coast can be foggy and is strewn with islands and rocky outcrops that can ensnare ships. When Sam was just ten years old he witnessed the aftermath of the shipwreck of the frigate *La Tribune* which ran aground at Thrum Cap Shoals in a storm. It was very close to the shore and the cries of those on board could be clearly heard but the bad conditions made it impossible to rescue everyone and 240 men, women and children were lost. Just eight were saved. This first hand illustration of the dangers of the sea would have a profound effect on Sam in later life.

Sam was educated at home with a few years at grammar school where he was good at figures but didn't really want to spend time on subjects such as Latin preferring to increasingly concentrate on the most important thing in his life, after his family, that of making some money.

```
Interesting point: The school Sam went to,
Halifax Grammar School, amongst other
things paid great store to "training up the
pupils in a just pronunciation and graceful
elocution." Could it be that this is
something that helped him in his later
business life? He did seem to be able to
```

```
mix happily with people of all social
classes and, whoever he was dealing with,
he usually seemed to be able to get his own
way!
```

Sam decided very early on that he was intended for a life in business. People paid him to run errands and later he graduated to buying small items of cargo at the wharves and selling them door to door.

Meanwhile Abraham and Margaret carried on with their reasonably comfortable life, not exactly rich but certainly comfortable enough to have servants. But they were nothing like as comfortable as Abraham's ancestors had been in Pennsylvania. Sam heard stories about those days and it is thought that this encouraged him to develop a successful business life.

When he was seventeen Sam left school and, after a few years helping his father in the timber yard, he headed for Boston where his father had arranged a placement in a ship broker's office. Sam spent three years in Boston reportedly having a fine time, making friends and partying but still finding time to learn about the business. When he returned to Halifax, not yet twenty one, he knew pretty well all there was to know about ships and shipping. The seeds of the Cunard transatlantic empire had now been sown.

Abraham by now had retired from the timber yard and had built a landing wharf at the base of Cunard Hill. He ordered a small schooner from Margaret's brother, Tom Murphy, which he named *Margaret* and a second vessel, the *Nancy*, soon joined the fleet. The vessels operated under the firm of A. Cunard & Son (the son, of course, being Sam).

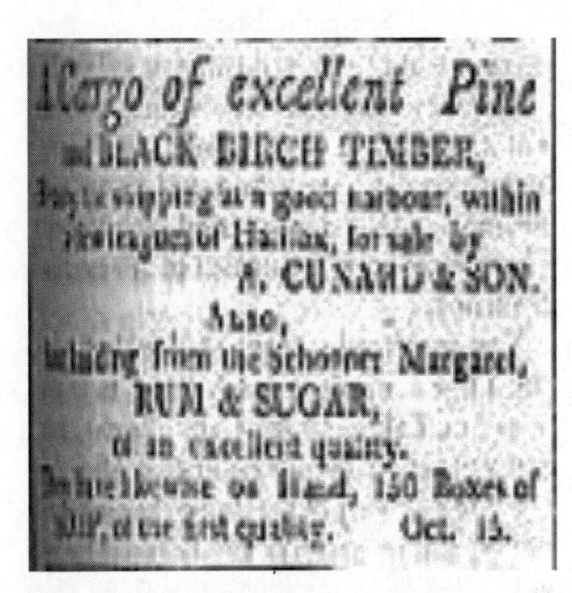

3 The first known Cunard newspaper advertisement
(Courtesy and copyright of the Nova Scotia Archives)

Abraham's health was not good by now and the death of his daughter, Mary, put great strain on him and Margaret and Sam gradually took over day to day running of the business.

In 1812, President Madison declared war on Britain and it was feared that this would mean the end for the many small ships trading between Halifax and the United States. However, New England refused to take part in the war and safe passage was granted to "neutral" ships of both countries. Sam was not one to be last in the queue for anything and he made sure that Cunard was one of the first to be granted a neutral permit which enabled the company to steer its ships safely around the British and American warships and privateers.

At this time Halifax was expanding rapidly, doubling its population within a year. Many vessels captured by privateers were brought to Halifax and, in 1813, the Cunard firm acquired a square rigger at a bargain price. She was renamed the *White Oak* and began a service to London. Another vessel was purchased and made its way to the West Indies with a cargo of dried fish to be traded for sugar.

The firm was now doing really well trading actively in sugar and coffee in the West Indies. Sam was becoming increasingly known on the waterfront as a very canny businessman who knew what he wanted and was usually able to get it. This was in no small part due to his commitment to his businesses, his attention to detail and his readiness to keep pushing until he got the desired result.

Sam now turned his attention to the girl he wanted to marry, Susan Duffus, the daughter of William Duffus, an influential Halifax merchant. In the summer of 1814, at the age of twenty seven, Sam became engaged to Susan and, the following February, they were married.

However, Sam's marriage coincided with big changes for the town of Halifax. Wellington had been victorious at Waterloo and now Britain had no major wars to deal with. The naval force at Halifax was reduced considerably and many troops went home leaving much fewer trade opportunities for Sam Cunard and the merchants.

Fortunately Sam wasn't one to wait around for something to happen. He made his way to London and secured a contract to carry Royal Mail between Britain and Bermuda. During the 1812 war, the mail had been delivered to Bermuda with traders taking the mail on to Halifax when possible. When the war had ended the packets reverted to their original programme of delivering mail directly to Halifax and New York with mail being sent on to Bermuda only during the winter months. Cunard's packet service gave Bermuda a more reliable service, calling at Halifax on the way. Maintaining a set schedule was however impossible as the packet boats could not set sail unless they had enough passengers and the crossing from Falmouth to Halifax could take up to twelve weeks.

Early in 1816, Cunard's contract was amended to include delivery of mail to Boston as well as Bermuda. Getting Cunard's name known in Boston would certainly turn out to be a good idea although no-one realised it at the time.

The following year, things went really downhill for the people of Halifax. There was hardly any work and many people were forced to beg on the streets. People who arrived at the wharves, having immigrated for the chance of a better life, would have been horrified by what they saw and many probably wished they had stayed at home. Rather than finding opportunities in Halifax they only ended up adding to the problem.

Sam's wife, Susan, was appalled at the plight of the ordinary people and she, and the Governor's wife, the Countess of Dalhousie, did much to help the town's paupers including helping with the establishment of soup kitchens.

During this time a frequent visitor to Sam and Susan was Lieutenant William Parry of the Royal Navy who was a friend of Susan's brother, James. No one knew it at the time but, in years to come, this acquaintance would prove to be a key factor in the future success of the Cunard Line.

Something else the family did not know when they accompanied Lt. Parry to the harbour to join his ship, and something perhaps they could never have imagined, was that one day, on the horizon, would be a steamship that had just arrived from Britain.

●●●

Chapter 4

The Power of Steam

Many people have grown up thinking that James Watt invented the steam engine after watching the power of steam lifting the lid of the kettle boiling on the hob and that no-one else was involved; all nonsense of course. The kettle story may in part be true and could have been something that he noticed as a child but he didn't actually invent the steam engine, it was already in use when he appeared. But, and it is a big but, he did make improvements to the basic concept which would have a dramatic effect on the development of the steam engine and the development of practical steam navigation. His contribution to Britain's industrial revolution would prove to be momentous and would change the world. However the principle and potential of steam power was realised a long time before Watt came on the scene.

Sometime around 120 B.C. the Greek engineer Hero of Alexandria was living in Roman Egypt and drew up a detailed design for a steam turbine, the *Aeolipile* in a work called "*Spiritalia Seu Pneumatica*". Around this time many works, covering literature, medicine, art and science, were held at the Library and Museum of Alexandria. These works were made by engraving onto a clay tablet which was then fired thus producing a library of ceramic "books". A large staff of scribes was maintained to transfer the works to another medium. During the reign of Caesar, Roman troops are said to have destroyed around 700,000 of these valuable works. The ancient Greeks had some of the greatest minds on earth at that time and the loss of this library would hold back intellectual thinking for centuries. Hero's machine consisted of a pivoted ball filled with water and suspended over a fire. Nozzles on opposite sides of the ball would expel the steam that built up and turn the ball. Whether Hero actually built this machine is not known but a model of it was constructed recently to test the theory and it did work with the ball eventually turning very quickly, at least until the machine started to come apart. But this could only ever have been a novelty; it was uncontrollable and the technology to convert the idea into a useful application was just not available at the time. Nevertheless Hero was way ahead of his time in devising a way of using the power of steam as a motive power source. It would be well over another thousand years before the idea would resurface in any meaningful way.

During the 16th century some understanding of steam and its potential started to develop. Cardan is said to have applied the principle of Hero's Aeolipile to drive a spit, referred to as a "smoke-jack" and Jacob Besson, a Professor of Mathematics at Orleans published a scientific tract which showed a great understanding of the properties of steam. But these were just their thoughts in writing as was the book by the Italian engineer, Agostino Ramelli. Producing a useful working steam engine was not for this time.

During the 17th century, more people gave thought to the harnessing of steam power and their knowledge was improving all the time as was the technology.

In 1601, Giovanni Battista della Porta of Naples, in a work called "*Spiritali*", described an apparatus that would raise water by the power of steam. Once again, this was only a speculative work based on the earlier work of Hero and did not lead to a working steam engine. But Battista, although little known today, was indeed a very clever man and is credited with inventing, amongst other things, the magic lantern and the camera obscura, both of which some artists would find very useful in the future.

In 1615, the French engineer Salomon de Caus published a work in Franfurt describing a way that "Water will, by the aid of fire, mount higher than its source" - once again just describing something, not actually building the item.

In 1629 Giovanni Branca of Loretto in Italy published a work describing, amongst other devices, a system using steam to turn a "windmill" and thus provide power for all kinds of applications. An ingenious idea but it could never have worked; the power output would have been far too low. Yet another example of the increasing understanding of the power of steam but finding a way to harness it was proving very elusive.

It was at this time that people in Britain got interested in steam power with the first authentic record being in a patent granted by Charles I to David Ramseye. The patent covered many steam powered inventions including pumping water from mines, powering mills, weaving; all big ideas but that was all. If they had been practical at the time, the industrial revolution would have been brought forward 100 years and would have changed the future of the world.

Britain now took over as the centre of steam engine research and development. In 1661 the Marquis of Worcester is said to have made a working steam pump to move water between the floors of his castle and to power his fountains. It is difficult to know whether this actually happened or not. The Marquis produced a book "*A Century of the names and scantlings of Inventions by me already practised*" in 1663 giving details of his "inventions" but it is clear they are often no more than ideas and it may be that these stories of a steam pump originated from that. Certainly it would have been difficult at that time to find someone who could actually make a steam pump or a pumping system. However the Marquis was definitely an ingenious man and some of his ideas were very advanced for the time. For instance, in his book, he mentions stenography, telegraphy, combination locks and speaking statues, whatever they were meant to be. Perhaps he did make a working steam pump or perhaps he was in the mould of Leonardo da Vinci who, despite all his acclaim as an inventor, was usually just an ideas man (and a skilled artist and anatomist), not really an inventor at all. Few of his ideas, admittedly very advanced for the time, would have worked using his plans although it has to be said that a couple of minor designs did lead to something. In fairness to the Marquis though, it has to be acknowledged that some writers do believe that he made steam work for him and that he really did use an engine to supply water to the inhabitants of Vauxhall, London. It is all a bit uncertain at the moment. A clearly interesting man, the Marquis seemed to regard himself as an expert on everything and Boyman in 1840 describes the Marquis as referring to himself in his writings as "*the never to be sufficiently admired*" - egotism par excellence!

There were many ideas and many patents but steam is a powerful and dangerous force and harnessing it and putting it to good use continued to be beyond the wit of man until.....

4   Thomas Savery   *(Thurston)*

...... Thomas Savery came on the scene. He was born to a well-to-do family in Shilston, Devon around 1650. As his father and mother looked lovingly at the new addition to their family, they would never have realised that, when their baby son grew up, he would begin a process that would transform life and prosperity in Britain, and that would eventually lead to a revolution in land and sea transport.

After completing his education, Savery became a military engineer, rising to the rank of captain and he spent some of his time in Dartmouth. He had a resourceful mind and put it to use trying to produce some useful inventions but at first with very limited success. But in Cornwall there was a big problem that provided an opportunity for Savery's inventive mind to find a solution. Mining of tin and copper was very important in the area and supported much of the population. Many of the mines were close to or actually ran under the sea and flooding was an ongoing problem which prevented the mines being sunk too deeply.

Savery turned his agile mind to the mine flooding problem and in 1698 came up with a way of using steam power to raise water from the mines. He demonstrated it to the Royal Society and described it in his book "The Miner's Friend" which was published in 1702. Savery had great hopes for his machine and suggested his "Fire engine" could even be used to pump water for towns, to drain marshes, to power ships and also to power mills, although his design would not have easily lent itself to providing a motive power source.

5   Savery's Engine
(Lardner)

In simple terms the machine worked by creating a vacuum which sucked water upwards, in principle not dissimilar to, and possibly based on, the design of the Marquis of Worcester. This was the basis for removing water from mines but, in practice, it had severe limitations. It could only draw water up to about 30 feet and, as mines needed to be dug deeper all the time, it was necessary to have extra engines on different levels. A further problem, and a big one, was that the engine consumed enormous amounts of fuel and, although it did the job, it cost a lot of money to make it pump water out of the mines. But there was an even bigger problem. The engine used high pressure steam as part of its cycle (when pumping from deep levels) and it did not have a safety valve although this had been invented by Denis Papin in 1681 and had been used by another steam pioneer, J. T. Desaguliers. Strong containers were just not available at that time and an explosion at Broad Waters in Wednesbury around 1705 put an end to Savery's engine as originally designed. Despite this, one early writer described Savery as one of the most ingenious men of his age. He may not be well known today but his "Fire engine" was probably the first practical steam engine, really a steam water pump, ever built and was used in many Cornish tin and copper mines and in some coal mines at other locations, as well as for raising water to supply towns.

However Savery had taken his pioneering steam engine as far as he could, the design having too many limitations. What was needed now was for someone to come on the scene who would have the potential to take the process to the second stage.

Then along came Thomas Newcomen who was born around 1664 in Dartmouth. He became a blacksmith and ironmonger and carried out work for the tin and copper mines in the area. He knew full well the problems caused by flooding especially as the mines got bigger and extended under the sea bed. Newcomen believed that a better version of Savery's engine could be made by using a piston, as suggested by Papin, and an overhead beam. He thought this would produce a better pumping action than Savery's and could clear water from a much greater depth. Around 1705, with his assistant John Calley, he produced a working model of what he called an "atmospheric steam engine". This was the first really practical and commercially useful and reliable design and gave us the familiar rocking beam we all associate with the early steam engines. It seems that Newcomen worked with Savery but to what extent is not certain. Some accounts suggest a passing collaboration whilst others suggest they were in partnership and produced the "Newcomen" engine together. They were both based in Dartmouth and they were both interested in steam pumping from mines so they would either have worked together as partners or they would have been strong rivals, it would certainly have been one or the other.

The principle of the Newcomen engine was very simple. Expanding steam would enter a cylinder where its pressure would force up a piston, then cold water is sprayed into the cylinder which immediately condenses the steam and forms a vacuum with atmospheric pressure causing the piston to move back down ready for the process to be repeated. This causes an overhead beam to move up and down in a regular motion and allows a container of water to be raised from the mine.

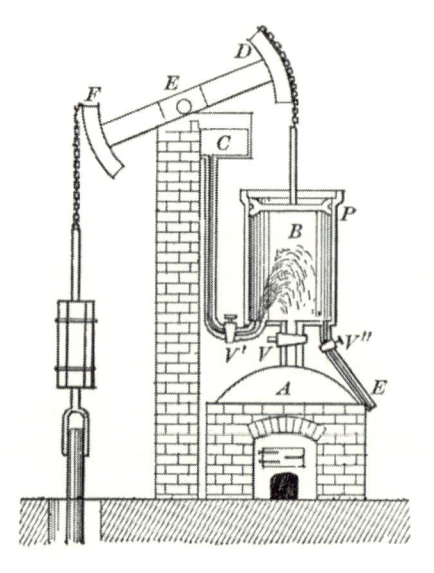

6 Newcomen's Engine
(BB-BY - 1923)

One of the big benefits of Newcomen's design was that it was not subject to the 30 feet height restriction and, around 1711, his engines began to be installed in mines in the West Country and by twelve years later were in common use in collieries. In 1725, an engine was installed in a coalmine at Dudley Castle. This was a substantial engine with a cylinder 21 inches and eight feet long. It could raise 10 gallons of water from a depth of 156 feet, way beyond the capabilities of a Savery machine. Remains of many of Newcomen's engines have been lost and we don't know the exact number that were put into use but it is probably over 100 with engines being installed in mines in the Midlands, the

North of England, Wales as well as the West Country. However, despite their success, they still had the same problem that Savery's machines had, and it was a problem that would dog steam engine designers for years to come, they used vast amounts of fuel, not such a problem for pumping water out of a colliery but in Cornwall, where coal was not readily available, it made the operation very costly. Where coal was available though, such as the Midlands and North of England it allowed Newcomen engines to be made larger and more powerful - and the Industrial Revolution was now under way.

The basic Newcomen engine remained in use until the early part of the 19th century with some improvements to the design of this, and the original Savery engine, being made by other steam pioneers.

Now we return to James Watt who powered the steam engine's design to its third and crucial stage.

He may not have invented the steam engine but the improvements he made to the latest (Newcomen) design had such far reaching consequences that he is credited with the invention of the "modern steam engine", a title he richly deserves.

Watt was born in 1736 at Crawfordsdyke, near Greenock, Scotland, the son of a prominent local schoolmaster and town treasurer. He was a bright but sickly child and could not attend school regularly but his parents ensured that he had plenty to occupy his mind at home. When he could eventually go to school regularly his progress was very slow at first but in his early teens he started to develop and began to excel at mathematics. At home he became adept at sketching technical drawings, working with nautical instruments and making ingenious models and musical instruments. When adulthood arrived, he, not surprisingly, became an instrument maker, often doing work for Glasgow University. A Newcomen engine was put into use in Glasgow and this attracted the interest of the young Watt who decided to do some research on the power of steam. Around 1763 the university had a model of a Newcomen engine which had ceased working.

This small engine, with a two inch diameter cylinder and a four inch stroke, was passed to Watt who set to work learning about steam power and getting the engine back into working use. But he was not impressed at all with its design.

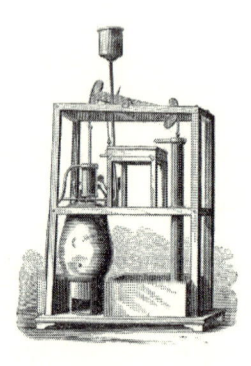

7 Model of Newcomen Engine
(Thurston)

He concluded that most of the steam entering the cylinder was wasted when it was condensed by the water spray on to the walls of the cylinder, which were then cooled. For the next cycle, time and heat had to be wasted heating up the cylinder and providing more steam. He solved this problem by adding a separate cold condenser to take the steam away after the piston had been raised. This enabled the main cylinder to be kept permanently hot, with the assistance of lagging, and it thus became much more efficient and used less fuel.

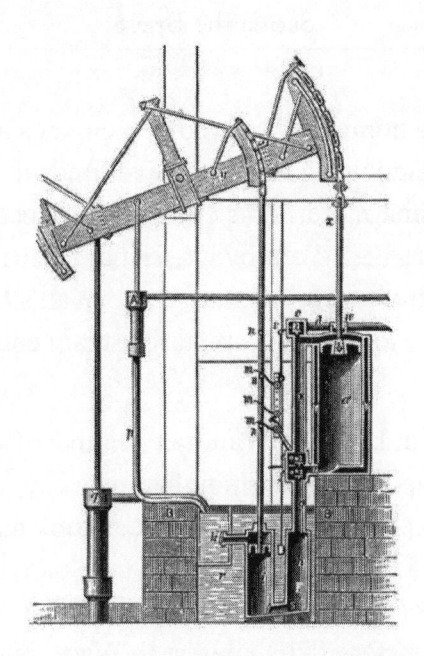

8   Watt's Double acting Engine
(Thurston)

Watt's engine also gave a faster, more efficient and smoother action than Newcomen's but it was still essentially a pumping engine. However converting the action into a motive power source was not in principle too difficult; the process of connecting a crank and a connecting rod to a treadle had been in use for many years to power a lathe. The problem for Watt was that the patent for using this system attached to a steam engine had been issued to James Pickard and if there was one person Watt didn't like, it was James Pickard who he thought was a plagiarist. Rather than have to come to terms with him, Watt designed his "sun and planet system" which gave continuous revolving motion to a shaft provided with a flywheel, a system which he used until Pickard's patent expired. The impact of this development on Britain's industrial revolution is incalculable. Steam could now be used to power machinery anywhere and to do so in a much more efficient way than could be provided by windmills or water wheels.

Watt acquired a number of Newcomen engines and tried to improve their design using all of his own funds in doing so and borrowing more and more. This eventually reduced him to poverty but he was bailed out by his friend, Dr. Roebuck, a physician and entrepreneur, who assumed Watt's liabilities up to £1,000 and agreed to provide capital for steam engine development.

In 1768, when in London, Watt met Matthew Boulton, who had a successful factory on Birmingham working on silverware. The two men hit it off right away and each took a great interest in the other's work. They decided to set up a partnership. At this time Dr. Roebuck had fallen onto hard times and, in the need to raise funds, he transferred his interest in Watt's business to Boulton and a new member of the Boulton and Watt operation, a Dr. Small.

In 1774, Watt completed and successfully trialled his Kinncil engine which would become the benchmark for future steam engine developments. Although Newcomen engines would continue to be built for many years, developers of new steam engines would tend to base their work on the Boulton and Watt engine, which they considered the best so far. But Watt did not take a back seat, he continued to develop more and more advanced engines with other developers struggling to keep up. Some developments were very complicated while some, like the governor, or fly-ball governor, were very simple, yet incredibly important. The governor consists of two iron balls on a crosspiece which are connected to the engine and turn with it. As the speed of the engine changes, the crosspiece holding the two balls move up and down, thus automatically regulating the supply of steam to the engine. In this way, the speed of the engine is kept relatively stable. A similar principle was already in use to regulate the speed of water wheels and windmills but

Watt was the first to apply it to steam engines. You often see these simple devices on steam engines; that is because they were one of the greatest inventions in the history of the steam engine.

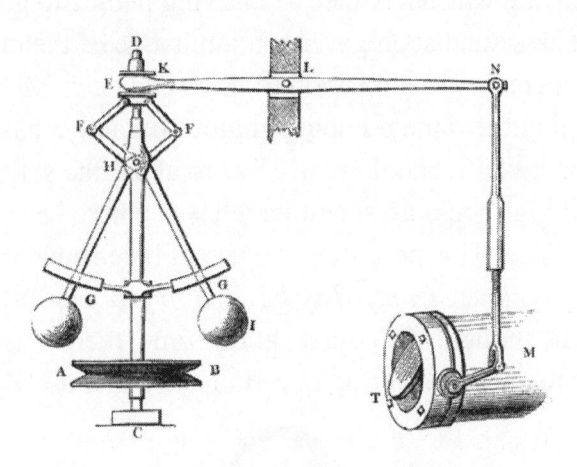

9   Ball Valve Governor
(Lardner)

One final word about James Watt. As well being wrongly credited as the sole inventor of the steam engine, he is also credited with inventing the term "horse power" for engineering use. Well, he didn't but, as with the steam engine, he did make an "improvement" and defined "horse power" in precise terms as "the rate at which work is done when 33,000 lbs. are raised one foot in one minute".

Who originally used the term "horse power"? It was the pioneer, Thomas Savery.

For the fourth and final stage of steam engine design which powered the industrial revolution, we go back to the West Country.

In 1771, in Cornwall, Richard Trevithick was born, the son of a mining official and a miner's daughter. From an early age he learned about tin and copper mining and watched the early steam machines pumping water from the mines. He did not do well at school but grew to become a tall, powerful and tough man, with wrestling as a hobby. He was not someone to be messed with and was not averse to bullying people to get his way. His background soon got him a job in one of the mines where he progressed to a position of mine engineer. Modifying and developing the mine pumping engines became a passion and he improved boiler technology in 1799 to allow the safe, or safer, use of high pressure steam which was where he scored over James Watt. This permitted the use of much smaller and less weighty engines. *Could they be used to propel road carriages?* he thought. Of course, at this time, there was only one answer to any engineering question and that was "*Yes*".

10   Richard Trevithick
(Thurston)

But Trevithick was not going to be the first.

In 1769, a little before Trevithick was born, Nicolas-Joseph Cugnot, a French inventor and military engineer, constructed a three wheel steam driven vehicle, probably the first, which he thought could be used to transport cannons. This fearsome looking machine did work, to some extent, but it wasn't very practical and did not really lead to anything.

11   Cugnot's Steam Vehicle
(Thurston)

Even before then, around 1687, Isaac Newton displayed some understanding of the power of steam by designing a carriage which would be propelled forward by a jet of steam exiting the rear.

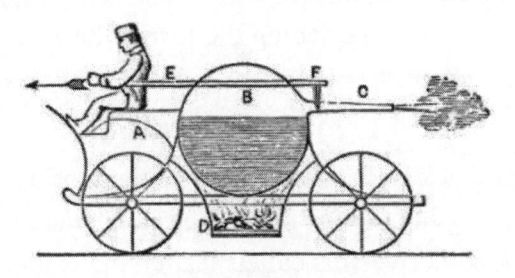

12   Newton's Steam Carriage
(Thurston)

But it was only what we would term today "a concept car". It would never have worked; the power of exiting steam would be way below that necessary to move the vehicle, which is probably just as well as anyone standing behind when the carriage moved off would have been subjected to a highly dangerous blast of hot steam. Perhaps Newton's understanding of steam power wasn't that great after all.

Now forward to the early 19th century, a time when "it all happened".

In 1801, in Camborne, Trevithick built his first steam vehicle, the "Puffing Billy", a very functional looking vehicle that resembled a boiler on wheels. The vehicle did work but it was a terror to operate and the roads at the time were not of course built for such heavy road vehicles. Unfortunately, a few days after it was first brought into use, it broke down and was left with its fire burning whilst the operators retired to a nearby public house. When they eventually returned, the "Puffing Billy" had been badly damaged. Not one to give in, Trevithick constructed another steam powered vehicle in 1803 which he called the "London Carriage". This enormous three wheeled carriage was demonstrated in London but it wasn't a success. However he had more success with one of his engines which was mounted on rails and towed coal at the Pen-y-Darran colliery in South Wales, replacing the former horse powered tramway. Later he constructed a few more locomotives for colliery use.

In 1808, Trevithick built what would be the world's first passenger carrying railway on a small circular track in Euston, London. The locomotive was called "Catch me if you can" and was built by John Urpeth Rastrick at Bridgnorth. Few people at the time had the ability to construct a locomotive and Trevithick was lucky that he had someone like Rastrick to call on. The locomotive weighed eight tons and operated at about eight miles per hour, which was quite fast for the diameter of the track. However it didn't operate for too long because the track was built on soggy ground and eventually started to give way. It was shored up with timber but then failed again causing the engine to topple over. Not surprisingly that was the end of the "Catch me if you can experience", nothing wrong with the engine though.

In 1825 the success of the Stockton and Darlington rail service, using strong wrought iron rails on oak or stone blocks, showed what could be done. Originally intended as a way of getting coal to the people of Stockton and Darlington, the line was soon seen as a way of making some additional money from carrying passengers. The opening day was set for 27th September 1825 and the first train consisted of 6 wagons containing coal and goods, the Railway Committee in the company's coach, 6 wagons with seats, 14 wagons for workmen and 6 coal wagons that were to be left at Darlington. Three hundred tickets were issued to travel on the train but on the day the crowds were enormous and many people clambered on to the train whether they had a ticket or not. Contemporary reports tell of up to 600 people in the wagons or hanging on to the sides. The train was hauled by Robert Stephenson's *Locomotion* and it was a great tribute to his engineering skills that the locomotive was able to haul such an overweight train for nearly four hours. Investors saw right away the potential of steam railways and by 1830 the 30 mile long Liverpool to Manchester line was in use, the first two cities anywhere to be linked by rail. But it was only the beginning; by 1842 Britain would have a rail network extending nearly 2,000 miles and many other countries were laying track as fast as they could. The age of the train had begun.

```
Interesting point. In Britain we use the
term railway to describe our rail system
whilst in America the term railroad has
always been used. Readers may be surprised
to learn that, in the early days, British
"railways" were in fact described as
"railroads" or "rail-roads". So our American
cousins have been right all along!
```

Trevithick went on to produce more designs for pumping engines and new applications for steam including a design for a steam hammer. His skills were in great demand and he went to South America and organised the removal of water from copper and silver mines.

Ingenious though Trevithick was, he was never good at handling his finances. He died in Dartford on the 22nd April

1833, penniless, without the support of friends or family, and was buried in an unmarked grave at East Hill in Dartford.

But even before steam locomotives started to revolutionise land travel, there were some far sighted people who thought that the main benefit of steam engines would be on the sea. Towards the end of the 18th century and the beginning of the 19th century, the thoughts of more and more engineers started to turn to steam powered ships. What a prize that would be - the holy grail for shipping - the ability to travel on rivers and oceans without being subject to the vagaries of the wind and without having to wait for the right wind before you could even set sail. Unfortunately this was not going to be easy. Steam engines could be temperamental, the vessel needed to carry a lot of fuel for them which took up passenger and cargo space and they were known to blow up occasionally. But, in those days, nothing seemed to hold people back. This was the time of the industrial revolution; problems were there to be overcome and that was all there was to it.

But before we look at the development of steam navigation, let's consider an important question - who did invent the steam engine, that is, *really* invent the steam engine? Inventing something is not just a case of coming up with an idea or a design or a working model. It is all of those things plus, the crucial element, putting the item into productive use. It is no use designing something if it serves no useful purpose, an invention has to be or do something useful. It doesn't have to be perfect, in fact all inventions are improved over time but it does have to work. On this basis the steam engine was not invented by one person, it was invented by four - Thomas Savery, Thomas Newcomen, James Watt and Richard Trevithick. Each of these men took the existing steam engine idea, made a major contribution to its development, and put the new engine into productive use. The work they did was interlinked and, if any of these men had not existed, the development of the steam engine, and the consequent industrial revolution in Britain would have been at best delayed and at worst compromised with it possibly even taking place in another country. The future of the whole world would have been different. It is acknowledged that there were many other steam pioneers and even these four men had assistance from others when they were designing and producing their engines. However the fact is that Messrs. Savery, Newcomen, Watt and Trevithick were the ones with the foresight, backed up by their drive and enthusiasm, to make steam work and, in Britain, we all owe them a big debt. However it has to be recognised that the biggest debt is probably due to Mr Watt.

But what about the Marquis of Worcester? Well the problem with the Marquis is that it is not certain if his plans actually led to anything; they may have been just ideas. If he did really succeed in making a working and useful steam engine, even if it was only to pump water around his country house or to power his ornate garden fountains, he would qualify as the fifth man in the steam engine hall of fame. In fairness though, it has to be said that, even if he did not actually construct working steam engines, he does merit some recognition for the fact that Savery is believed to have been influenced by his plans. But at this stage the jury is still out on the Marquis of Worcester.

Scotia the Brave

Chapter 5

Steam Navigation

Even before anyone had thought that a machine to pump water out of mines was a good idea, some visionaries had speculated that a steam engine could be developed to power ships.

As far back as the 13th century, Roger Bacon, the learned Franciscan monk, may well have foretold the use of marine steam power when he wrote: *"I will now mention some wonderful works of art and nature, in which there is nothing of magic, and which magic could not perform. Instruments may be made by which the largest ships, with only one man guiding them, will be carried with greater velocity than if they were full of sailors."*

In 1543, a Spaniard, Blasco de Garay, is said to have propelled *La Trinidad*, a 200 ton vessel, by steam in the presence of the Emperor Charles V. A number of early writers have referred to this quoting ancient documents held in Catalonia. It is really difficult to believe that this actually happened, the technology being way beyond knowledge or materials in the 16th century. Some other old Spanish documents tell of two vessels, one driven by paddle wheels powered by 25 men and the other driven by paddle wheels driven by 40 men, steam power not being mentioned at all. It seems that Blasco had a vessel with a furnace on board which may have been connected to some form of machinery but this was kept hidden from observers. Although this story is often mentioned by early and some more recent writers, it is clear that the whole thing is a load of nonsense, particularly as the story didn't originally appear until around 1825 when steam navigation was already in use. If he did actually use steam to power *La Trinidad,* Blasco de Garry would have to have been one the cleverest men in history.

In 1618, David Ramsey obtained a patent for an invention *"to make boates for carriages running upon the water as swift in calmes and more safe in stormes than boates full sayled in great windes"* and in 1630 he patented a plan *"to make boates, ships and barges to goe against the wind and tide"*. Similar patents were filed by Francis Lin in 1637 and Edward Ford in 1646.

The Marquis of Worcester didn't overlook steam navigation in his "Century of Inventions" talking of "*a way how to make a boat work against itself against wind and tide; yea, both without the help of man or beast*". Once again, only one of his ideas, nothing became of it.

In 1699 Jonathan Hulls was born in Campden, Gloucestershire. A thoughtful and studious man, he earned his living as a clock maker and repairer. He was very inventive and developed an interest in steam power. In 1736, when aged 37, with assistance from a Mr Freeman, he drew up a patent for a "*machine for carrying ships and vessels out of or into any harbour or river against wind or tide*". This was described in a pamphlet he published the following year entitled "*A Description and Draught of a new-invented machine for carrying vessels or ship out of or into any harbour, port or river against wind or tide or in a calm*". Obviously short, snappy book titles were not in vogue at that time! In this well-considered work, Hulls showed a full understanding of how to power a vessel by steam and paddle wheels. It is possible that he actually used a steam engine to propel a boat by driving a stern wheel and, if this true, it may be the first successful use of a steamboat and the first use of a stern driven vessel. But there is a lot of doubt as to whether this really happened, not least because

Hulls was seen as someone with a lot of ideas but not much in the way in the way of success, apart from repairing clocks. In fact, there was a street ditty around at the time which recorded his "achievements"

Jonathan Hulls,

With his patent skulls

Invented a machine

To go against wind and stream

But, he, being an ass

Couldn't bring it to pass

And so was ashamed to be seen

Hulls is said to have moved to London where, like many steam developers, he died in poverty not having been recognised for his contribution to steam navigation.

Steam technology had developed so far that it was time for some clever people to think about designing a steam powered boat that really worked. But they knew it wasn't going to be easy and, even if they could make something that worked, they only expected steam power to be applied to small river or canal boats. After all, a boat would have to carry a large, heavy steam engine, plus its stock of fuel and the thought of having a raging fire on board to heat the boiler would not endear the idea to passengers. But as the 18th century got under way, things started to fall into place.

Denis Papin had described way back in 1690 *"a steam cylinder in which a piston descends by atmospheric pressure when the steam below is condensed"*. He had clearly developed an understanding of the vacuum. In 1707 he adapted the engine to power a model boat on the Fulda at Cassel. In this trial he used a steam pumping engine to force water up a water-wheel which in turn drove paddles, an interesting blend of current (water-wheel) and new (steam) technologies. His application to build and use a full size ship for freight was turned down by the local officials, no doubt heeding the concerns of the local boatmen who thought that they would lose their livelihood. A lot of antagonism built up towards Papin and his boat was attacked and destroyed overnight and he was lucky to escape with his life. This incident plus the fact that he was subject to persecution for being a protestant caused him to flee to England, where he prospered and became a Fellow of the Royal Society. He died three years later.

In 1729 Dr. John Allen drew up a patent for a boat propelled by a water jet. Good idea, we use water jet powered boats today. Unfortunately his energy source for powering the water jet was far from ideal; it was gunpowder. This may seem a strange suggestion but there were other proposals around the time for powering a boat by the use of gunpowder. People were of course working at the limits of scientific knowledge at the time and science is all about learning.

In 1778 the Marquis de Jouffroy is reported to have begun experimenting with steam power and in 1781 built a massive steamboat, 140 feet long by 40 feet wide that was said to work. The intervention of the French Revolution put an end to his work.

In 1783 the Frenchman, d'Abbas, is said to have steamed his paddler, Pyroscaphe, a vessel of 182 tons displacement, for fifteen minutes until it disintegrated.

On 27th July 1786 John Fitch successfully propelled the first steam boat in the U.S. along the Delaware River. This strange looking craft was powered by a system of vertical oars, perhaps inspired by the canoes of the native Americans. Each revolution moved 12 oars about 5 feet with six oars entering the water as six came out. Fitch was seen as an eccentric, and often worse, but he was a very clever man and constructed a number of small steamboats including one driven by a screw propeller and one driven by rear paddles. In fact it is said that his first design was for a vessel powered by a form of screw propeller but it didn't work in trials and, whilst pondering over the problem one night, Fitch came up with the idea of steam driven oars. His vessels did actually work but it has to be said that these were all only really novelties, although fairly good ones. There was little if any support for taking his ideas further in the United States at that time. Fitch died in 1787 still thinking, despite what others thought, that one day steam vessels would cross the oceans.

13   Fitch's Steamer
(Thurston)

In 1786 James Rumsey had more success and drove a boat on the Potomac River at around 4 mph, reportedly in the presence of George Washington. Crowds lined the banks of the river to see the spectacle of this awesome vessel as it noisily made its way through the water belching smoke and probably looking as if it was going to explode or be consumed by flame at any moment. The method of propulsion was to use a steam engine to pump water under great pressure aft of the vessel thus propelling it forward, a propulsion system that has been re-invented many times since and that is in use today, albeit without the steam engine! Those watching would probably never have even seen a stationary steam engine before so this must have been an incredible sight and, for many people, quite a frightening one. Later newspaper accounts probably gave a good description of what it would have been like *"[the vessel] moved into the stream, the steam connection hissing at the joints, the crude machinery thumping and groaning, the wheels splashing and the smokestack belching like a volcano"* and *"the monster moving on the water, defying the waves and tide, and breathing flames and smoke"*

In 1788 Rumsey moved to England where he saw a bigger future for his steamboat. He met up with a wealthy American merchant and they agreed to build a vessel powered by Rumsey's water jet system. Rumsey died before the vessel was completed but his partner carried on with the work and eventually, in 1793, the boat was launched on the Thames and did some useful work.

In 1790, Earl Stanhope patented his *Ambi-navigator* driven by a rear-mounted propeller in the shape of a duck's foot which was powered by a 12 h.p. steam engine. Not surprisingly, the experiment was not a great success and the vessel was soon laid up. But it didn't end there. The Earl didn't give up on the idea and, three years later, constructed another vessel, this time driven by two enormous duck's feet paddles, fitted either side of the vessel, which opened and closed like giant umbrellas. Amazingly the duck's feet moved the vessel at a rate of three miles per hour! Fulton became aware of the experiment and contacted the Earl suggesting that paddle wheels would be a better idea but of course Earls always know better than the common people and rejected the idea. Clearly this was not a ground-breaking step in the development of steam navigation - the world just wasn't ready for duck's feet powered steamers!

In Britain steam navigation development was going ahead. In 1787 Patrick Miller of Dalswinton, Scotland experimented with boats powered by paddle wheels turned by men, not surprisingly with limited success. Millar worked with James Taylor on the possible use of steam power to power boats instead of men. A young engineer, William Symington, who was working at the lead mines at Wanlockhead, Dumfrieshire and who had been a schoolmate of Taylor, had produced a small working steam engine. In fact he is also said to have produced a model of a steam carriage which Millar is believed is to have seen and been impressed with.

Symington was brought into the project and, the following year, his little two cylinder engine was placed in a 25 feet long and 7 feet beam pleasure boat and driven on Loch Dalswinton at 5 m.p.h. The vessel was an unusual design with the paddle wheel situated in the centre of the boat with the engine one side and the boiler the other. Despite the momentous nature of this event in the development of steam navigation, it was apparently barely reported in local newspapers.

The following year, Symington built a larger vessel with a cylinder 18 inches in diameter powering paddle wheels which drove the boat at 7 m.p.h. Despite the success of these vessels, Millar and Taylor lost interest in steam navigation and withdrew funding, Millar no doubt conscious of the fact that he had spent so much of his own fortune on the project and was receiving little in the way of reward or recognition.

Symington still had more to do in the development of steam navigation but it would be some years before his services were called upon again. In 1801 Lord Dundas, who was a large shareholder in the Forth and Clyde Canal Company, employed him to design a steamboat to tow vessels on the Forth and Clyde Canal and put up £7,000 to fund the scheme. Symington had designed a new engine incorporating some of Watt's improvements and, in early 1802, the rear paddle wheel driven *Charlotte Dundas,* named after the daughter of Lord Dundas, took to the water for her trials. Despite having to drive into gale force winds, she towed two 70 ton barges for twenty miles along the canal in six hours, a feat that a sail driven boat couldn't even begin to contemplate. Lord Dundas and the invited guests on board were delighted, as were the hundreds of people who lined the canal banks and who had definitely never seen the like before. The *Charlotte Dundas* is considered by many to be the first practical steamboat.

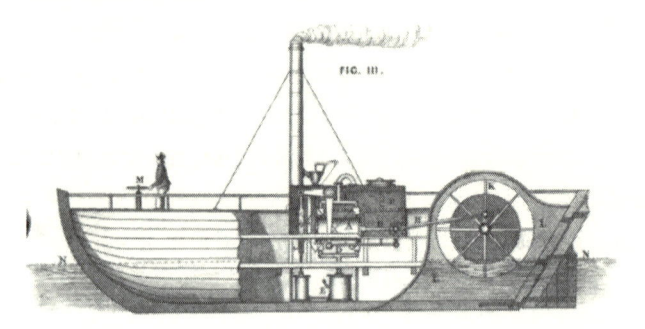

14   The Charlotte Dundas
(Thurston)

Lord Dundas wrote to the Duke of Bridgewater telling him about the successful trial of the *Charlotte Dundas*. His lordship was almost immediately smitten by the idea of steam boats and said that eight boats would be ordered for use on the canal. The struggling Symington would have been ecstatic, he was about to find fame and fortune. But then it all went wrong. The Duke of Bridgewater died suddenly and the committee which took over from him decided that the wash from steam boats would damage the canal and the project was cancelled.

Symington's contribution to steam navigation was never fully appreciated by the government and he received just £150 for his contribution whilst many others, whose inventions or discoveries had not been so important, had received much more. He died in March 1831, an impoverished and broken man believing that few people realised what he had done and that others were getting the benefit from his work.

The *Charlotte Dundas* was similarly unrecognised and, instead or being preserved as the world's first really practical steamboat, she was laid up in a creek to rot away.

But one person who did recognise the achievements of Symington and the *Charlotte Dundas* was the American marine pioneer, Robert Fulton. Born in Pennsylvania in 1765, he developed a love of fine arts and, when still a young man, moved to Britain and immersed himself in the art scene. But water navigation became a developing interest and, perhaps because of his art leanings, he was very prepared to think outside the box and come up with ideas that no-one else had thought of. But first he had to learn about steam navigation which some people thought could be the future, if it could be made to work. Although not too widely reported, he heard about Symington's boat and in July 1801, he visited Symington and was taken for a four mile trip on board the *Charlotte Dundas* and was allowed to make drawings of the vessel. He then decided to try some new ideas and moved to France where he developed a submarine armed with a gunpowder torpedo. In tests for the French and British governments, the submarine and its torpedoes were surprisingly successful, for the time, but the ideas were amazingly not taken up.

Fulton then returned to the United States and drew up a design for a steam boat, doubtless based on the *Charlotte Dundas* .

The *Clermont* was built at the Charles Brown yard on the East Hudson. The vessel was 30 feet long and 18 feet beam and was driven by 15 feet diameter paddle wheels. The low pressure engines were supplied by Boulton and Watt in England and had 24 inch cylinders and a 3 feet stroke. In 1807 he steered the *Clermont* up the Hudson River, exactly two hundred years after Hendrick Hudson first sailed the river in his Dutch barque, the *Half-moon*, much to the amazement of the local native Americans. Fulton's vessel though was quite difficult to handle due to the large boiler, carrying a huge amount of water, and the heavy masonry it was set in. The *Clermont* used dry pine wood for fuel which caused flames and black smoke to rise a considerable distance above the smoke stack. The sight of this, combined with the noise of the engine and paddles, resulted in some panic amongst the crews of vessels on the river as the "great monster" approached them. Despite this, the voyage was deemed a great success and the vessel was enlarged, to 43 feet by 16.5 feet, and two cabins were added. She was now ready for carrying passengers and a regular service between New York and Albany was inaugurated, a distance of around 125 miles, much to the annoyance of the operators of the sailing ships and ferries on the Hudson.

Interestingly, Fulton didn't seem to think that much of his steamboats. Boyman, in his book "Steam Navigation, its rise and progress", recounts that Fulton, in a letter to Joel Barclay in 1807 recalling the success of his *North River* steamer, says *"However, I will not admit that it is half so important as the torpedo system of attack and defence"*.

Despite the preference for his torpedoes, Fulton built on his success and constructed more steamers for use on the river. But his inventive, and sometimes warlike, mind was not resting and he is credited with designing the first ever steam warship. On

20th June 1814, the vessel was launched from the yard of Adam and Noah Brow watched over by a vast crowd and a number of bedecked sail powered men o'war. In May 1815, her engines were installed but, before her sea trials could take place, Fulton died. He was seen by some as the inventor of the real steamboat but by many others as just a follower of Symington. The reality is perhaps that they were both first. Symington was the first to construct a really practical steam boat and Fulton was the first to make a steam boat a real commercial success.

In Britain, in 1812, Henry Bell, influenced by Symington's *Charlotte Dundas,* produced the *Comet.* Bell was born in Linlithgow in 1767 and progressed to shipbuilding after first learning about stone masonry and carpentry. He moved to Helensburgh in 1808 where his wife is said to have kept the Bath's Inn, leaving Bell time to develop his interest in mechanics. Helensburgh was a popular watering-place on the Clyde but getting there from Glasgow by rowing/sailing boat took up to six hours. Bell thought the journey ideal for a steamer and that it would be a good business opportunity. He contracted with John Wood to build the *Comet,* a 40 feet by 10.5 feet paddle steamer, using an engine locally produced by Bell and a boiler built by James Watt. She was perhaps an odd looking vessel with a single very tall funnel which could also act as a mast. To the reporter from the Liverpool Mercury, however, she was a *"beautiful and commodious boat".*

15   The Comet on the Clyde
(Thurston)

The 25 ton vessel did her intended job, with varying degrees of financial success, carrying passengers up and down the Clyde at 3 m.p.h. and was the first passenger steamboat built in Europe.

Travelling on the *Comet* would have been a tremendously exciting experience for people at the time but what they would not have known was that the design was much more dangerous than that adopted by Symington. In Symington's *Charlotte Dundas*, the furnace was contained safely within the boiler rather than around the outside as in the case on the *Comet*. Nevertheless she worked safely on the Clyde for many years.

Advertisement for the *Comet in the Greenock Advertiser*

"STEAM PASSAGE BOAT,
"THE *COMET*",
BETWEEN GLASGOW,
GREENOCK, AND HELENSBURGH
FOR PASSENGERS ONLY.

"The Subscriber having, at much expense, fitted up a handsome vessel to ply upon the river Clyde, between Glasgow and Greenock, to sail by the power of wind, air and steam, he intends that the vessel shall leave the Broomielaw on Tuesdays, Thursdays, and Saturdays about mid-day, or at such hour thereafter as may answer from the state of the tide; and to leave Greenock on Mondays, Wednesdays, and Fridays in the morning, to suit the tide.

The elegance, comfort, safety, and speed of this vessel requires only to be proved to meet the approbation of the public; and the proprietor is determined to do everything in his power to merit public encouragement.

The terms are for the present fixed at four shillings for the best cabin, and three shillings for the second, but beyond these rates nothing is to be allowed to servants or any other person employed about the vessel.

The subscriber continues his establishment at HELENSBURGH BATHS, the same as for years past, and a vessel will be in readiness to convey passengers to the *Comet* from Greenock to Helensburgh

HENRY BELL

HELENSBURGH BATHS, 5th August 1812

In 1818 the *Comet* was lengthened to 60 feet and fitted with a more powerful engine built by John Robertson of Glasgow, which took her speed up to 6 m.p.h. This enabled her to travel further afield, with a service to Oban and also to Fort William via the Crinan Canal, the first steamer to complete the canal journey. In 1820, following an ill-advised attempt at making the journey from Oban in bad weather, she was wrecked en route but everyone on board escaped injury. In 1821 she was replaced by another steamer, a vessel of the same name, which worked around the south west coast of Scotland until 1825 when she collided with another steamer off Gourock and over sixty or more of those on board perished. It wasn't the end for the new *Comet* though; she was raised, re-rigged as a schooner, re-named *Anne* and carried on with her coastal trade for many years.

> A replica of the *Comet*, built by Clyde shipyard apprentices, is on display at Port Glasgow.

But the Comet did not have a free hand on the Clyde. She was followed almost immediately by other steamers. In 1813, the *Elizabeth* took station on the Clyde, a much bigger and better vessel than the *Comet*. She was 51 feet by 12 feet and carried up to 100 passengers daily on the 27 mile journey between Glasgow and Greenock in some comfort.

In the years after the *Elizabeth* was built, almost year on year, new Clyde built steamers appeared, initially as Clyde passenger steamers and then as longer distance passenger or freight steamers. Glasgow and the rapidly expanding Clyde shipbuilders started to set the pace in the construction of steamers, not just in Britain but worldwide.

In 1815, there were 10 steamers operating on the Clyde and they were also appearing further south with a Leeds-built steamer operating between Norwich and Yarmouth on the River Yare in 1813 and in 1814 a steamer set off from Hull for Gainsborough and is said to have reached the unprecedented speed of fourteen miles per hour. In 1814 a 40 ton steamer was introduced on to the Thames via the canal at Limehouse and was capable of carrying over 200 persons. More steamers soon followed.

In May 1815, a Clyde-built steamer made her way to Liverpool, the first steamer on the Mersey, after calling at the Isle of Man on the way, another first.

In 1816 the many ferry routes across the River Mersey were supplemented by the steamer *Etna* which crossed to Tranmere. Even by the standards of the early steamers, this vessel looked strange. She consisted of two separate 63 feet long hulls joined together by beams with a paddle wheel in the centre covered by a 28 feet wide deck. Today a catamaran may be considered fairly normal but this vessel must have looked peculiar at the time. Better designed steamers soon followed on the ferry crossings.

In 1818, the *Rob Roy,* 90 tons, made the first steam voyage across the Irish Sea from Glasgow to Belfast and she would be the first steamer in Europe or North America to provide a regular service, carrying mails, across the sea although only for a short passage. This was the first sea-going vessel from the yard of William Denny. The engineer on board was David Tod who had learned about steam navigation in the yard of David Napier. Tod later became a partner in Clyde shipbuilders, Tod and Macgregor, who built the first vessels for the highly successful Inman Line which had been set up by Liverpool-based William Inman. Inman was the son of Charles Inman who, having retired from the haulage firm of Pickfords, where he was a partner, moved to Liverpool. Tod is said to have been instrumental in persuading Inman that the new vessels should be constructed with iron hulls and screw propellers which, in 1850, was certainly a very progressive, and risky, step for a new company.

In 1826, the first of the big ships arrived, the 160 foot long, 26 feet beam *United Kingdom* with 200 h.p. engines. Built by Robert Steele of Greenock, she would run between London and Leith. The writer Henry Fry believes the *Royal William*, which would be laid down in Quebec in 1830 and which would subsequently find fame on the Atlantic, is based on the *United Kingdom.*

While the engineers were working hard on their steamboats in Britain and the United States, they would have been amazed to learn what was happening many miles away, in Canada. It is claimed that, as far back, as 1809, a passenger carrying steamboat was operating between Quebec and Montreal, a full three years ahead of such an event in Britain. This ship was the *Accommodation,* an 85 feet long vessel which was doubtless copied from Fulton's *Clermont* which had itself been based on the *Charlotte Dundas.* The ship was powered by a Boulton and Watt six h.p. engine and, driven by open-spoked paddles, is reported to have travelled at a creditable 5 m.p.h.

It was now clear to everyone that steam boats were a practical proposition and they were starting to appear in many parts of Britain, carrying passengers on rivers and canals and soon becoming popular taking families on a day trip to a coastal resort. But it didn't stop there. Steam boat fever soon resulted in steamers that could cross the Irish Sea, the Straits of Dover and even the North Sea. These vessels however were fairly rudimentary steamboats relying on the support of sails. In the U.S. things developed in a similar way with the eastern seaboard towns being linked by steamers and the rear paddle steamers appearing on the wide rivers.

But this was just the beginning and thoughts increasingly turned to the Atlantic Ocean. Could a steamboat cross three thousand miles of open sea? Well, in the opinion of most people, the answer was most definitely "no". A steam vessel covering such a great distance would have to carry so much fuel that it would be impossible. Fortunately, at the time, many people did not seem to understand the meaning of the word.

In 1818 the Savannah Steam Ship Company was formed to show that it was time for steam to conquer the Atlantic. The company acquired a 110 feet long sailing vessel under construction by Crockett and Pickett in New York which had been originally designed to run as a sailing packet from New York to Havre. She was fitted with iron paddle wheels and a single auxiliary steam engine of 90 h.p., which was quite big at 40 in. diameter and a stroke of 5 feet. It operated at a pressure of 10 lbs. which was high pressure for the time. On 22nd May 1819 she set out to cross the Atlantic from Savannah, Georgia to St. Petersburg via Liverpool. She carried no passengers and her cargo hold was filled with coal and firewood. Twenty nine days later she reached the coast of Ireland and her captain decided to get up some steam using the last of the ship's fuel stocks. This caused some distress to those on shore who thought the vessel was on fire and a cutter was sent out to help. After refuelling in Ireland, the *Savannah* set sail for Liverpool where she was received with great acclaim after completing what was considered an heroic journey and her captain, Moses Roger, was regarded as a steamship pioneer, some considering him to be on a par with Columbus. As soon as news of her safe arrival reached New York there was jubilation – steam had conquered the Atlantic. A new company was formed, the Ocean Steam Ship Company, and plans were announced to build a fleet of ocean steamers. But when the full facts of the *Savannah's* voyage came through, a different view was taken and the company quietly folded. The Savannah was in fact a full rigged sailing ship and had only used her steam engine for 85 hours, at the beginning and end of her journey. Most of the time her paddle wheels had been stored on the ship's deck, it only taking thirty minutes or so to take them on board. Her engine, although well made, was only really designed to be used when the ship encountered calm conditions to keep her moving and not for extensive use. She could only carry 80 tons of coal and some wood so was never able to steam the entire distance. On top of that she had taken longer to reach Liverpool than the sailing ships of the Black Ball line. Perhaps not much of an advantage really. At St. Petersburg her engine and boiler were removed and she returned to New York under sail alone where she was probably soon forgotten. In fairness, though, she should be remembered as a trailblazer. She had steamed, to some extent, into open water and the captain and crew would have known how risky the crossing could be. Many people were convinced it would be a suicide mission with the engine being certain to explode on the way. So, not the first to steam across the Atlantic but the first to enter the unknown and make a brave, if limited, attempt.

In 1821 the *Rising Star,* commissioned by Thomas Cochrane, Earl of Dundonald, for the Chilean Navy was one of the first naval steamers and was converted from an earlier ship at Rotherhithe by Brents. The 428 ton vessel had engines fitted by Maudslay, Son and Field and, unusually, had internal retractable paddle wheels. This seemed like a good idea because the main factor that held back development of paddle steamers for naval use was their exposure to damage and fitting them internally gave a degree of protection from damage. But the design wasn't that successful and the *Rising Star* was much more a sailing ship than a steamer. Her voyage from Gravesend to Chile in 1822 is recorded as the first east to west crossing of the Atlantic by a steamer but the reality is that she could only have steamed a very small distance not being able to carry anything like enough fuel to steam all the way.

As the *Savannah* had shown, there was still a little way to go in the development of steam navigation across the oceans. However in Britain there was concern about both the advance of steam, and the Americans getting a lead ahead. This quotation from Ackerman's Depository illustrated the fear of many people:

O! That I should live to see the day when a British line-of-battle was led by the nose by a floating tea-kettle....The Americans have beat us on our own element. Men-of-war have made way for steam vessels. With a chimney for a nest and a column of smoke for a pedant. Naval-officers command them with a thermometer for a speaking trumpet; the Captain stands over the boiler and directs the paddles. The glory of the British navy evaporates in steam, or is it condensed in a bucket, and the safety of a gallant crew lies in a valve.

At around the same time, the French were still gloating at Britain's poor performance in the War of 1812 and, when they heard about the voyage of the *Savannah*, some came to the conclusion that Britain was about to go downhill and that the United States would take over as the front runner.

Despite what was being said though, interest in transatlantic steam navigation remained very limited, especially in the United States where it would not be until 1845 that another American steamer, the *Massachusetts,* would make the crossing.

In 1825 the French naval steamer, *Caroline,* crossed the Atlantic to French Guiana while two years later the Dutch paddler *Curacao,* a sizeable steamer of 428 tones, would cross to the Dutch West Indies from Rotterdam, a journey taking twenty eight days. Built in Dover, the *Curacao* was sold to the Dutch Government for use as a man-of-war but was employed on the mail service to the Dutch West Indies and became the first steamer to make regular crossings of the Atlantic which she did until 1830.

Despite Britain's position as a major maritime nation, it would be another five years after the crossing by the French naval steamer *Caroline* before a Royal Navy steamer would cross the Atlantic. This was the Royal Navy's *Rhadamanthus* which crossed from Plymouth to Barbados in 1832 but, even then, naval interest remained limited. The Royal Navy had much the same view of steam paddlers as it would have about iron clad ships – they were unproven, susceptible to damage and it didn't really like them. The main problem for the steamers, which were virtually all paddle driven at the time, was, of course, that just one direct hit on one of the paddle wheels and the vessel was helpless. And when ironclad vessels appeared the Navy feared damage to the iron hull during battle which couldn't be repaired. For fighting ships, the Royal Navy thought that it would be best to stay with sailing men o'war at least for the time being. However the Admiralty took a different view with regard to steam tugs with the first one the *Comet*, not the vessel earlier mentioned, being built in 1819. Steam paddle tugs would be built to tow British naval sailing ships for many years and the scene is immortalised in Turner's masterpiece "The Fighting Temeraire".

In less than ten years, great progress had been made in steaming across the Atlantic. Admittedly there were only a handful of ships that could do it and even then could only steam a small part of the way. But this was advanced technology for the time. The shipbuilders and ships' crews were really stretching the boundaries in what could be done and, more importantly, what could be done safely. Some people thought it would only be a matter of time before steam travel across the Atlantic was a practical proposition and that sailing ships would eventually be confined to history. There were many doom mongers, however, who did all they could to dampen enthusiasm. As far as they were concerned it would be impossible for a vessel to steam across the Atlantic regularly. Quite simply, they would not be able to carry enough coal - end of story. But they were wrong - this story still had quite a way to go.

Some people may think that steam power is something from the past and that it has been replaced by more modern methods. They couldn't be more wrong. Each time we switch on a light or a computer or the television or ride on electric train or a tram, the chances are that we will be using electricity that has, at least in a major part, been generated by steam. The power of steam is just as important today as it was in the 19th century, if not more so.

Meanwhile, back in Nova Scotia......

● ● ●

Chapter 6

Developments in Nova Scotia

By 1820, the worst of the post war depression was over and the fortunes of Halifax and Nova Scotia were beginning to improve, albeit slowly. Britain had made Bermuda its North American naval headquarters and Halifax became a subsidiary naval base providing extra income for the town.

Unfortunately things were not going well for William Duffus, Sam's father-in-law, who was not able to make it through the slump and went bankrupt. Sam wanted to help but this was declined by Mrs Duffus who, instead, decided to turn her big house into a lodging house to raise funds. Eventually Mrs Duffus relented and accepted an allowance from Sam who always remembered his friends and extended family.

Meanwhile his immediate family was getting bigger at a regular rate. Edward had been born in 1815 and by 1821 four girls had been added. Later there would be three more girls and another boy, a big family perhaps but not at all unusual at that time, many families were even bigger.

Mrs Duffus became a great help to Sam's wife, Susan, when he was on one of his many trips, the role of the grandmother as important then, as it is today.

In 1820 Abraham Cunard retired to the Murphy farm in Rawdon where he died in 1823, two years after he lost his wife, Margaret. This left Sam as the family head as well as being the prime mover of an increasingly big business empire. He reorganised the family firm, changing the name to S. Cunard & Co., and Edward and Joseph became partners with other family members holding junior positions. The Cunard empire was now a force to be reckoned with and operated thirty ships all carrying the Cunard flag, a blue pennant with a white cross in the centre. They carried fish, timber, rum, hides, sugar and coffee and sailed to the United States, the West Indies and South America with big square riggers crossing the Atlantic to Britain. Passengers were also carried on the Boston and Bermuda trips.

Samuel Cunard was now an increasingly wealthy man with interests in many businesses. He had achieved great respect in the local community, just like his ancestor, Thomas Cunard, and it was all down to his hard work and business acumen, plus of course some guidance and encouragement that his father had bestowed upon him.

Sam followed the developing timber market with great interest. The rapidly growing economy in Britain, together with its expanding shipbuilding industry, produced an insatiable need for timber. Britain had a limited stock of timber whilst North America had vast quantities. Sam established three agents in Britain, in London, Liverpool and Glasgow, and visited them periodically, sailing on one of his traders. Most of the timber (and fish) exported on Cunard vessels came from the area around the River Miramichi.

In Britain, building ships in oak was considered best but it was expensive and supplies were limited. The Glasgow firm, Pollok, Gilmour & Co. set up a branch at Douglastown, on the banks of the Miramichi, to handle export of tamarack, a buoyant softwood, that could be used to build ships. They sent two employees, Alexander Rankin and James Gilmour, over to run the operation. Ever watchful of business opportunities, Sam acquired timber rights in the area and sent Joseph and Henry to run the business and soon had gangs of lumberjacks felling trees and raftsmen taking the timber downriver. In 1825 a major fire destroyed seven thousand square miles of forest, destroying settlements and killing around 500 people. The fire moved down from the north but when it reached the wide Miramichi it was stopped in its tracks and a vast area of forest was left untouched. Rankin and Gilmour lost their homes and their business premises while the Cunard brother's premises, located on the south side of the river, were left untouched. Once again, an example of the Cunard lucky streak. But Rankin and Gilmour were strong characters and they soon got busy rebuilding their lives. Within a year they were back in business, stronger than ever, and ready to compete again with the Cunard brothers.

While Joseph and Henry were running the timber operation, Sam turned his attention to a new business opportunity he had spotted – tea. Britain's colonies were not allowed to trade directly with China and trade had been through the East India Company. Even when the company's monopoly had been abolished, it still effectively controlled the China trade for some time. Word reached Halifax that overseas agencies were to be established and, in 1824, Sam set off for London to meet up with representatives of the East India Company, determined to acquire the distributorship for North America.

```
Memo to prospective entrepreneurs: Be on
the lookout for new business opportunities
and make sure you get in there first.  Sam
Cunard was not the only one who wanted the
tea contract.  Another Halifax businessman,
Enos Collins, also wanted it but, while he
was thinking about what to do to gain the
distributorship, Sam was already on the
boat to England. Typical Samuel Cunard,
just do it.
```

It took five months for a decision to be made but in the end Sam was successful. During this time he had to kick his heels in London but he took the opportunity to touch base with people he knew in the Government and with Lombard Street bankers. He knew the value of contacts and communication and took every opportunity to touch base with people who could be useful in the future.

A year later the first shipment of tea arrived from China. During this time Sam, as usual, was busy investing in other businesses. With other investors he set up the colony's first bank which proved to very profitable. The same group then invested in a small iron mine and set up a blast furnace making household items but this venture was not a great success.

Around 1825, steamboat fever again hit America following rumours of a planned service from Britain to New York via Ireland and Halifax. This possibility certainly concentrated the minds of a number of people in Halifax. The town was the nearest seaport to Europe on the North American eastern seaboard and this was an opportunity to transform its fortunes. What could hold the town back though was the problem of linking with Quebec with sailing vessels currently taking a month to complete what was often a very unpleasant journey. A steamer could do it in a week. Sam, as usual, was ready to step in. He formed the Quebec and Halifax Steam Navigation Company with himself, Joe and Edward as the main shareholders and the intention to set up a steam service between the two towns. This would fully integrate Halifax and Quebec into any new Atlantic steamboat service.

Then the idea of an Atlantic steam service suddenly faded, with the doom mongers once again pointing it that it would be impossible for a steamer to carry enough coal for the journey. The Quebec and Halifax Steam Navigation Company scrapped its plans and went into hibernation much to the disgust of the local newspapers. In 1826 *The Novascotian* declared "*It does seem a stain upon our enterprise that upon the harbors and estuaries of this province we have yet received no advantage from the most gigantic improvement of modern times – navigation by steam"*

A Halifax newspaperman, Joseph Howe, was a great champion of steam. He had visited Britain and had been more than impressed by the use of steam vessels. He had noted that sailing vessels had great trouble getting out of the River Mersey when the winds were blowing upriver but steamers were on hand to help. He recorded that *"an American packet which wishes to sail from Liverpool on a certain day, in place of waiting for a fair wind, employs a steam boat to tow her round the Rock – a service which it performed for £5, and hence the admirable regularity with which these vessels arrive and depart. There are upwards of 70 steamboats on the Clyde and 50 on the Mersey."* He described the latest coaster, the *United Kingdom*, launched at Greenock as a *"stupendous vessel"*. This paddle steamer was 175 feet long and had two 100 horsepower engines built by Robert Napier who was rapidly turning into Britain's marine steam engine's expert. The vessel had a spacious sleeping cabin and a ladies' cabin with, according to Howe, *"every convenience that luxury could invent"*.

This illustrates the progress that was being made in Britain in developing steam navigation.

But things were very different in Nova Scotia where the colony had to try and cope with the geography of the area. Ships carrying goods to the towns at the head of the Bay of Fundy had to travel five hundred miles around the rocky coast to reach an area that was fifty miles away by land. There were a number of small lakes between Halifax and the headwaters of the Shubenacadie River and all that needed to be done was to construct a number of canal links to join up these lakes. This would enable one small steamer to tow four schooners up the canal in a day rather than spending a week going around the coast. The Shubenacadie Canal Company was formed to undertake the project and Sam was appointed vice-president.

In 1826 the East Indiaman *Countess of Harcourt* berthed at Cunard's Wharf with the first consignment of tea. It was as if the whole of Halifax was there to greet her. The 6,715 chests of tea she brought would be enough to supply the whole of North America for a year. We may take tea for granted now but, at that time, having tea available, and at reasonable prices, was something very special and no doubt Samuel Cunard was well praised for getting it to Nova Scotia. Traders were soon taking supplies to Bermuda, the West Indies and Canada helping the Cunard tea agency to remain very successful for many years – yet another profit centre for Sam.

Samuel Cunard was now so wealthy with a fleet of over forty vessels that he probably had more money than he would ever need. His business ventures were not always successful but most were and the failures were soon pushed into the background. What drove him on to work and work? It was probably the fact that he enjoyed just being a businessman. He was one of those lucky people who could wake up on a Monday morning and think "Great! Time for work! Which business should I concentrate on today? What new opportunities are there? Should I arrange a trip to England or New York or perhaps Bermuda?" How many of us would like to be able to do that? And he could do all that in the knowledge that it was all down to his own honest efforts. He hadn't stolen. He hadn't cheated. He had just been a wily businessman, watching for opportunities and always trying to get in there first with the best deal. Admittedly not everything had gone according to plan and some people lost out which they held Sam responsible for but this was a time of major business opportunities where fortunes were made and, sometimes, lost.

Around this time, a company, The General Mining Association (G.M.A.) was formed to handle development of the vast Nova Scotia coal fields. The company had enough capital to finance purchase and use of the latest steam engines to pump water out of the mines, something that was not currently available in Nova Scotia. In 1827 Sam set out for England and came back with a host of steam pumping equipment which was soon put to work in the mines. This was thought to be the first time that steam engines had been used on Nova Scotian soil. Sam was the distributor for G.M.A. and this turned out to be another very profitable enterprise.

Sam was often away from home dealing with his businesses and sometimes was away for months at a time when on his long sea trips. But he tried not to neglect his civic duties. He was a committee member of the Poor Society, the Public Library and the Mechanic's Institute besides being a fire warden. While he was away, Susan had her children and a large circle of friends and family to occupy her, as well as her own civic duties.

Like anyone else, Sam sometimes had his family tragedies to deal with, He lost his second, daughter, Susie, and then, within two years, he lost both his mother and father. But sadly there was more to come. In 1828, Susan gave birth to their ninth child, Elizabeth, but the elation felt at the new addition to the family soon turned to tragedy. Just ten days after the birth, Susan died. The large Cunard and Duffus families rallied round to help raise the children while Sam faced up to life and business without the help and support of his wife of 13 years.

● ● ●

Chapter 7

Life without Susan

Following the death of Susan, Sam threw himself into his many business enterprises, probably with even greater intensity than before. But, perhaps regretting the time he had spent away from Susan, he gave up travelling for many months to spend more time with his children and to oversee their religious upbringing. The following summer, 1830, he began making short voyages to local ports and usually took the older girls and Ned with him.

Within two years, Sam had decided that it was time to move on. He started to travel again, often on long journeys, confident that the children's grandmother, Mrs Duffus, would look after them although quite often he took some or even all of the children with him. He didn't neglect his civic duties though. In 1830 he became a member of the crown-appointed council which worked with the Nova Scotia elected assembly and had some powers over it.

Joseph Howe, who had since purchased the *Novascotian* newspaper, had a lot of issues with the activities of the council and wrote editorials lampooning it. He saw it as jobs for the boys and a way of getting some of the financial perks that went with it. Howe was a cultured and gifted man but he could be blunt and outspoken. He was very different to Samuel Cunard in many ways but, despite that, the two men became good friends. They were both supportive of British influence and were dedicated to Nova Scotia and wanted the colony to be the most important in British North America. It may have been an unlikely alliance but the seeds were being set for the greatest revolution in transatlantic travel so far.

For twenty years, Sam headed the Lighthouse Commission of Nova Scotia. It was an honour to hold this position but it was a very important and onerous job. The rocky coast of Nova Scotia was treacherous for ships. When Sam first took up the post, there were only half a dozen beacons along the shore. Under Sam's direction, new lighthouses were built at the rate of about one a year and he introduced the custom of painting each in a different way to serve as markers.

One of the most important beacons was erected, in 1831, at Seal Island, sixteen miles off the southwest coast of Nova Scotia. This small island was often obscured by fog and was really treacherous. Each year dozens of small schooners were lost on the surrounding rocks. The beacon reduced the risk but the danger still remained.

Meanwhile, Joseph Howe had become increasingly concerned about Nova Scotia being left behind in the development of steam navigation. He had noted that steam vessels were in operation on rivers and coastal waters in Britain, America and Canada while in Nova Scotia there was only one steamer in operation, between Halifax and Dartmouth. He really did not want Halifax and Nova Scotia to be left behind and was probably, at that time, a greater exponent of steam navigation than the legendary Samuel Cunard. He really wanted Nova Scotia to join the steam navigation revolution and was about to get his wish.

That year, 1831, the Quebec and Halifax Steam Navigation Company, headed by the Cunard brothers and formed in 1825 but lying dormant since, finally decided to enter the world of steam navigation. This decision would have a major impact on the future of ocean shipping. Mail for Quebec, which arrived on the sailing packets from Falmouth, was transferred to a coastal sailing vessel which could take a month to get around the rocky and inhospitable coast. A steamer could do the journey much more quickly. The company constructed the *Royal William*, a 363 ton paddle steamer, 160 feet long and 29 feet beam between the paddles. She had two eighty horse-power engines and was barque-rigged as were all the early steamers, except the Mississippi rear-wheelers. A spacious vessel, she could carry twenty cabin passengers and seventy in steerage together with a lot of freight. She was built by James Goudie, a Scottish immigrant, who had learned about shipbuilding in Greenock, and was launched at Three Rivers near Quebec on 27th April 1831. The launch was a really big event, military bands were playing and other vessels in the harbour were decked out with bunting. The vessel was christened by Lady Aylmer, the governor's wife, who named her after the reigning monarch. Despite all the celebrations, no one knew at the time what a famous vessel the *Royal William* would turn out to be.

The ship was then towed to Montreal to have her 200 h.p. British-built engines fitted and then underwent very satisfactory sea trials. She then steamed back to Quebec ready for her first big test - a run from Quebec to Halifax. On 24th August 1831, she set off reaching Halifax, after stopovers at Miramichi and Pictou, six and a half days later. Her cabins and holds were filled to capacity. There was a big celebration in Halifax when she docked at Cunard's Wharf and the sight of her made a big impression on Sam who spent a long time questioning those on board about technical details of the craft and its performance.

Earlier that year, Sam had visited England and had made his first journey on a train on the newly opened Manchester to Liverpool railway. This made a big impression on him and the performance of the *Royal William* convinced him that *"steamers, properly built and manned, might start and arrive at their destinations with the same punctuality of railway trains on land".*

This was a momentous year for Samuel Cunard. He had seen, at first hand, what a paddle steamer could do and he had understood how steam navigation could enable ships to serve a timetable without having to rely too much on the wind. However he would probably have just been thinking about local steam journeys in North America, steaming across the Atlantic was something else altogether.

Sam decided to order two steamers – the *Pocahontas* and the *Cape Breton* - for his own fleet to support a weekly mail contract between Pictou and Charlottetown on Prince Edward Island. Both vessels were built in England and were sailed over to Nova Scotia. The *Pocahontas* began service in 1832 and, in the following year, was leased to G.M.A. while the larger *Cape Breton* took over.

Meanwhile the *Royal William* continued her regular runs to Quebec until December 1831 when ice closed the seaway and the vessel was trapped there during the winter. The following spring a cholera epidemic stopped sailings until June but, when the ship finally sailed, she still carried the disease and was put in quarantine. In spring 1833 the vessel was ready for use again but by then the lost income had bankrupted the company. The *Royal William* was put up for sale and she was bought by some of the original company owners who paid just £5,000 for a vessel that not too long before had cost £16,000 to build. Nevertheless they eventually came to the conclusion that they could not make any money with her in Nova Scotia and decided to steam her across the Atlantic where they thought they could get a better price.

On 4th August 1833 the *Royal William* set out for her long trip under the command of Captain John McDougall, a native of Oban. She carried thirty six crew members, seven passengers, who had paid £20 each, 330 tons of coal and - a box of stuffed birds. After a partly stormy but otherwise uneventful voyage, she arrived safely on the Isle of Wight. Her voyage took either seventeen days, nineteen days, twenty five days or even forty days, depending on which early writer you believe. Such is the problem of interpreting historical "facts". The journey probably took twenty days.

This journey is accepted as the first (almost) real west to east steam North Atlantic crossing. It wasn't constant steaming, however, as the engines had to be shut down every fourth day to allow salt to be cleared from the boiler and during this time she continued just under sail. Encrustation of the boilers of marine engines would be a major problem for sea going paddlers and even paddlers operating on inland waters were badly affected by impurities such as mud and lime. Despite this problem, the ship's performance caused a bit of a stir in the shipping industry but the achievement was tempered a little by the arrival of an American sailing packet in Liverpool which had made the journey in a slightly shorter time, although helped by following winds. The performance of the *Royal William* was impressive but interest soon started to wane and things went a bit quiet on the Atlantic steam navigation front for the next few years. The vessel was sold for £10,000 to Portugal and then to Spain for use as a warship and so turned out to be a nice little earner for her Canadian owners, who had only spent £5,000 for her. As well as making the first real steam crossing of the North Atlantic, the *Royal William*, when enlisted in the Spanish navy as the *Ysabel Secunda,* achieved another historical first, she is said to have been the first steam driven vessel to fire a gun in anger.

The Canadian Parliament was very proud of the Royal William's achievement as a transatlantic steam pioneer, and rightly so, and a brass tablet was commissioned to record her feat.

IN HONOUR OF THE MEN
by whose enterprise, courage, and skill
THE
ROYAL WILLIAM
The first Vessel to Cross the Atlantic by Steam Power was wholly constructed in Canada and navigated to England in 1833. The Pioneer of Those Mighty Fleets of Ocean Steamers by which Passengers and Merchandise of all Nations are now conveyed on every sea throughout the World.
ORDERED BY THE PARLIAMENT OF CANADA. JUNE 13 15 1894

16 Facsimile of the Memorial Brass

Meanwhile Sam continued running his business empire. The Boston and Bermuda mail runs were increasingly profitable but the abolition of slavery had made the cost of running the plantations very high and trade in sugar was starting to tail off. Tea was now the big thing and gave a real lift to the Cunard coffers as did the performance of the G.M.A. coal distributorship. In fact output from the Albion Mine was so high that it was decided to build a railroad for steam locomotives to take the coal from the pithead to the docks at Pictou, six miles away. Meanwhile Sam's brother, Joe, became more and more involved in the family business and developed some enterprises on his own account. Some people thought that Joe was taking over from Sam as the Cunard driving force, but the big event was yet to come.

● ● ●

Chapter 8

Race to be first

It is now 1836 and marine traffic on the Atlantic is much the same as it has been for years with many sailing packets plying their trade and their captains hoping that each day would bring a favourable wind. A few small paddle steamers have made the journey across the Atlantic but these were just one-off voyages and they relied on their sails for at least part of the way. But on the waterways and around the coasts of Britain and North America things were very different with new steamers appearing almost every week. Boyman estimated that in 1836 there were 800 steamers in use in the United States, 811 in Britain and the Empire but just 211 in the rest of the world combined. Many people thought that the practicalities and potential of steam navigation had now been proved and, in Britain, some thought it was now time for someone to set up a regular steam service to the United States using some specially designed vessels.

Three British shipping companies took up the challenge - the Great Western Steamship Company would build the *Great Western* in Bristol, the British and American Steamship Company would build the *British Queen* on the Thames and the Transatlantic Steamship Company would build the *Liverpool* on the Mersey.

Each of the companies was determined to be the first to send a steamer to New York despite grave warnings from people such as the eminent scientific writer, Dr. Dionysius Lardner, who firmly believed that it was impossible since a vessel could not carry enough coal for a journey east to west against the prevailing winds. Not only that, thought Dr. Lardner, the firemen would be so exhausted that they would die at their posts. As was pretty normal at the time, the ship owners and engineers ignored such warnings and carried on regardless.

The paddle steamer *Great Western* was the product of the ingenious, and sometimes successful, engineer Isambard Kingdom Brunel. Although heavily involved in his railway career, he still devoted some time to ships, an interest which he no doubt inherited from his father, Marc Brunel, who helped in the development of some early steam engines, including devising an improved version of the governor and a surface condenser to obviate the need for using sea or river water in the boilers (a practice which required the boiler to be regularly put out of action to be cleaned).

Unlike his father, however, Isambard thought that steamships were not just something for rivers and canals and that large steamers could be built for use on the oceans. The view of the "experts" at the time was that this was not possible; in simple terms, if the size of the hull was doubled, then twice the power of the engines would be needed which would mean that the vessel would have to carry twice as much coal. Eventually the ship would have to carry so much coal that there would not be any room for passengers or cargo! Brunel realised that the key factor was that the resistance it encounters as it drives through the water does not increase at the same rate as the size of the vessel and building big paddle steamers was not a problem.

In 1835, at a meeting of the Great Western Railway, the proposed railway line between London and Bristol was discussed and Brunel suggested making it longer by linking it with a steamboat service to New York.

What a silly idea everyone thought, except for Thomas Guppy who took the idea on board and set up the Great Western Steamship Company to provide the Atlantic link. Funds were organised and, in 1836, the yard of William Patterson in Bristol was contracted to build this revolutionary new vessel which would be named, not surprisingly, the *Great Western*. At 235 feet long and 1,340 tons gross, she would be the biggest steamer so far and her fittings, for the first class only passengers, would be luxurious for the day. She would be built of traditional oak construction but would be immensely strong with closely trussed iron bracing. Her two side lever engines had two cylinders of 74 in. diameter with a stroke of seven feet producing a total of 750 h.p. They were built by Maudslay, Son and Field of London. This firm was originally founded by Henry Maudslay who was a brilliant designer and manufacturer of machine tools and his successful company progressed further when he was joined by his sons and Joshua Field, an Admiralty design engineer. Gradually, the design and manufacture of marine steam engines became a major part of the business and the first steam vessel commissioned for the Royal Navy was powered by one of their engines. Henry Maudslay is said to have trained many key British engineers including Joseph Whitworth, developer of the famous Whitworth Thread. The contribution Henry Maudslay made to Britain's industrial revolution is perhaps not always fully appreciated today. In his early years, he was employed by Joseph Bramah and assisted him in the development of the hydraulic press and later, on his own account, he designed and manufactured metal lathes and milling machines which allowed others to play a great part in the Industrial Revolution. Although Henry Maudslay is little known today, it is a fact that some industrial equipment, crucial to Britain's industrial development during the 19th century, might never have seen the light of day without Maudslay's design and manufacturing skills.

But to get to this stage in transatlantic steam travel, a lot of faith had needed to be shown by Brunel and his supporters because there were still many who poured cold water on the idea, especially the infamous Dr. Dionysius Lardner. Dr. Lardner was a Dublin-born academic who knew, or thought he knew, about everything including all aspects of mathematics, mechanics, steam engines and even bees. Although much lampooned by contemporary and even more recent writers, he was undoubtedly a very clever man but, unlike the practical engineers of his day, he was a theorist and, in his many technical works, he liked to produce lists of figures to prove his point and his point was often that something was impossible. Perhaps he suffered from the affliction that affects some scientists even today whereby they start with their own or another's assumption that something is true, or is believed to be true, then begin research or the preparation of data which just happens to prove that something is true. Research data, in fact or in timing, that does not prove the point may be ignored. Perhaps some might say that this "reverse research" happens today in the field of research into man-made climate change and some areas of medical research, such as the health benefits of red wine - but that's another story.

In December 1835 Dr. Lardner had continued his policy of pouring scorn on the idea of transatlantic steam navigation at a meeting of the Royal Institution in Liverpool at which he stated *"As to the project however, which has been announced in the newspapers of making the voyage directly from New York to Liverpool, they might as well talk of making a voyage from New York or Liverpool to the moon".* Soon afterwards he denied making any reference to the moon but the reporters of the Liverpool Albion had recorded his comments in great detail and the Doctor was once again left with egg on his face.

While the *Great Western* was being constructed, Dr. Lardner arrived in Bristol to give a lecture to the British Association on the subject of transatlantic steam navigation during which he, once again, produced figures to show the impossibility of it. Brunel was in the audience and Dr. Lardner's comments were like a red flag to a bull. Brunel's railway project had been put in jeopardy in the past by Dr. Lardner's uninformed comments about the proposed Box Tunnel and his comments on this occasion so incensed Brunel that the good doctor came close to getting a punch on the nose!

Nevertheless, and despite Dr. Lardner's best efforts, the *Great Western's* hull was completed and, in July 1837, she was floated out of Patterson's dock and 300 dignitaries were invited on board to a luncheon in her fine saloon.

On 17th August, she set out for London to have her engines fitted and for some general fitting out. Crowds flocked the banks of the Thames at Blackwall to admire *'her magnificent proportions and stupendous machinery.'* They were seeing the biggest ship ever built so they would certainly have been impressed.

However, some people were not so impressed with the *Great Western.* The city fathers in London, as the capital city, and Liverpool, a city expanding at a phenomenal rate, were not at all happy. They were very concerned that this great ship could mean that Bristol would become once again a major port and would take trade away from their two cities. But two companies, the British and American Steamship Company of London, who laid down the *British Queen* and the Transatlantic Steamship Company of Liverpool who purchased the not yet completed steamer *Liverpool,* had plans to put a stop to Bristol's ambitions.

In February 1838, Samuel Cunard arrived in England on one of his frequent trips. At this time the small *Liverpool* and the large 1,320 ton luxury *Great Western* had already been launched and Sam travelled to see them.

While Dr. Lardner was having trouble "making friends and influencing people" in Bristol, the *British Queen* was still progressing slowly on the stocks of Curling and Young on the Thames and would clearly not be ready in time to join the race to cross the Atlantic, in fact she was likely to be twelve months or more behind.

The vessel may have been out of the race but her owners were not going to give up on their "one chance to make a first impression". They got together and came up with a plan; they would charter another vessel to make the trip and the vessel they came up with was the *Sirius*, a paddle steamer which had only been designed to run between London and Cork and, at 703 tons and 178 long by 25 feet beam, was much smaller than the *British Queen* although still a fairly big steamer for her day. She was one of the first to be fitted with a condenser instead of using salt water in her boilers which helped overcome the problem of salt encrustation in her boilers. She was built by Menzies of Leith and was fitted with Wingate side-lever engines with 60 inch diameter cylinders and a stroke of 6 feet. Her paddle wheels were 24 feet in diameter. Although quite a big vessel for a coastal steamer, she wasn't that big for a passenger carrying journey across the Atlantic and planning to send her at short notice was quite adventurous. It was also potentially hazardous but the owners might not have seen it that way as they were not planning to be on board. On 4th April she set out on her transatlantic voyage from Cork, where she had taken on 450 tons of coal, after first loading in London. She carried forty passengers.

In March the *Great Western* was completed and on the 31st she set sail for Bristol to start her maiden voyage. But what should have been a routine voyage nearly turned to tragedy. After about two hours sailing there was a fire in the engine room when some felt lagging the boiler got too hot and burst into flames and this spread to some deck boards. This fire almost cost Brunel his life. Captain Claxton had gone down into the engine room with Brunel following at a later stage. When Brunel was descending the stairway, a rung gave way and Brunel dropped 18 feet into a dark expense of water which had accumulated there from the fire hoses. Brunel was quite badly injured and could well have drowned if Caxton hadn't been on hand to rescue him. Brunel was taken off the *Great Western* to Canvey Island where he spent three weeks recovering from his injuries.

Damage to the *Great Western* was quickly repaired and she continued her journey to Bristol. Unfortunately the press soon got hold of the story and gave the impression that the fire had been much more serious than it actually was. This caused 50 of those who had booked a passage to cancel and, when the *Great Western* set out from Bristol for New York on 8th April, she had just seven passengers. The *Sirius* had set out four days earlier and that was from Cork which was a whole day's sailing nearer New York. If those on board the *Great Western* had known the position of the *Sirius*, they would probably have thought that the outcome of the race was a foregone conclusion; and so it turned out to be.

17 The Paddle Steamer Sirius
(Unknown/G. Atkinson)

On 23rd April, she *Sirius* steamed along the Hudson River to a tumultuous welcome from crowds on the river banks and aboard a host of small vessels. She had taken 18 days 14 hours to make the journey at an average speed of 8 knots and had steamed all the way. It had been a close run thing though with the *Sirius* having to power against strong headwinds for most of the journey and when she arrived in New York, there were only 15 tons of coal left in her bunkers. In fact, the conditions had been so bad that the crew came close to mutiny when they confronted the captain and demanded that the little ship turns back; the passengers were none too pleased either. The Captain, Lieutenant Roberts, R.N., thought the best way to deal with the problem was to display some loaded firearms which soon succeeded in putting the crew into a much calmer and more co-operative frame of mind.

Crowds of people were on hand to see the amazing sight of the little *Sirius* entering the harbour but they were even more amazed when, a few hours later, smoke on the horizon signalled the arrival of another steamer, the *Great Western*. She had made much better time than the *Sirius* but steamed in second and, in many people's eyes, second is nowhere. In addition she only brought seven passengers, the *Sirius* had forty so the *Sirius* and her crew were the heroes of the day. But attitudes soon changed when people realised that the *Great Western* was actually a much faster ship as well as being bigger and more luxurious. She had steamed directly from Bristol and had not stopped off in Ireland to refuel as the *Sirius* had and, despite facing the same headwinds, had arrived with 200 tons of coal still unused.

So, who had really won the race to be the first to carry passengers across the north Atlantic to the New World?

Well, actually, they had both won. The *Sirius* undoubtedly arrived first but, having coaled in Ireland on the way, this made her first to cross from the British Isles. The *Great Western* had steamed all the way from Bristol so she was the first to cross from Great Britain.

But effectively it was the *Great Western* that took the prize as this was the vessel that most people wanted to travel on and, of course, she was the first real trans-Atlantic liner, being specially built for the purpose. The *Sirius* was a converted coastal/Irish Sea ferry and couldn't possibly compete with the *Great Western*. Nevertheless her journey across the Atlantic was heroic and in the true traditions of early sea travel. After celebrating her Atlantic crossing, she went back home to become an Irish Sea ferry once again as the *British Queen* was ready to take over.

The *British Queen,* also a side paddle steamer, was constructed for the British and American Steam Navigation Company by Curling and Young on the Thames, and fitted with Napier engines after the preferred engine supplier went bankrupt. At 1,850 tons and a length of 245 feet and a beam of 40 feet, she would be the biggest ship in the world when launched. As with the *Great Western* and the *Liverpool,* her hull would be made of wood with iron bracing, and she was designed to carry over 200 passengers. Her side lever engines had cylinders of 6 feet diameter and a 7 feet stroke and were rated at 700 h.p. and, to get the big ship moving, she was fitted with huge 30 feet diameter paddle wheels.

The *British Queen* set out on her maiden voyage from Portsmouth on 12th July 1839 and made nine trans-Atlantic trips with her speed competing with that of the *Great Western* at first but then failing to make the grade. She was sold to the Belgian Government in 1841 for an Antwerp-Cowes-New York service but this was not very successful and she was laid up after just three trips.

The British and American Steamship Company ordered a sister ship to the *British Queen*, the *President,* but with larger engines fitted by the specialist marine engineers Fawcett and Preston of Liverpool. She was an opulent vessel but her performance wasn't that good and she would struggle to compete with the other steamers. Lt. Roberts, who so ably took the *Sirius* across the Atlantic, was given command of the luxury vessel. On 17th July 1840 the *President* sailed from the Mersey for New York and went on to make a further two successful voyages, but after leaving New York on 11th March 1841, she is believed to have been caught in a gale in mid-Atlantic and all 135 on board, including Lt. Roberts, were lost.

As with the *British Queen,* the *Liverpool* was not going to ready to challenge the *Great Western,* so her owners chartered the *Royal William*, not the Quebec-built vessel mentioned earlier but an Irish Sea ferry, to make the trip. She did successfully make her way to New York but her voyage took place a few months after the *Sirius* and the *Great Western*. After a further successful voyage, she went back to her Irish ferry job as the *Liverpool* steamer was ready to take over the Atlantic route with her first crossing of 16 days 17 hours from Cork. She would make six more return crossings but could never match the performance of the *Great Western* and lost money on every trip. Her owner, the Transatlantic Steamship Company, was never a commercial success and was wound up in 1840 with the *Liverpool* being sold to P & O.

After her successful maiden voyage, the *Great Western* headed back to Bristol, this time with 68 passengers on board. When she got back to Bristol, 15 days later, most of the city seemed to be on hand to welcome her, church bells rang and there was lots of rejoicing. Everyone felt that the *Great Western* would mean that Bristol would become the main British link with the New World. To some extent they were right. The increasingly popular well built *Great Western* would make a further 67 successful journeys with an average crossing from Bristol to New York of 13½ days. But her owners did not want to risk her on a winter crossing and she was laid up as soon as the autumn weather started to get bad.

Despite her popularity though, life on board the *Great Western* was not necessarily very comfortable.

A collection of correspondence from people who had sailed on the *Great Western* gives some idea of what conditions were like. Although the passengers weren't impressed with it, food on board was perhaps not unreasonable for a ship on a long journey at that time. Livestock was carried to provide meat, milk and eggs and a baker prepared bread every day. Unfortunately, when the food got to the table, it was not very appetising and there were complaints about greasy toast for breakfast and a choice of cold meat or cold meat for dinner. The journey could take up to perhaps 22 days and, the longer the voyage, the greater the strain on food stocks. If the journey took a really long time, those who liked pea soup and pea pie were definitely in for a treat. The conditions the livestock were carried in were appalling and even concerned an on board butcher. One of his two cows on board had stopped providing milk and he said he was not surprised, the cows being kept in a padded stall on deck, unable to lie down and constantly wet due to the salt waves or the spray from the paddle wheels. The butcher wrote something which said a lot about social standards of the time "*We have a great deal of company on board, consisting of 200 men and women, 2 cows, 10 pigs, besides fowls and mulatto girls. One of these women isn't a bad looking heifer either ...*" Other correspondents have mentioned the mulatto girls but what they were on board for has not been disclosed. Perhaps it's best not to ask!

But if you didn't like the food, there was an emergency plan, you could retire to the bar which was always well stocked with brandy. At least you could until 10 p.m. when the bar would close and all of the lamps and candles below deck would be extinguished whether you liked it or not. Fire was considered a real risk to the vessel. When you got back to your cabin you could, if you were a sole traveller, be faced with a big problem, a cabin mate whose standards and personal hygiene left a lot to be desired. One stateroom passenger wrote about having to share with such a passenger in his poorly ventilated stateroom which became much more of a problem when the passenger had a bout of seasickness. It wasn't even possible to go into the adjoining saloon during the night for some relief because that was where the servants slept, on the floor, and the atmosphere there was even worse!

A big problem for passengers though, often referred to in correspondence, was the surly and unhelpful attitude of the waiters and stewards. Technology and business may have been moving forward at a phenomenal rate at that time but clearly the concept of "customer service" had not yet been invented!

A cadet, whose cadetship had been arranged by his mother, wrote to her asking to relieved from serving on the vessel. He complained about life on board, of being very hot when downstairs because the crew lived next to the engine room and the boilers, of his head being covered in bumps and of being smutty all of the time, like a chimney sweep. Whether his mother removed him from the vessel, is not recorded but it is extremely unlikely as she had just paid £300, a lot of money at the time, to get him the three year cadetship. Almost certainly he was in for the long haul but he probably soon toughened up because that was the way it was at the time for everyone unless they were wealthy. People usually had to work long hours and often in difficult conditions. If you weren't tough and prepared to work you would not survive whether on board or on shore.

One of the cadet's jobs was to lower the chip log over the stern of the ship. This was a length of string with a weight, which would float on the surface of the water, and with knots in the string at regular intervals. The cadet would allow the string to pay out and the number of knots that would pass through his fingers in a set time would give an indication of the speed of the ship. This is thought to have been surprisingly accurate. Now you know why a nautical mile per hour is referred to as a knot!

While those on board the *Great Western* were learning to cope with their daily trials and tribulations, the people of Bristol continued to rejoice in the knowledge that the vessel, operating out of their town, would surely improve the town's declining fortunes. Bristol must be on course to get back its title as England's second city. But they had missed one important point - while Bristol had largely waited for something to turn up and had only made limited improvements to its dock structure, the Corporation and people of Liverpool had, for some time, been extending and updating their dock system and developing the city's infrastructure, and the city was more than ready to take on a rejuvenated Bristol. The Bristolians were heading for disappointment.

● ● ●

Chapter 9

Rise of Liverpool

The Port of Liverpool, together with the shipyards of Glasgow, played a crucial role in the creation of wealth in Great Britain in the nineteenth century and in the establishment and success of the Cunard Line. But it was much more than that. The rapid development of the United States during the same period was heavily linked with, and largely depended on, Liverpool. This comment by respected American ship owner E. K Collins in 1841 to friends in New York after seeing the ill-fated *President* steamer pass one of his sailing ships "*I will do my utmost to promote a line of steamers to cross to Liverpool in ten days*" illustrates the importance of the city in the eyes of Americans at the time, Liverpool not London, Bristol, Britain or England being mentioned by name. Indeed, if Liverpool, and the shipyards of the Clyde, had not existed, history could have taken a very different course indeed.

So what was it that turned this insignificant little settlement on the edge of the known world in the Middle Ages into one of the world's greatest and best known ports? It seems so obvious today - Liverpool's position in the centre of a country, with excellent communications, and a wide frontage on to a deep river able to handle the biggest ships - a perfect place to build a port. But going back in history, the question might have been "Why on earth build a port there?" Up until the end of the first millennium, what is now Liverpool was part of a sparsely populated area with its only perceived asset being an inland creek that was useful for safely berthing the few small fishing boats that the settlers used. There was no need for a port to be built because there was one just thirty miles away, Chester, which had been in use since Roman times and which would remain a largely naval port through Saxon and Norman times. Having one port was certainly enough for the area especially as to the west there was only war-torn Ireland and ice covered Iceland and Greenland. For a long time most people thought that if they travelled too far west they would fall off the edge of the earth so, apart from trade with Ireland, England's trade routes were pointing east and, as today, most of the country's wealth and power lay in the south east of the country. "Liverpool's" links overland were practically non-existent, with its location being surrounded to the north and east by a large wooded area that would become known as the West Derbyshire Forest, an extension of the vast forest that covered the area north of the River Trent. And where there wasn't forest, there were meres or areas of moss or rough moorland. Getting to what would become Liverpool by overland means would prove to be very difficult for many years. In fact it wouldn't be until the middle of the 18th century that Liverpool would have a road link that would enable stage coaches from the south to travel further than Warrington. Travelling by water was also problematic. The upper reaches beyond Runcorn were barely navigable and beyond Warrington the river was even less navigable. The navigable section, west of Runcorn, was often not for the faint-hearted with its exposure to strong winds and its fast moving tides. Up until the Middle Ages the River Alt is thought to have been navigable as far as Croxteth on the outskirts of Liverpool but vessels of any size would have found it difficult. And when settlers did manage to find their way to the site that would become Liverpool, what did they find? - just a patch of inhospitable sandy soil on a continuous slope of sandstone lying at the head of a small unproductive river valley. Perhaps the fact that the river was teeming with fish, including salmon, helped them face up to the problems they would have to deal with!

Looking at all of these drawbacks, it seems amazing that Liverpool ever managed to develop and prosper.

So what was it that first put Liverpool on the map?

In the past, and increasingly in recent years, it has been suggested that it was all down to the city's involvement in the slave trade. It is true to say that in the eighteenth century the city became heavily involved in the trade; in fact it became by far Britain's biggest slave trade port, having taken over from London and Bristol. It is also true to say that this brought some wealth into the city. But is it true, or is it fair, to suggest that, without the slave trade, Liverpool would never have become a great port and a great city?

Let's follow Liverpool's history from the early days to see what the facts are.

```
But first, where did the name come from?

There have been many suggestions for the
origin of "Liverpool" It has been suggested
that the town's name is based on the LEVER,
a fanciful heraldic bird which some of the
important 16th century families in Lancashire
used on their crest but this doesn't seem to
make sense as the name Litherpool, or
something similar, was in use before the
town became a borough and adopted the
mythical Lever, now called, the Liver bird,
on its seal. It has also been suggested that
the name arises from the LIVER, a plant said
to exist in some pools and that gives its
name to other towns such as Liversedge. This
suggestion fails because the Pool of
Liverpool was a salt-water pool where the
plant would not have thrived. These
suggestions are clearly nonsense and owe a
```

lot to nineteenth century imagination. In earlier history the city's name was not as we know it today. Various spellings have been recorded including Lyrpul, Lytherpul, Lytherpole, Lierpole, Liverpul, Leverpool and more. So what could the real derivation be? Well we'll never know for certain but there are a few contenders –

1) The pool or pul part relates to the tidal pool which was used as a harbour until being filled in to form the area facing Castle Street. The Liver or Lyrpool element could be a reference to the ancient British word Lir meaning sea. A "Sea pool" would be a good description of a tidal inlet. This sounds a very plausible derivation.

2) Possibly Liver could be a reference to a word meaning lower and the tidal inlet could be referred to as the Lowerpool or Liverpool. This also sounds very plausible with "Lither" being a local dialect interpretation of "lower" and is used in the name of the local area of Litherland. In Henry IIs charter the town if referred to as *"which the Lyrpul men call Litherpul"* This is a very good candidate as most towns probably owe their name to some local feature and in modern day Liverpool, the name of its district of Everton is almost certainly derived from its position of "Higher Town". Of course, if Liverpool was named after its lower pool, it begs the question "Where is or was its higher pool?!

3) There is another possibility which sounds reasonable. The ancient Norse word Hlithar-Pollr means pool on the slopes and, although it does not always seem so now because the city is so built up, the land does gradually slope towards the river. So perhaps the Norsemen can take the prize.

Having said all that, the oft-repeated assumption that the "pool" in Liverpool relates to its former tidal inlet could well be suspect and ignores the fact that other towns have "pool" in their name. What about places such as Blackpool, Hartlepool. Do they have a small pool? And what about Poole in Dorset which, rather than a small pool, has a huge harbour. Or did the name come about because they are near water? Could it be that the "pool" in Liverpool actually relates to the estuarine section of the River Mersey to the west of Runcorn rather than its tidal inlet. Perhaps "Liverpool" was originally more of a generic term covering a larger area than that which King John would define in his famous charter. This suggestion does meet with a problem however; Liverpool's tidal creek is referred to as "The Pool" in early maps and also had a Pool Lane running to it but this was hundreds of years after the town had been given its name so this doesn't necessarily prove that the town was named after the tidal creek. Something to think about!

Further reading. If any reader would like a detailed review of how Liverpool's name could have originated, I recommend "The Place Names of the Liverpool District" by Henry Harrison published in 1898. It provides a twelve page precise and exacting narrative of all the options. If you thought you knew where the name came from, prepare to be amazed (or confused). The fact is that we will never know for sure but that is all part of the city's interesting history.

Now where did it all start; well certainly not with anything of great importance and, in historical terms, not that long ago. It is not mentioned at all in any Roman Itinera and some writers think that Roman visits to the South West Lancashire were few and far between and that they didn't leave much in the way of any legacy. However the writer Henry Smithers in 1825 refers to the arrival of the Romans, led by Agricola, in Lancashire in A.D. 79. Certainly the Romans set up a base in Manchester, which was already a populated area, and further west in Warrington but whether they made great inroads into south west

Lancashire and what is now Liverpool is very doubtful. Much of the area would have been left in the hands of the tribes of Celts who are said to have been there for over 500 years. After 400 years, the Romans left and in the eighth century, small colonies of Norsemen settled on both sides of the river but settlements were small and the whole area remained sparsely populated. It would be some time before Liverpool, or whatever early name it had, actually existed.

> The fact that the Romans do not seem to have mentioned the existence of the River Mersey, or indeed the fledgling Liverpool, in their Itinera seems surprising. They certainly mentioned Preston and the River Ribble, and Chester and the River Dee although of course they had settlements there. However they did have a settlement at Warrington and, with their liking for fish, it seems likely that they would have fished the fertile waters of downstream River Mersey. There is a possible explanation for this though. They may have thought that, like some people today, the area to the west of Warrington, certainly to the west of Runcorn, that we think of as part of the River Mersey, is really part of the estuary and not part of the river at all. The Romans may have thought that the "real" River Mersey to the east of Warrington is so insignificant that it wasn't considered worthy of mention - an interesting hypothesis!

Not just the Liverpool area but the whole of Lancashire between the River Mersey and the River Ribble, had little going for it. This was an age, that would continue for some time into the future, where agriculture was the main part of life and the two main commodities were wool and grain. The huge forests, mosses and heath lands of Lancashire made growing corn or raising sheep next to impossible and, when the Domesday Book was completed, the amount of arable land recorded in South

Lancashire was less than any other area in England of comparative size. However there were pockets of developed land around the area's manor houses where the often peaty soils produced good crops and were found to be ideal for raising cattle which produced prized dairy products. The rich farmlands we see today in South Lancashire are largely due to the Dutch drainage experts who arrived in the Middle Ages. Before then the area was seen as a barren and inhospitable place, the back of beyond - plus a bit further!

Just north of what is now Liverpool was the manor of West Derby with its Lord in command of much of the area. The manor had five or six "berewicks", subordinate manors, and it is believed "Liverpool" was one of these but as far as the Domesday commissioners were concerned the settlement wasn't even worthy of a name. However small villages such as Litherland, Formby and Everton were mentioned by name. This was Liverpool at the time - a total non-entity. By contrast, its neighbours, Chester and Manchester, not too far away, had built on their positions as Roman settlements and were thriving whilst "Liverpool" comprised a handful of fields owned by the Lord of the Manor of West Derbyfield which were worked by serfs.

After the Norman Conquest, the area was granted by William to Roger de Poictiers, the first Norman Lord of Lancashire, together with all the land between the Mersey and the River Ribble. Around the year 1089, he built a castle at nearby West Derby and appointed Vivian de Molines, the ancestor of the Earl of Sefton, its castellan. This was a traditional Norman style motte and bailey castle and said to be largely of wooden construction. This is thought to be about the time that Liverpool got its name. After various forfeitures, the little hamlet of Liverpool was handed by Henry II to Warine de Lancaster in a deed said to be dated 1173, although the deed does not survive and its date is not certain. It is also claimed that this is the first time that the name Liverpool, in one of its early forms, has been recorded in history, it being referred to as a place "which the men of Lyrpul call Litherpool". This would seem to be the first time that "Liverpool" was recognised as a district separate to West Derby. In a deed executed around 1191 by John, Count of Mortain, later King John, he confirms Henry Fitzwarine as in possession of "Liverpool". Once again the name of the town, in one of its early forms, is mentioned in writing. It needs to be borne in mind though that the facts involving Henry I and Henry II regarding Liverpool are far from certain and the story about the 1173 charter, and possibly an earlier one, is thought by some to be a complete fabrication. What is certain though is that, in 1207, King John re-acquired the small settlement of Liverpool, giving the town of English Lea, near Preston, in exchange. John needed a base for his adventures in Ireland and later in Wales and, Liverpool, with its tidal pool which could provide a safe harbour for the largest vessels of the day, seemed ideal. In addition this would be an alternative to the port of Chester which was at the time under the domain of the Earl of Chester who had semi-independent palatine powers and the King felt he could not fully rely on the services of the port. Just five days after re-acquiring the settlement, he issued letters of patent granting Liverpool the same status as that of any other free borough upon the sea. This was the real birth of the township of Liverpool and, in its creation, King John had made a momentous decision that would eventually change the face of Britain and in fact the rest of the world.

John had used his royal prerogative to create the borough of Liverpool, almost on a whim. This was unusual as the creation of boroughs normally took place because a settlement had achieved importance by becoming a key administrative or trading area and borough status was part of a natural progression. It was very different for Liverpool which didn't fit into any of these categories, in fact it barely existed at all and, other than in the eyes of King John, it had no conceivable importance. But John saw the small settlement differently and showed tremendous foresight.

It was clear to the King right away that Liverpool was lacking something that a successful town needs - enough people. He offered inducements to settlers to build there, including freedom from tolls and no requirement to provide agricultural services to the king although they did have to pay rent – one shilling per year. They also had the right to organize themselves into a guild merchant, a right confirmed in 1229 by the charter of Henry III. The guild merchant controlled trade into the town and laid down mooring fees for visiting ships. In order to exercise their powers, the burgesses appointed a number of officials, including a mayor, valuer of goods, a warehouse keeper and a water bailiff. Liverpool was now a real town and could make its own decisions. But there was a price to be paid for this freedom. Being a free borough meant that responsibilities to the king had to be met when required. In 1208 King John summoned all of Liverpool's ships to Ilfracombe for some reason and gave this precise instruction to the ship owners *"Know for certain that if you act contrary to this we will cause you and the masters of your vessels to be hanged, and all your goods seized for our use"*. No confusion there, then!

Advice to entrepreneurs. Be precise in your communications but perhaps write in more moderate terms!

Liverpool was now a town, albeit small, of strategic importance and needed something to reflect that - a castle. Some time before 1235, William de Ferrers built Liverpool's castle on a rocky promontory, currently the site of Queen Victoria's monument, between the Town Hall in Castle Street and the inlet of the pool which flowed on to where Paradise Street and

Whitechapel now stand. The castle at West Derby was still extant at the time but would soon fall into decay. Contemporary images and designs of Liverpool's castle do not now exist but it was just an ordinary Norman castle and its main features are fairly certain. It was not that big being built on an artificial plateau about 50 yds. square but held a commanding position with two of its four walls overlooking the pool and one wall overlooking the River Mersey. It had a circular tower at each corner and a strong tower and gatehouse facing Castle Street. It was surrounded by a deep ditch which may or may not have incorporated a moat and the castle was connected to the river by a covered protected walkway.

By the early 18th century, the castle had been demolished by Cromwell's troops although ruins remained until 1721. In 1715, Queen Anne granted the site to the corporation who erected St. George's church on it.

Liverpool was now starting to look like a real town and the people got organised and set up a weekly market, an annual fair and the erection of a mill. But, for exchequer purposes, it still came under the control of West Derby.

The town steadily turned into an important naval base, together with Chester, supplying stores and reinforcements to Ireland and Wales for King John but otherwise trade developed slowly during this time and, in the great scheme of things, Liverpool still remained pretty insignificant. After an early spurt, it struggled to compete with Preston which took over the bulk of the Irish trade.

However traffic between Liverpool and the Wirral was increasing and a ferry across the Mersey was first established in King John's reign. Bad weather on the river sometimes left passengers stranded on the Wirral side and Edward II granted a charter to "Byrkehaved" – Birkenhead – to erect lodging houses for the stranded travellers.

The 14th century started badly for the people of Liverpool. Turbulent times in the country resulted in much disorder on the town's streets punctuated by riots and considerable violence. But, despite this, the town's prosperity started to improve as it benefitted from King Edward III's increasing requirement to send men and supplies to fight wars with the Scots and the Irish. By this time the town had three or four mills and the large number of troops billeted in the area gave opportunities for providing them with food and supplies. By the middle of the century, the town's population had increased to around 1,100 persons. Trade with Ireland was developing with cattle and hides being imported and manufactured goods and iron being exported. There was also some trading with Wales and Scotland but otherwise international trade was largely negligible although some wine did manage to make it from France. Liverpool missed out on one of the key imports at the time, salted fish from Iceland, which was taken to Bristol, Hull or Scarborough.

Edward III accession to the throne in 1327 did not result in any measures to help Liverpool. A particular problem was his law that regulated trading in the "staple" products of wool, hides and lead with only designated towns being able to market them and only designated ports, including London, Boston and Southampton being able to ship them. Liverpool was left out in the cold and, although the law was later relaxed, it had helped the designated towns to prosper whilst Liverpool didn't. However Liverpool was doing well in one product and people would travel many miles to the town to stock up on this important food. The product was - honey. At least the heaths and meadows of Lancashire were useful for something.

Around 1331 Liverpool became sufficiently important to be featured on a map for the first time - only to be ignored on most future maps for some time, a brief moment of fame. Around 1360, the Black Death arrived and carried off a large part of the population and this left the town impoverished. At that time most of the town's inhabitants were clustered in a small area between the pool inlet and the river and this promoted the establishment and spread of plague, a problem that would haunt Liverpool for many years to come.

The 15th century brought new opportunities for England as its trade with continental Europe started to develop. Many towns, including Norwich, York and Bristol started to become rich but Liverpool headed in just one direction - downwards. The town had still not established itself as an important commercial centre and then it got caught up in the War of the Roses which brought poverty and turbulence to much of Lancashire. Despite many other towns prospering, Liverpool was still a small town with only a few streets including Castle Street, Dale Street, Bonke (now Water) Street and Chapel Street. It was a difficult time for the town but it managed to cling to its trade with Ireland which largely amounted just the import of hides, fish and linen.

The 16th century didn't get off to a good start for the town and many of the previous century's problems continued. Another outbreak of plague around 1540 almost de-populated the whole town. But, by the middle of the century, things had started to improve. In 1558, the Elizabethan traveller, Leland, visited and seemed happy with the town describing it as a paved town, much frequented by Irish merchants and as an importer of Irish yarn. However his description of a paved town, very unusual at the time, doesn't agree with comments by many future travellers about the state of, or non-existence of, Liverpool's paving. Perhaps Leland had been sampling too much mead made from the highly prized Lancashire honey! At this time the town is reported to have had a population of around 690 living in 138 houses, a fair sized township, but then the plague arrived again and killed a reported 240 persons. Not surprisingly the town seems to have then declined and it became increasingly poor as trade with Ireland reduced. This was despite the fact that Lancashire was booming with many towns, particularly Manchester, doing well with the manufacture of wool and linen cloths. These towns are thought to have preferred to send their cloths to eastern ports for export to the continent rather than Liverpool. This seems strange but at the time Liverpool had few ships to carry the goods abroad. In 1565, it had just twelve barques and the biggest, the Eagle, was only 40 tons and had a crew of twelve men and one boy. The other vessels were mostly much smaller and more akin to fishing boats, fishing being more important locally than is today. Even then it was not possible to catch enough fish to meet local demand and herrings were often brought down by Scottish ships. What trade there was from Liverpool would have been primarily serving towns not too far away such as Preston, Lancaster and those in Wales.

The level of poverty in the town encouraged some ship owners to turn to piracy with a Spaniard complaining to the Privy Council in 1555 of being robbed by the "pirates of Liverpool and Chester". In Elizabeth's reign some ship owners did much the same thing but on a legal basis by becoming privateers and brought the ships and goods they had captured into the Mersey.

```
Privateer: A privately owned armed vessel
which could be commissioned by the government
to operate against the enemy in wartime.
Common into the nineteenth century. Really a
legalised pirate ship.
```

In 1570 the Mayor and civic officials got together and drew up plans to bring some sort of order to the lives of the local people including setting price controls on ale, wool, geese and bread and a reduction in the strength of ale because of the high cost of corn. To improve safety on the streets, new regulations were brought in including a reduction in the number of alehouses and a requirement for them to be licensed, a ban on cudgels being carried in the street, a requirement for those suspected of carrying plague to be removed to huts on the common where they had to stay until they recovered or died and - obviously an important rule! - a ban on bachelors being allowed on the streets after 9.00 p.m. unless with very good reason. They dealt with the problem of bigamy by requiring any man with two wives to leave the town right away - and to take his second wife with him!

In 1571, the inhabitants petitioned the Queen to be relieved from a subsidy imposed on them and described the town as *"Her Majesty's poor decayed town of Liverpool"*. The town had started off badly and now seemed to be going even further downhill, on a number of occasions being referred to as *"the poor town of Liverpool"*.

Towards the end of the century, things started to improve a little for Liverpool. War with the Irish provided some income from the provision of transport and the need to garrison troops in the town although the local people often had to cope with their riotous behaviour. But Chester, as the perceived main port, did best out of the arrangement. Most of Liverpool's sea-borne trade was with Ireland and it wasn't just military transport. During 1586 ships arrived in the town from Irish ports including Dublin and Drogheda bringing shipments of linen and hides; the linen went to Manchester and the hides were processed in Liverpool. But exports out of the town were much more varied and gave an indication of what was to come. They included textiles from Manchester and Kendal, woollens from Yorkshire and knives from Sheffield. But getting the goods to Liverpool for export was a major operation and required teams of pack horses and a lot of hard work.

So things were improving - but there was still a long way to go. By 1590 the population had increased to around 1,000 which was only about the same as it had been 150 years before. The town was still poor, but perhaps not as poor as it had been. Some industrial development had taken place but it had been limited. The main industry, as with many other towns, was milling although tailoring and brewing were developing in the town. In its early days Liverpool had been unlucky in many ways - remoteness, accessibility, lack of agricultural land - but as industry started to build, it faced another problem, a lack of suitable streams to power water wheels. The town had a few water mills, which reduced in number when one fell into the creek, and there was one at Bootle Springs but Manchester, with a number of fast flowing streams, surged ahead as a manufacturing centre and Liverpool was left floundering - at least until steam power arrived.

Despite its problems, Liverpool managed to end the century a little bigger than when it started. It now had seven streets including Castle Street, Water Street, Chapel Street, Juggler Street, More (now Tithebarn) Street and Mylne (now Old Hall) Street.

As the 17th century got under way, things started to fall into place for Liverpool and, slowly but steadily, it started to progress. It still had a mountain to climb though and its importance at the time was illustrated in 1630 when Charles I issued writs for the levying of ship money. Liverpool was rated at only £26 while Bristol was rated at £1,000, an indication of the relevant wealth of the two communities. Even by the middle of the century, there were still only fifteen ships with an aggregate tonnage of 259 tons operating out of the port.

However this small decaying town had now reached its nadir and was about to expand as its fortunes began to change and the Liverpool we know today started to build. Shipping to and from

Liverpool had primarily consisted of coastal and Irish trade plus some journeys to the continent but, around this time, Liverpool began trading with the New World and the genie was now out of the bottle. As soon as tobacco and sugar arrived in England there was a big demand for more and soon extensive imports of tobacco from America and sugar from the West Indies led to a big increase in shipping in Liverpool. At the same time manufacturing in South Lancashire was growing and the once bigger port of Chester was starting to struggle as the River Dee began to silt up and the town ended up with only a few small ships. If there had not been problems with access on the Dee, Chester would have had a bright future as a commercial port with its link with the Cheshire salt mines via the River Weaver and a Roman road, and agricultural output from the local rich farmlands. But it wasn't to be and Liverpool was the first to benefit.

Liverpool had now became the main port serving Ireland which coincided with peace coming to that country and a rapid increase in trade. At the same time trade with France and Spain started to become regular. This sudden increase in shipping put a tremendous strain on Liverpool's port facilities both on the river and around the Pool and chaos often ensued. The Water Bailiff, with the authority of his silver oar, struggled to keep some sort of order on the waterfront.

Despite the increase in shipping, the town's population had hardly increased since the 16th century and, around 1650, was estimated at about 775 persons. For some time Liverpool had drawn the poor and unemployed from a wide area in the hope of finding work. The slow growth in population may not suggest this but the incomers had periods of disease and plague to contend with and many people died. The Black Death took 200 hundred lives around 1651 and all the victims were buried communally in appropriately named Sickmans Lane, which is now known as Addison Street.

18   Liverpool 1650
Smith's Stranger's Guide 1843

Then 1660 came and this could be said to be the time that Liverpool really "arrived". In that year it was recognised by the Surveyor General of Customs to be *"distinct and absolute, of its own selfe"* The town now existed as a significant community not just locally but also nationally. In fact, it was even considered bigger than it actually was, the town being defined as *"the whole of the River Mersey and the shores on both sides"*.

This was time that Liverpool really began its transformation. In the second half of the 17th century the city started to become the place to be and many people made their way there. By the turn of the century the population had increased to 4,240 with many coming from Ireland attracted by the booming trade between the two countries. Unfortunately Liverpool was not, for many, the promised land they had hoped for. There was a lot of work available but just not enough for the numbers that were coming and many took the opportunity to emigrate to the New World instead.

Up to then, London and Bristol had carried out extensive commerce to many parts of the globe while Liverpool had remained in relative obscurity. But that was now changing. It was as if the town and all of its inhabitants had decided to show the world how to turn a small town into a booming city, how to create a great international port and soon, it has to be said, how to create a highly efficient slave trading operation. The town still controlled most of the Irish trade and had built up major trade routes with France, Spain, Denmark and Norway. But the most important trade which would gradually turn Liverpool into one of the world's greatest ports had been established and was now being developed at a fast rate - the cotton, tobacco and sugar trade with the plantations of the West Indies and Virginia. Suddenly everything started to fall into place for Liverpool. The Great Fire of London and an outbreak of plague caused some of the wealthy merchants of London to move to Liverpool where they saw business opportunities and wealth and expertise flowed into the town. And it got better following the outbreak of war with France in 1689 as this encouraged merchants to look at Liverpool as a safer base for operations rather than southern and south eastern ports.

The town expanded rapidly as local industries were created and more and more ships used the port. This caused considerable resentment amongst the merchants in Chester, London and Bristol as they lost trade. By now the Mersey was becoming busier all the time and there was more and more congestion on the quays as ships tried to load and unload. The river often became a scene of chaos. The longer it took for ships to be tied up, the more money it cost in lost trade and there was also the risk of vessels turning over if they were still tied up during high tidal movements. A plan was needed to deal with the problem. Then someone had a clever idea; why not build a dock with gates that could be opened to let the tide in and then closed to maintain the water level. Ships would be able to dock and load or unload whatever the state of the tide.

The plan was finalised and in 1709 the engineer, Thomas Speers of London, began work on the project. The dock, which later became known as the Old Dock, was constructed by extending the dock walls into the town's tidal creek, a revolutionary method for the time as dry docks for shipbuilding and ship repair were previously constructed by digging out the ground at the side of a watercourse. In 1715, the Old Dock was opened and would be a real first for Liverpool; neither Bristol or London had anything like it. This would be the first commercial wet dock in the world and, a couple of years after it was built, Thomas Speers became Liverpool's first Dock Master.

The impact of the Old Dock was enormous. Overnight Liverpool was able to handle shipping traffic in a way that no other English port could even contemplate. The dock could hold up to 100 ships and would ensure a slick and rapid turnaround of vessels which turned the civic officials and merchants of other ports, including London, Bristol and Chester, green with envy. They weren't happy at all and many took the opportunity to heap scorn on the town and people of Liverpool under any pretext they could think of. By 1737, the tonnage of vessels using Liverpool would almost double.

But, a little before the Old Dock idea came up, Liverpool had started to be affected by something that was becoming important in the British economy - African slavery. Slavery had been established in many parts of the world for centuries even, in some forms, in Britain. For many years slaves had been taken from central Africa to northern African countries but it was some time before European countries became involved. It was a long journey for ships of the day and the stories emanating from the African continent even frightened some of the sailors who did not want to risk going there. They even thought the high seas contained monsters that would rise up and devour them and their ship. Eventually better ships became available and, led by the Portuguese, and soon followed by the Spanish and French and then other countries, the European/African slave trade began with the slaves being transferred to European colonies in the Caribbean and South America. Contemporary reports speak of great cruelty being inflicted on the slaves, particularly by the Portuguese traders, and many did not survive.

But the African slave was slow to get established in Britain. Spain and Portugal had been involved in the African slave trade since the 15th century but, although the first British slavers left Portsmouth around 1553, Britain only dabbled lightly in the trade. It was only in the second half of the 17th century that Britain started to become significantly involved when the country had acquired the West Indian colonies with their sugar plantations which needed a large supply of labour. The establishment of cotton and tobacco plantations in the New World created even more demand for labour. Acquiring slaves in West Africa seemed an ideal way of providing a labour force and, in turn, of providing Britain with a regular supply of sugar and cotton. People didn't see anything wrong with the trade because the slaves were only "primitive Africans" and, in some people's eyes, barely human. They were just a commodity, like any other, and the whole idea was fully supported by the British Government.

As the slave trade got under way, London took over as the British slave capital but Bristol was not far behind. Slave ships also sailed from many other English ports including Lancaster, Exeter and Hull but they couldn't compete with London or Bristol. By 1700, Liverpool had latched on to the African slave trade with one of its ships, the *Liverpool Merchant,* carrying 200 slaves to Barbados, but the slave trade through London and Bristol was well organised and Liverpool could not really compete and by 1709, the town was only handling around 1%, if that, of the trade.

It is a little known fact that Liverpool was involved in a form of white slavery before entering the Africa slave trade. Records suggest that as early as 1648, Civil War orphans were transferred to the New World in exchange for tobacco. Later that century ships took adults, probably with free passage, to America to be used as servants and the Norrises, of Liverpool's Speke Hall, were certainly involved in this trade around 1693. The Norrises are said to have inaugurated the famous and efficient first triangular run when one of the their ships, the *Blessing,* sailed from Liverpool to West Africa to pick up slaves, then to the West Indies to sell the slaves and pick up sugar, and then back home.

Another form of white slavery developed during the 18th century when poor orphans were transported to the New World to live as indentured servants, a life they would have found difficult to break away from. A number of Liverpool sea captains got together and funded the Blue Coat Charity School to give these orphans a new chance in life.

Although Liverpool was only handling 1% of the slave trade in 1709, in other areas it was doing very well and 334 ships cleared the town in that year carrying 12,636 tons of non-slave cargo. This was 35% of total English trade and shows how important Liverpool had become even without a contribution from the slave trade.

But then the slave trade began to concentrate the minds of the Liverpool merchants and the local dignitaries. London was doing very well out of trade with India, via the East India Company, but other English ports couldn't get a look in. Now there was an opportunity for Liverpool to make it big especially as the town had its new Old Dock. This was an opportunity for many people - ship owners, ship captains and investors - to make a killing.

Meanwhile London's slave trade decreased rapidly as Bristol put up increasingly strong competition. The capital's slave ships decreased from 104 in 1701 to only 30 in 1707 as Bristol took over as the main centre for the trade. By 1720, slave trading had ceased in London. But Bristol's dominance did not last long. Liverpool increasingly took over most of the slave trade helped by its Old Dock, which became the heart of Britain's sugar industry, and by its position as the hub of the triangular trade.

In 1730 just 15 slave ships set out for Africa from Liverpool. By 1751 this had increased to 53 and then it increased further as Bristol's trade started to fade. In 1764 Liverpool sent 74 slavers to Africa while Bristol could only manage 32. Liverpool gradually took over the trade and by 1792 there were 136 slavers operating out of the town. It was now seen as big business with around thirty shipping lines involved, some with just one ship and some with up to four. It should be remembered however that there were more people involved in England than just the ship owners and the crews in Liverpool and the other slaving ports. The slaving expeditions could take up to nine months or more and were expensive to set up. People would invest on a share-holding basis, perhaps between six and twelve shares of which the captain would hold at least one.

By 1790 Liverpool was by far the key player and handled about 80% of the British slave trade, and Britain was the key player in Europe as this table shows:

Slaves transported 1790

Britain	*38,000*
France	*20,000*
Portugal	*10,000*
Holland	*4,000*
Denmark	*10,000*

But despite Liverpool's expanding role as the hub of the British slave trade, the town was actually developing at a fast rate with non-slave traffic. Liverpool's non-slave trade with America and the West Indies was expanding at an unprecedented rate. Manchester had taken over from France and Spain as a manufacturer of fine textiles and these were shipped across the Atlantic with the vessels returning with sugar, cotton and tobacco. Suddenly everything was falling into place for the town - but the assistance provided by the slave trade cannot be denied.

The volume of slaves being transported to the Americas is difficult now to comprehend. Between 1680 and 1786 it is believed to have been as high as 13 million with 610,000 being transported to Jamaica alone. Losses on the Atlantic crossings and failure by many to adapt to their new life meant that only around 50% would become useful labourers in the fields.

So how did the trade work?

The first part of the slaving trip was a journey of around six weeks to West Africa. It is easy now to imagine the scene where the heavily armed crew of the ship, usually from Liverpool, would make their way into the jungle and come back with dozens or hundreds of terrified African slaves, all roped together and driven forward by crew members with whips. A popular view held by many people today but that's not how it was at all, at least not when Britain became actively involved in the slave trade. Slavery had existed throughout the African continent for centuries and millions of people were enslaved. It took many forms, from comparatively benign domestic servitude or serfdom to full-blown work until you dropped. During the sixteenth and seventeenth centuries, the Portuguese and Spanish slavers arrived to find workers for their American colonies and the West African export slave trade became established. In some ways, the British slavers had it easy, the infrastructure was already up and running and all they had to do was bring goods to barter with the African slave masters at the huge slave markets in exchange for slaves. The trade was under the control of the self-styled kings and princes who controlled the markets such as those in Salaga, in Northern Ghana, and Bonny on the Niger Delta. To get to the slave markets, many slaves would have endured a long forced march from the African interior after capture or purchase by other Africans. They would have been in a dreadful state when they reached the slave markets but their captors had a system for preparing them for sale. They would feed then up and just before putting them on display they would wash them and smear their bodies with palm oil. Trading at the slave markets would have been brisk as African and European traders tried to make some good deals.

Popular goods that the Europeans brought with them for bartering were textiles, pots, beads and muskets. But the slave masters did not want any old rubbish. They were well practised businessmen and wanted the best quality textiles, and the best beads from Italy. Similarly the slaving ship captains, weren't just looking for any old slaves, they wanted fit young men and youngish women who would all be capable of hard work.

Obtaining enough slaves "*of good quality that would fetch the best prices*" to fill the vessel meant that the slaving ships could be berthed in West Africa a month or more and each day spent there carried big risks for the crew. Tropical diseases, such as yellow fever, were rife and many crew members, especially those on their first trip who had not acquired any immunity, would succumb and die before the ship even set sail or would become sick on board resulting in them being unable to crew the ship properly. Paradoxically this would often provide opportunities for the slaves and some would be enlisted as crew members and be paid accordingly. In fact a few would go on to build successful careers as seafarers. But for most though it was a very different story; they would have to face a two to four month journey crossing the Atlantic Ocean, most of the time living below in dreadful conditions, all to be followed by a very uncertain future. They were, however, provided with enough food and water to try and keep them in good condition for sale. If any of the slaves died en voyage, they would unceremoniously be pitched over the side and those who became ill would probably suffer the same fate because of the risk that the rest of the "cargo" would become infected. It was normal for the slaves to be taken on deck daily to be fed and they could remain there from some hours if the weather was fine. This would be an opportunity for the holds to be cleaned which would have been in an unimaginable state. They were still chained though to prevent them jumping over the side or attacking the crew. This was often a time when the crew would have some fun at the slaves' expense and they would be made to sing and dance whether they wanted to or not. This may have been bad but, for the younger female slaves, things would be much worse and they would be subjected to considerable abuse. If the weather was bad the slaves would only be brought up in small batches for a short time to be fed, perhaps just for fifteen minutes. If the weather was really bad, they would have to stay battened down in the ship's holds and many would die. Slaves who weren't compliant and who caused trouble were punished severely as an example to the other slaves who would have greatly outnumbered the ship's crew and, given the right circumstances, could take over the vessel. On occasions this did happen. On 12th January 1759 the Liverpool slaver *Perfect* loaded 100 slaves at Mana but, before the vessel left the harbour, the slaves rebelled, killed the captain and all of the crew, ran the ship aground and made off. However most slaves didn't get the opportunity to escape and had to face the gruelling Atlantic crossing. Some slaves would put an end to it all by throwing themselves overboard much to the consternation of the captain who would have been a shareholder in the enterprise and would not have been pleased to see his profit being reduced. The captain would have done what he considered necessary to keep the slaves under control and if they suffered, well so be it. The ships carried some simple little devices to help deal with intransigent slaves such as thumb screws which were easy to use and which caused considerable pain. If they wanted to end it all by refusing to eat, the ship's captain had a device to deal with that as well. An example of the cruelty inflicted on the slaves is illustrated by Gomer Williams in his book on Liverpool privateers and the Slave Trade in which he recounts a story, which may be apocryphal, where a slave trader captain told, at a large gathering in Buxton, of a concern he had about the health of a slave because she was fretting about her infant child which she had brought with her. He claimed to have dealt with the problem by smashing the child's head against the side of the ship and then throwing it overboard. The captain seemed quite proud of the way he had dealt with the situation. Although terrible punishments could be inflicted on the slaves, it has to be borne in mind that punishments for crew members who transgressed could be just as severe.

Around 10% of slaves, sometimes more, would not survive the Atlantic crossing and in 1789 an Act of Parliament was passed which required each slave ship to carry a doctor. A Liverpool doctor, James Currie, who was a fierce opponent of the trade, was a member of the Liverpool licensing board for surgeons and selected surgeons to serve on the slavers. He was dismayed to see that most of the surgeons who applied just saw it as a way to make some good money and did not see anything wrong with the slave trade. Many of those who became surgeons on the slavers were just starting out as doctors and were a bit naive about the risks involved. Their exposure to tropical diseases would be even greater than the crew members and many would not survive their first voyage.

> As wealth from the slave trade flowed into Liverpool, the slave traders invested their vast gains in property and many of Liverpool's fine buildings, which still exist today, were built on the back of the slaves. This is what has been documented for many years. But is it all true? Were the profits that great? Did the traders make vast fortunes to fund their great buildings? Or did it all build from this comment by the actor George Cooke who was booed off the stage of Liverpool's Theatre Royal after a drunken performance in 1772 and made an insulting comment which is recorded by early writers as either "there is not a brick in your dirty town but what is cemented by the blood of a negro" or "I have not come here to be insulted by a set of wretches, every brick in whose infernal town is cemented with an African's blood"? Whatever was actually said, the inference is clear. I will return to this later.

Meanwhile the effect of the Old Dock on Liverpool's fortunes was dramatic. In 1709 Liverpool possessed 84 ships totalling

5789 tons; by 1737 this had increased to 171 ships totalling 12,016 tons and the number of ships sailing from the port increased from 335 in 1709 to 435 in 1737 with tonnage doubling. The merchants in Bristol and London would have watched developments with total horror.

It wasn't just international trade that was developing, coastal shipping was increasing all the time with vessels from the town carrying coal, Cheshire cheese and Cheshire salt to London and many other towns including those on the south coast. But despite this, coastal shipping became a reducing part of Liverpool's overall trade as overseas trade, including with trade Ireland, increased even more rapidly.

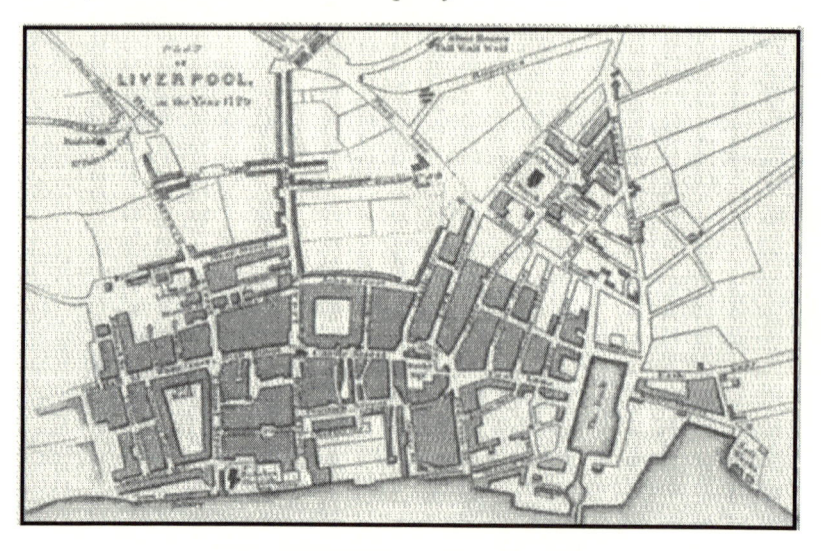

19   Map of Liverpool 1729
Smith's Stranger's Guide   1843

Lots of wealth was coming into the town and funds were available to build the new Town Hall, which is still in existence, although it now includes later additions. More importantly funds were available to build the town's second dock, the South Dock, later known as the Salthouse Dock. Construction began in 1734 but it took nineteen years to complete. Why "Salthouse Dock"? Well, whilst we take it for granted today, salt in those days was greatly prized. Salt had been produced since Roman times with brine pans being established in coastal areas to produce salt by evaporation. Liverpool already had brine pans to the south of the Pool and was an exporter of the product. At the time salt formed the basis of trade with Newfoundland where it was exchanged for cod, which was often taken to the West Indies to be exchanged for sugar and coffee. Some Liverpool merchants did not like the developing slave trade and preferred this northern triangular run. Chester too had brine springs and salt had been a valuable export for the town, especially after the discovery of vast quantities of rock salt under Northwich and surrounding towns, but the gradual silting up of the River Dee took the edge off the trade. But everything changed in 1720 when the River Weaver was made a navigable waterway and Cheshire salt could easily be transferred to Liverpool. By 1732, eighty sloops were operating on the Weaver carrying salt to Liverpool for export and the trade continued to expand considerably. Hence the decision to build the South Dock. By the end of the eighteenth century salt exports had increased ten times and the product was being sent all over the world from Liverpool.

Although Liverpool's sea trade was increasing rapidly during the early 18th century, the town was still held back by its poor mainland links. But that was about to change. In 1720 the River Douglas was made navigable from Wigan to the River Ribble. This enabled coal to be transferred by boat from the Wigan coalfields to Liverpool, a much easier and cheaper option. A couple of years later, work began on deepening the Mersey and Irwell beyond Warrington which enabled barges to travel as far as Manchester.

Liverpool's population increased rapidly from 5,000 at the beginning of the century to around 25,000 by the middle of the century but there were still many problems. The physical size of the town did not increase at the same rate and many people lived in unhealthy, overcrowded conditions. The town had narrow, badly kept streets and "roads" outside the town were very poor and often impassable. The stage coach services from other parts of the country could only run as far as Warrington until 1758 when the unfinished road between Prescot and Warrington was completed and Liverpool had its first proper road link with the rest of the country. A weekly stage coach service, starting from the Golden Lion in Dale Street, was set up to take passengers to Warrington where they could join the Warrington Flying Stagecoach to take them on to London, a two or three day journey but usually taking a day longer in the winter.

More and more people were attracted to Liverpool by the new industries that were developing including ship-building, sugar refining, rope making and iron smelting, all aided by the ready availability of coal as a result of the Wigan canal link. But the town was also developing specialist precision industries and became a centre for watch making and turning out top quality "delft" china. But many of those who moved to the town were very poor people looking for work rather than bringing in wealth and this led to much drunken disorder on the streets although the street watchmen, and police with cutlasses, kept street robberies and burglaries to very low levels.

By then Liverpool had become England's second port, surpassing Bristol, and it was an important centre for overseas trade particularly with the West Indies. Almost all of the Irish trade went through the town and silting had put Chester out of the running although Parkgate, on the lower reaches of the River Dee, was still able to act as a port for the time being.

Manchester's rapid development as a centre for the production of textiles helped Liverpool enormously with the town handling the export of the manufactured wool and cotton goods, advantage being taken of the new road and canal links.

During the seven years war, from 1756, Liverpool's privateers were once against in action as were French privateers targeting Liverpool ships with many seizures on both sides. A successful local privateer was Captain William Hutchinson who became a borough councillor and dock master. He was a skilled seaman and he used his knowledge to provide practical benefits to the mariners using the Mersey including the establishment of lighthouse and a series of observations on the tides which provided the basis for Holden's tide tables. He also invented reflecting mirrors for lighthouses. The most famous lighthouse he was associated with was at Bidston which commenced in 1771. When a ship arrived in the Mersey, a semaphore signal and the flag of the owners was displayed so that owners and families knew of the vessel's arrival, another example of how shipping on the Mersey was becoming more and more organised.

During and in the years following the Seven Years War, Liverpool continued to prosper. The development of the industrial revolution, with Lancashire being highly involved, affected Liverpool greatly. Canals were bringing manufactured goods for export and raw materials such as cotton were streaming in. The opening of the Wigan link on to the Leeds and Liverpool Canal in 1774 enabled coal to be transferred easily and cheaply to Liverpool where it powered local industry and was sent abroad with coal exports increasing ten times from 1770 to 1791. The town continued with its traditional imports which also increased at a fast rate. Between 1700 and 1790, sugar imports increased fivefold and rum and tobacco threefold.

The increase in imports of cotton, however, was phenomenal with imports increasing by fifty times in this period.

In 1760 the town was visited by Samuel Derrick from Bath, apparently a very noble and distinguished person. He found the town to be opulent with some elegant buildings but generally narrow, poor streets, and on the whole not as nice as Bristol. Nevertheless he found the people welcoming and enjoyed his visit and would have had the opportunity to read Liverpool's first newspaper, Williamson's Advertiser, which had commenced publication a few years earlier.

At this time the Liverpool dock system was extensive and could hold up to five or six hundred vessels although many would not have been as big as those that would appear after the turn of the century. But still it wasn't enough and new docks were deemed necessary. In 1788 King's Dock was opened followed by the Queen's Dock eight years later. In 1795 a massive Tobacco Warehouse was opened at King's Dock to hold 7,000 hogsheads of tobacco followed in 1812 by an even larger one.

```
Just in case anyone doesn't know - a
hogshead is a barrel used for storing
liquid, usually alcohol. In the United
States it was applied to a barrel used for
storing and transporting tobacco and thought
to have held around 1,000 lbs. of the
product.
```

It was all going well but then, once again, Liverpool's fortunes went downhill. The American War of Independence started (1775 - 1782) and Liverpool's trade with the New World reduced overnight. Customs revenues dropped from £274,655 in 1775 to £188,830 within five years and the tonnage of Liverpool's ships fell as some American privateers, with little enthusiasm, and later their French and Spanish allies, with great enthusiasm, took action against British, often Liverpool, vessels.

England stood alone against the world and traders setting out from Liverpool had to run the gauntlet of marauding French and Spanish warships and privateers with the Royal Navy having lost control of much of the sea around Britain. Liverpool responded to the nation's plight and, in 1778, raised a regiment of 1,100 troops, the Liverpool Blues. The regiment was sent to garrison Jamaica but, unused to the climate, only 84 men survived the posting and were able to return home.

Times were difficult for Liverpool's sea traders but, never ones to miss an opportunity, some made plans to turn the situation to their advantage. This was the time for some active privateering and 120 vessels were fitted out to target any French vessels that were spotted. Within five weeks of the campaign starting the privateers had brought prizes worth £100,000 to Liverpool and later a chance encounter with a French East Indiaman produced a prize of a box diamonds worth £135,000, an incredible sum at the time. Many people, of all classes, jumped at the chance to invest in privateering but it was risky, there could be good rewards or there could be none. There was a price to pay though with the crews of the privateers thinking they were a law unto themselves and their riotous behaviour was a common problem.

Some of the privateers may have been doing well but for the ordinary people and the merchants, things were not looking so good. Ever since Liverpool was founded it has experienced regular problems, be it plague, trade issues or some kind of hostilities. Each time the town would struggle back to its feet and become successful and then something else would happen.

But this time it would be different. When the American War of Independence ended, the town didn't exactly struggle to its feet, it surged forward with a tremendous increase in trade and prosperity. It was as if someone had turned on a tap that released ships on to the River Mersey at an unprecedented rate. Trade with the United States and the rest of the world boomed and Liverpool was taking the lion's share. In 1716 the town had shipped only 18,371 tons of cargo out of a total of 456,309 tons (4.0%) from all English ports; in 1792 the town shipped 260,380 out of an English total of 1,565,154 tons (16.7%). In 1791, 350 vessels were recorded as leaving the town on one tide. No wonder merchants in other English ports were worried.

The rapid development of the Lancashire cotton industry produced increasing imports of cotton from all parts of the world but mainly the United States. In 1791 the total number of cotton bales imported into England was 68,404. Within forty years this had increased by nearly ten times with most of the product being shipped to Liverpool before being transferred to Manchester.

By the end of the 18th century, Liverpool had turned into a very different town compared with 1700. It was much bigger with twelve times as many houses, its population had also increased twelve times, it now had over 400 streets, a Theatre had been opened in Drury Lane, it had extra dock facilities and shipping was now greater than Bristol's with the number of ships entering of leaving increasing by around 40%. Communications with inland towns were better than they had ever been and, as well as countless stage wagons operating, there were also many daily stage coach services including four to London, two to Manchester and one to York, Bolton and Lancaster.

Considerable wealth was now coming in to the town, making a number of people rich and providing employment for the thousands who flocked to the town. Much of the incoming wealth was put to good use with the construction of many fine buildings. Among the new buildings was the Infirmary (1748), the Painting Academy (1777), the Asylum for the Blind, the Workhouse (1770), the Athenaeum Library (1798), the Blue Coat Hospital (1798). Towards the end of the century there was an increasing interest in art and the promotion of knowledge with many schools being set up, including Sunday schools in 1784.

In 1775 the Drury Lane Theatre was opened, a substantial building with a stage wider than that of Covent Garden on a site that is now part of Williamson Square. At its opening this prologue by Dr. Aitkin was read:

Where Mersey's stream long winding o'er the plain,
Pours his full tribute to the circling main,
A band of fishers chose their humble seat;
Contented labour blessed the far retreat;
Inured to hardship, patient, bold, and rude,
They braved the billows for precarious food;
Their struggling huts were ranged along the shore,
Their nets and little boats their only store.

At length, fair Commerce found the chosen place,
And smiled approving on the industrious race.
Lo! as she waves her hand, what wonder's rise,
Stupendous buildings strike the astonished eyes:
The hollowed rock receives the briny tide,
And the huge ships secure from Neptune ride;
With busy toil the crowded streets rebound,
And wealth, and arts, and plenty spread around.

In 1803 the frontage of the building was replaced by this imposing semi-circular shape.

The theatre became very popular but it was only open during the summer months when the London theatres were closed. It is said that the success of the theatre was due, in part, to its "respectable" performers.

In 1785, perhaps to accommodate "less respectable" performers, the Music Hall in Bold Street was opened. Despite its unimposing exterior, the building was well featured internally with huge glass chandeliers, a secluded gallery, a fine organ and orchestra space. It could accommodate up to thirteen hundred persons.

While many people were enjoying themselves in the Liverpool scene, there were those who gave thought to scourge of the age - slavery and Britain's involvement. Even during its heyday in the eighteenth century, many people had been against it including such luminaries as Adam Smith, Dr. Johnson and Josiah Wedgwood. But as Liverpool approached the end of the 18th century, more and more people questioned the morality of it. But it was a difficult thing to publicly condemn. The trade was well supported, not just in Liverpool but also in Bristol and London, the British government giving tacit encouragement, and the churches were not too bothered with some churchmen even claiming that it was supported by the bible. It took brave people to put forward a different view.

Looking back now it is difficult to believe that Liverpool, and indeed any part of Britain, was ever involved in the slave trade but the reality is that, for most, it was a very different way of life and standards were very different to those we expect today. On the one level we had the very wealthy who could afford to construct many country houses during the 18th century and comfortably pay to staff them. Then we had the engineers, writers and artists, such as, Liverpool born George Stubbs. At the bottom of the heap we had the common people, who were in the majority and to whom life was cheap. This was a time when if you were not able to produce any income, you would not eat and would not have somewhere to live. Medical care, such as it was, was limited or not available, penalties for transgressions were severe and many people lived on a day-to-day basis. For entertainment people, at all levels and both sexes, thought it good fun to visit a public execution. Bull-baiting and cock-fighting were popular and were well supported in Liverpool where this form of "entertainment" was well organised, something to take the children to see on a Sunday afternoon or on market day. Many of the institutions had been at least been partly funded by public subscription with the opulent merchants who enjoyed the bull-baiting and cock-fighting, or who had made money out of slavery, no doubt contributing to these good works. A paradox which is now difficult to understand. The plight of slaves needs to be seen in relation to this way of life.

But what about the ordinary seaman who served on the slave trading ships? How could they do it? Conditions for the slaves were horrendous and they were mainly chained and packed like sardines below decks for weeks on end in conditions that can hardly be imagined. How could the seamen voluntarily sign on to face seeing the slaves in those conditions every day, and to some extent face living in similar conditions themselves? Well the fact is that these seamen were incredibly tough men and they were often offenders trying to escape justice. One of the few slave trader captains who is regarded as more humane, Hugh Crow, recounts how he found many slave trader crewmen to be the "very dregs of the community". Also, as Chandler in his book "Liverpool Shipping" points out, they probably saw nothing wrong with the trade. They would not have seen things as we see them today. They were living life on a day to day basis and each time they set sail they knew that they were taking terrible risks and may not return. Their vessel could be lost in a storm, they could succumb to serious or fatal diseases or injury, or they could be shipwrecked on rocks in unchartered waters. Even if they managed to avoid all those dangers, they still faced a threat from their own countrymen as they approached home waters. They had to get past the south western coast of England without becoming prey to the Cornish wreckers who would place false lights to lure any passing ship onto rocks so that their cargo could be seized. But even if they got home safely, they still had risks to face. The first thing that crew members would do after being paid was, not surprisingly, head for the Alehouses, particularly around Pool Lane and South Castle Street in Liverpool, where there would be people ready to deprive them, by whatever means, of their pay. It didn't even end there; drunken seamen were always at risk of being press-ganged into the Royal Navy, with Liverpool being such an important hunting ground for the naval press gangs that a naval "recruitment ship" was almost permanently berthed on the river.

But what the seamen really feared was being captured by Barbary Coast pirates which would mean them being taken into slavery and ending up in servitude with conditions at least as bad, and probably much worse, than the African slaves would face on the plantations. It is estimated that in the 250 years up to 1830, over one million European slaves ended up in hell-holes in North Africa. This risk was not just on the high seas, Barbary Coast pirates had been known to attack vessels in the Irish Sea and the Bristol Channel or even to come ashore on the south coast to seize slaves. As pirates go, these fierce buccaneers liked to operate at the upper end of wickedness and were something to be feared. They were well established in the 17th and 18th centuries and still continued into the 19th century until the French conquest of Algeria finally put an end to them.

Daily life for the mariners was an ordeal with poor food and dreadful living conditions. Discipline on board was often harsh and, in the case of some ship captains, it was brutal. Harsh conditions for crew members of early sailing ships have often been reflected in films and television drama, but, in some cases, the reality was even worse. In 1808 William Chapman, the Captain of a Liverpool slaver, was indicted for the murder of Robert Dunn, a crewman. Dunn was put on board by the ship's owners and Chapman took an early dislike to him, thinking he was a spy, and he was ill-treated from the start. Within a month of leaving Liverpool, he received twelve dozen lashes for spilling some molasses and for the remainder of the eighteen month journey he was subjected to regular abuse. Any minor transgressions were met with severe punishment including suspension by his heels for hours, starvation, being left naked on deck for hours and, towards the end, a severe beating with a hand-spike for resting where the pigs were kept. Dunn managed to crawl to a corner of the deck where he was covered with a tarpaulin. The Captain ordered that no-one should go to his aid. A few days later, he died and was thrown overboard. A doctor on board did nothing to help him and told the court that he feared for his life. Captain Chapman, who treated the court proceedings with some disdain, claimed in his defence that the crew were rebellious and that they had it in for him. He had to do what was necessary to ensure order on board. After a long deliberation, the jury acquitted him. Two other charges of murder of crewmen on the same voyage were not proceeded with as the evidence was much the same as for the Robert Dunn case. Such was the way of life on the high seas at the time. If you did what you were expected to do and didn't cause any trouble, you would have a hard journey but, if you were lucky, you would be paid for it and, if you were very lucky, you may receive some perks depending on the cargo carried and the places visited. But if you didn't do your job properly or if you crossed the Captain or the Officers, you could expect to be severely punished and there would be no-one to help you unless the rest of the crew mutinied which seldom happened. The crew normally accepted one of the number being punished because they knew that if they didn't they would be next and also because they realised that they were far from home on an unforgiving sea and their own lives depended on good ship discipline. And the ship's Captain knew that, if he lost control of the crew, he could well end up over the side, so he had to be tough. A soft Captain would soon lose the respect of the crew. In fact what crew members tended to prefer was a Captain who was very firm but fair since this would give them the best chance of getting home safely. Such was the way of life on ocean going vessels at the time; the crewmen are unlikely to have given much, if any, thought to the plight of any slaves they were carrying.

So it was very difficult for the slaves and it was very difficult for the seamen, but what was it like for the ship owners and the slave trader investors. It has long been assumed that they all did very well out of the trade - but is this true? Were the profits as high as people say? Gomer Williams gives an account of the *African* which crossed the Atlantic with 268 slaves, 197 male and 71 female in 1764. They were sold for a net amount of £8,131 which was a vast amount of money at that time. Obviously anyone hearing of sale proceeds such as these, today or at the time, would take the view that slave trading was a really big earner. But the costs involved in slave trading were massive. Williams tells of the goods that were traded for a single male slave at the Bonny slave market in 1801 (it was usual for slaves to be purchased individually or as a small group). The goods consisted of:

96 yards of various Manchester and Indian textiles
52 Handkerchiefs
5 Iron or Brass pots
2 Muskets
25 kegs of gunpowder
20 knives
4 Cutlasses
Beads
14 gallons of Brandy
Plus hats, flints and bags of shot

This is representative of the package of goods that would be traded for a slave and is estimated to have cost around £25. Buying goods to trade for slaves was the main cost of the exercise and, based on this example, it may have cost around £6,700 to acquire the 268 slaves that were transported by the *African*. There was also the cost of the crew to take into account. When it was a requirement to carry a doctor on board, the cost has been recorded as about £8 for the journey. On this basis, a crew of, say, forty might have cost around £200 for the journey. On top of this there was the cost of food for the crew and the slaves for what could have been up to a twelve month journey - perhaps £300. This would make the profit on the *African's* voyage £923, which was still a lot of money at the time. But there was another cost to meet - the cost of the vessel. Vessels were converted or specially built for the slave trade and this was expensive. They were fitted out with separate holds for the different slave sexes and were provided with shackles and slave collars. There was also the cost of protecting the ship's keel against attack by tropical worms. This would all have been a very big cost. Obviously, once built, the ship could undertake many journeys without further great expense but the ship could be lost at any time due to the weather or attack by pirates. Also there was a big risk when England was involved in hostilities with another country. During the seven years with France between 1756 and 1763, a number of slave traders were taken by the enemy or their privateers. This is a fairly simple look at the profits that the slave trader investors actually made and only highlights one journey of the *African* slave trader which may not be fully representative. Certainly some other accounts of profit from the slave trade show greater amounts being available to investors than that which is quoted here. However more recent analyses of slave trader accounts suggest that profits may not have been as high as has always been assumed and some have suggested that the average return on investment was only around 10%, still good but not massive. But until a full, and objective, forensic accounting exercise is carried out on the slave trader account books, many of which are said to still exist, we will never know for sure what the real profits were. What we do know, though, is that for most slave traders, the profits must have been good. Quite simply there were many traders and investors who got involved in the trade over many years and this would just not have happened if there hadn't been good money to be made out of it, or at least more money than would have made from other forms of trading.

But to what extent did Liverpool benefit from the slave trade? Was the town "built on the back of the slave trade" or did the slave "make a success of a struggling port", both allegations that have been made against the town? Clearly both comments show limited knowledge of the factors involved in the rise of the town. It is true to say that Liverpool had been a struggling port, in fact it often struggled to survive just as a town. But the fact is that when Liverpool started to become heavily involved in the slave trade, around the middle of the 18th century, the town had already turned the corner and was a bustling port with the Old Dock and the newer docks often bursting at the seams. Up to that time, Liverpool had only dabbled in the slave trade and Bristol and London were the key players. Even when Liverpool took over as the main slaver port, the trade was still not the dominant force in Liverpool shipping. In fact, despite what many people seem to think, most vessels travelling in and out of Liverpool, even up to around 75% at the height of the slave trade, were not slave ships.

However it is an undeniable fact that Liverpool and its people took to slave trading with gusto and, although slavers would remain in the minority of ships using the port, their impact certainly contributed significantly to the wealth of the town. It has been said that the slave trade needed Liverpool more than Liverpool needed the slave trade. This is undoubtedly true but the town certainly did well out of it. It became part of the town's, and its people's, psyche, and almost everyone thought it was important and that there was nothing wrong with it. The fact that it was wicked did not seem to occur to anyone or, if it did, the fact that, directly or indirectly, it provided some income was deemed to be more important.

Despite Liverpool's willing adoption of the slave trade, it should be borne in mind that many other ports would have been more than pleased to have a piece of the action, or a greater piece of the action. London merchants were peeved at losing the slave trade to Bristol and Bristol merchants were distraught at losing most of the trade to Liverpool. They would really have liked to have been more involved and other ports were also interested. Even a fine town like Lancaster had a real go at the slave trade in the middle of the 18th century but just couldn't compete with Liverpool. Other ports were finding it difficult to compete with Liverpool's entrepreneurial spirit, whether it was in the slave trade or in any other form of shipping. But it wasn't just the people of Liverpool who benefited from the slave trade, there were many others who made something out of it, including investors and manufacturers in various parts of the country. It could be said that the whole country benefited, sad fact though that is.

As the possibility of the abolition of the slave trade came closer, the people of Liverpool became increasingly bereft. They thought that abolition would not just mean a check on the town's economy, it would lead to total ruin, the smart new dock system would become empty and the town would once again become impoverished.

But the slave traders were determined to make as much money out of the trade as possible and kept it going until the last minute. In the twelve months before abolition in 1807, 185 slavers left Liverpool and transported 49,000 slaves.

Then the trade was abolished but unfortunately it didn't all cease right away. It was difficult for the Royal Navy to police thousands of square miles of ocean and some traders thought the penalty, a fine and confiscation of their ship, was worth the risk and, as long as they could safely complete one journey out of three, there was still money to be made. Another ruse was for slave traders to sail under a foreign flag. The Government decided that increased penalties were necessary and the threat of fourteen years transportation for offenders and later the classification of slave trading as piracy, which meant the "long drop" for those caught, soon did the trick and the slave trade rapidly tailed off.

So what became of Liverpool? All of that trade lost and then more disruption in 1812 when war with the United States seriously affected North American trade. Did the town go bankrupt? Well of course it didn't, the opposite happened. As in previous crises in the town's history, Liverpool bounced back but this time it was immediate and it was spectacular. It would move forward with a rate of growth that no British town or city had ever experienced before.

The factors which had held back Liverpool's growth in the past really were now confined to history. New factors came into play and Liverpool ticked all the boxes. It was the main port to handle the booming textile industry, it had an unsurpassed dock structure and shipping experience, it now had good internal links with manufacturing industry and it was right there to take advantage of the world's greatest opportunity during the 19th century - the rapid development of North America, especially the United States. And, if this wasn't enough, steam navigation was just about to take off in a big way and the ship builders of the Clyde, not too far away, knew how to build steamers and how to build them properly and, if anyone knew how to best make use of them, it was the people of Liverpool. And, unlike many ports, Liverpool had large supplies of coal locally available to power them.

In 1815 the first steam ship entered the Mersey and more soon followed. In 1816 the many ferry routes across the River Mersey were supplemented by the odd-looking double-hulled steamer *Etna* which crossed to Tranmere. The following year, trippers were able to enjoy the novelty of a steamer journey to see Chester Races, via the river and canal, a previously unimaginable experience. In 1819 the *Robert Bruce* gave Liverpool its first service to Glasgow and in the same year the

Savannah arrived having steamed a small part of the way across the Atlantic.

By 1832 there were 70 steamers operating out of Liverpool to Ireland, the Isle of Man, Wales, Scotland and Lancaster and 20 steamers providing local ferry services. In 1830 the world's first important railway was constructed between Liverpool and Manchester, a key manufacturing centre. In 1833 the first vessel to steam across the Atlantic, the *Royal William*, arrived in Liverpool. With steamers on the canals, there were now ways to move people and goods around the industrial hinterland of Lancashire and on the open sea without waiting for the right wind. Liverpool made the most of the opportunities and trade rocketed, particularly with the United States with imports of cotton reaching unprecedented levels. In 1791, the number of bales of cotton imported into was 68,404; in 1832, 774,937 bales were imported - into Liverpool alone, London could only manage 66,712 bales. The sugar trade with the West Indies became increasingly important and several refineries were established in Liverpool. The town also became part of the trade in spices when it was accepted as a port within the East India Company's charter. Trade with Ireland remained important with over 400,000 head of livestock being imported each year together with large quantities of agricultural produce especially wheat, oats and butter. In return, Liverpool despatched to Ireland manufactured goods and around 70,000 tons of salt and 50,000 tons of coal each year.

Cotton didn't just come from the United States, around 32,000 bales also came from Egypt plus some from the East Indies. After unloading at Liverpool docks, the cotton wool bales were sent on to Manchester and other Lancashire mill towns where they were converted into manufactured cotton goods which returned to Liverpool to be exported all over the world, in vast quantities. Britain was rapidly turning into the world's main centre of textile manufacture. Communications inland had always been a problem for Liverpool but the opening of a good road link and canals had improved links substantially. In 1830, they improved further, and dramatically, with the opening of the world's first important railway, between Liverpool and Manchester. By 1832, the number of stage coaches operating out of Liverpool had built to around 100 but numbers dropped dramatically as the Manchester railway became more and more important and was soon followed by other rail services.

There was nothing now to hold Liverpool back. In 1832 Liverpool's export value of manufactured cotton goods was £14 million, an incredible sum at that time, the rest of the country combined could only manage to export £3 million worth. In the same year Liverpool exported 100,000 crates and hogsheads of earthenware goods, many manufactured in the city, plus 300,000 tons of salt. Liverpool was providing a quarter of England's customs duties and had more ships registered than other towns except London and Newcastle and was now handling goods to and from most countries in the world with the United States, Canada and the West Indies the main links in the chain.

The rapid increase in Liverpool's trading just went on and on. From 1813 to 1857, imports of cotton increased five times, sugar and rum from the West Indies were up fifty per cent, wheat from North America went up ten times and exports of salt went up three times. In just thirty years, from 1796, the goods coming into Liverpool rose from 224,000 tons to over 1,200,000 tons.

As the town's shipping increased, so did its industrialisation. Manufacturing developed to handle the needs of the shippers, to process goods being imported and to provide goods for export. An eclectic mix of small and large factories were established to handle almost every type of product imaginable including sails,

Scotia the Brave

ropes, armaments, tools iron and brassware, tobacco, and corn. The big players though were the sugar refineries, the potteries, the tanneries and the shipbuilders. Another successful industry for Liverpool, which had begun during the early 18th century, was watch making with the town now turning out 11,000 timepieces a year, more than any other town except London.

Much wealth was now coming into the town and it was time for this to be reflected in its infrastructure and its layout. More and more workers were arriving, some poor but some bringing wealth and business acumen with them. The city expanded to meet the increasing population and the prosperous traders moved out to more salubrious parts with Everton village becoming popular with its pleasant vista over the river. For many though, living conditions were not that great but the local corporation, aided by the successful merchants who subscribed to many good works, did make some efforts to improve the town for everyone. The residents had the benefit of high quality water which was piped into the city from the springs in Bootle and Toxteth. It wasn't available every day though and, even when it was being piped, it was often only on tap for less than an hour a day. Nevertheless it was still much better than having to rely on water from contaminated wells all of the time but disease and uncleanliness would remain a big problem for Liverpool until 1857 when copious supplies of water were made available from a new reservoir at Rivington, later supplemented by further supplies from Lake Vyrnwy in North Wales. [handwritten: Surely Birmingham? and]

Despite the improvement in the town's fortunes, Liverpool was considered, up to around 1818, to be one of the worst lit and worst paved town's in England. One visitor from London, in January of that year, was so moved by having to walk on the city's sharp gravelly pavements in total darkness that he felt the need to pour his heart out in one of the capital's newspapers.

Apart from these problems, however, he was more than pleased with the town and its people. The response from Liverpool was almost immediate and later that same year gas lighting was installed near the Town Hall followed by nearby Castle Street and Lord Street in January 1819. Gas lighting was gradually extended throughout the whole town. Many libraries and learned institutions were set up due to the generosity of public subscribers around this time and, in 1823, the Marine Humane Society was established which paid rewards to those rescuing crewmen from vessels in distress in the river or around the coast.

But the rapid development of Liverpool came with its problems. Things were moving so fast that the town found it difficult to accommodate everything that was happening. More and more commercial premises were required and these were increasingly crammed into a small area near the river. The consequence of this was that uncontrolled fires were commonplace. The Spectator referred to Liverpool as The City of Fires and questioned why there did not seem to be a good system for extinguishing the fires when the buildings concerned were not far from the river. The newspaper even suggested that merchants should store their goods in other towns. Losses were enormous. In 1802 one million pounds worth of property in major warehouse fires and fires in 1836 and 1842 destroyed goods and buildings worth £700,000. During the early part of the nineteenth century, fire fighting in Liverpool was the under the control of the local corporation and insurance companies but in 1834 responsibility was transferred to the local Police Force and by 1836 this was a fully organised fire brigade with a staff of over sixty available to deal with any incidents. Staff joining the brigade from outside the Police Force were sworn in as special constables. They were initially equipped with three manual fire engines and a water cart. But this was clearly not enough to deal with the threat of fire, particularly in commercial premises and premises holding a lot of people, such as workhouses, and the brigade was regularly increased in size and within 25 years had over 140 fire officers operating from numerous fire stations around Liverpool. They were equipped with 17 manual fire engines, as many hose reel and ladder carts, and one 40 foot escape ladder. However these hand pumped engines would have struggled to cope with a fire in one of the many large warehouses which were springing up around the docks area and the arrival of steam pumped fire engines in the latter part of the 19th century would have been welcomed. Manual fire engines would still have a part to play though for some time.

Liverpool's Fire Brigade would remain under the control of the local Police Force until the outbreak of World War II and, on Merseyside, Fire Officers are still sometimes colloquially referred to as "Fire Bobbies".

Each year, the amount of traffic on the river was greater than the year before and more and more facilities were needed. In 1847 the 500 feet long George's Landing Stage was brought into use followed, ten years later, by the nearby 1,000 feet long Princes Landing Stage. The already extensive docks system proved increasingly inadequate and five new docks were opened in 1848 but these were soon overwhelmed and four more were opened just four years later. Across the river, the situation was the same with new docks and port facilities being established at Birkenhead.

Amongst the people though there was a price to pay for Liverpool's increasing prosperity - drunkenness. This had been a developing problem for some years and an early attempt at controlling it had been made by publishing a Drunkard's List every week in the local newspapers which listed those who had been convicted of being drunk and incapable. It was hoped that this would shame people into cutting down on alcohol. Unfortunately the practice had to be discontinued when the lists became too long and were taking up too much newspaper space! It was a good idea in principle but it became a bad advertisement for the town.

By 1858, the volume of cargo being shipped through Liverpool had reached the amazing figure of nearly 4.5 million tons.

```
Interesting Fact: Whoever prepared these
tonnage figures in 1858 could never have
imagined, even in their wildest dreams, that
exactly a century later the tonnage passing
through Liverpool Docks would be almost 27.5
million tons! Currently (2014) it is 29
million tons.
```

But shipping through Liverpool was not just cargo; it was also people and many thousands of them. Even before steam arrived Liverpool was a major port for passengers travelling to many parts of the world, in particular it was the main port for emigrants to North America. It was often a difficult journey though. There were many sailing packets available for the journey from the famous lines, such as, Black Ball and Dramatic etc., but they needed two things before they could set off - the right wind and the right tide. But transatlantic steam navigation would soon change that.

In 1840, one of the most important years in Liverpool's history, Samuel Cunard's first transatlantic steamer on a regular passenger and Royal Mail service, the *Unicorn*, would set out for North America. More vessels carrying the Cunard flag would soon follow and Liverpool would become synonymous with transatlantic passenger travel for more than the next hundred years.

In 1857 an Act of Parliament took away control of the docks from Liverpool Borough and created the independent Mersey

Docks and Harbour Board to run the docks on both sides of the river. The new board was required to pay Liverpool Corporation £1.5 million as compensation for loss of the power to levy duties and, at the same time, took over the Corporation's debts of £6 million and Birkenhead Dock Estate's debt of £1.4 million.

One of the Board's first jobs was to expand the docks which still couldn't cope with the vast increase in trade. In 1859 the Canada Dock was opened, its name reflecting increasing trade with the colony, followed by construction of the Herculaneum Dock which was named after Herculaneum Pottery, a major nearby pottery manufacturer until competition from Staffordshire and foreign potteries put an end to it.

The Board planned a big new dock in Birkenhead, the Great Float, which became an important port for emigrants to Australia to feed the gold rush. A large number of Liverpool shipping lines were established to meet the demand using sailing clippers, the distance being much too far for most steamers at the time. When the gold rush ended, some shipping lines went under, but others were able to continue with routes to Australia and the Far East becoming well developed. As the gold rush tapered off, the Governments in Australia came up with new ideas to encourage settlement, the Government of Queensland, for instance, offering settlers who travelled there on the Black Ball Line in 1861 a grant of good land worth £30, roughly the cost of a first class ticket.

A good illustration of how Liverpool had grown by the middle of the nineteenth century is provided by M Jackson and T Sulman who produced an aerial drawing of Liverpool and the River Mersey that was published in the Illustrated London News in 1865. The artists were suspended in a captive balloon above the river and produced a sequence of six drawings that could be placed together to form a panorama of the whole Liverpool waterfront. The drawings record 469 vessels on the river or in the Liverpool docks system. This does not include rowing boats, small personal sailing vessels, vessels in dry dock or under construction, vessels berthed on the Wirral side of the river or in the Birkenhead docks system, or vessels in the estuary.

Analysis of the vessels is as follows:

Screw Cargo/Passenger steamers	18
Military Screw Steamers	1
Screw driven Liners	2
Sailing Ships	385
Paddle Liners	2
Coastal Paddlers	16
Paddle Tugs/Ferries	45

All figures approximate

Further analysis of the drawings gives an indication of the level of industrialisation within the city. This shows that the city had at least 213 tall factory chimneys, not including those within the docks system, and still retained 7 windmills plus, interestingly, at least 2 oast houses and this was in a town that was still quite compact in size.

And so, after many trials and tribulations, Liverpool had made it, and had made it in a big way. That little settlement sitting on the northern sandstone bank of the Mersey that no-one, apart from King John, thought had any future had blossomed into Britain's second city and was a major force in international trade. It had become the most important British terminal for shipping, of goods and passengers, between Britain and North America and, importantly for this book, it had become the home of the world's finest, and last, paddle liner - the *Scotia*.

Chapter 10

Liverpool's bid to lead the Atlantic steam service

Despite high hopes, the Liverpool-based attempt to be the first to send a passenger steamer across the Atlantic to New York was not successful. The two contenders were way behind the *Sirius* and the *Great Western* but the two vessels did make their mark in history - the *Royal William,* which was the first to make the journey across the Atlantic from Liverpool, and the *Liverpool,* which was the first big steamer to carry the city's name. Therefore they deserve a chapter to themselves.

In 1838 the Transatlantic Steamship Company was formed and its aims are quite clear in the title. Their plan was to send a passenger steamer across the Atlantic ahead of the *Great Western* and the *British Queen* and the vessel they hoped would do this was the *Liverpool* which was under construction in Liverpool by Humble and Milcrest. The ship was actually being built for Sir John Tobin but the company agreed to buy her as soon as she was finished. Her dimensions were - length 240 feet, beam 35 feet, depth 21 feet, tonnage 1150. Her engines were built by Messrs. George Forrester and Co., of Liverpool, and were of 464 horse-power, giving an expected speed of ten knots.

However, with the *Liverpool* not yet complete, it soon became apparent that the company had no chance against the *Great Western* which had already been launched. As with the *British Queen*, the company came up with a rescue plan and chartered the *Royal William* to make the trip.

This was not the *Royal William* mentioned earlier but a vessel designed to cross the Irish Sea between Liverpool and Dublin and owned by the City of Dublin Steam-packet Company. She had been recently built by the Liverpool firm of Wilson and was 145 long by 28 feet broad and 17 feet deep and she displaced 617 tons. She was powered by two side-lever Fawcett, Preston and Co. engines having cylinders 48 inches in diameter with a five foot stroke, and 24 feet diameter paddle wheels. Her speed was expected to be 8 to 10 knots. The *Royal William* is said to be the first to be divided into watertight compartments by iron bulkheads, of which she had five.

Although ready built, she wasn't suitable for sailing the Atlantic immediately and needing some refitting to enable her to carry more coal and also to provide the passengers with facilities for a fifteen day journey across the Atlantic rather than a short hop across the Irish Sea.

By the time she left for New York, on 5th July 1838, the *Great Western* and the *British Queen's* substitute, the *Sirius*, had already reached the city and the *Royal William* was well out of the race. However she performed well and made a successful trip. She now needed passengers for her journey home and the following advertisement appeared in New York papers:

British Steamship Royal William, 617 tons.

Captain Swainson, R.N.R., Commander.

This fine steamer, having lately arrived, will be dispatched again to Liverpool on Saturday, August 4th, at 4 P.M. She is only sixteen months old, and from her peculiar construction (being divided into five sections, each watertight) she is considered one of the safest boats to England.

Her accommodations are capacious, and well arranged for comfort. The price of passage is fixed at 140 dollars, for which wine and stores of all kinds will be furnished. Letters will be taken at the rate of 25 cents for the single sheet, and in proportion for larger ones or one dollar per ounce weight. For further particulars apply to Abraham Bell and Co., or Jacob Harvey

Note the confident tone of the advertisement and the price - 140 dollars which must have been a fortune at the time.

The *Royal William* made a few more successful journeys to New York but then the *Liverpool* became available and she rejoined the very successful City of Dublin Steam Steam-Packet Company and her 20 ferry sisters on the Irish Sea routes, her long distance marathons now over. Eventually she was downgraded to being a coal hulk and then, in 1888, she was sold for just £11.

More transatlantic travellers now had more confidence in steam travel and passenger numbers on the existing steamers were increasing all the time although many still preferred the sailing packets and the newer clippers, many of which continued to operate. With the *Liverpool* now ready, the owners of the Transatlantic Steamship Company thought that they could make a killing and placed the following advertisement in the Liverpool Mercury to raise funds for two additional vessels:

" Applications for the unappropriated shares may be made to the Company's Bankers or Solicitors or at the offices of the Company in Liverpool, Dublin, and London or to D. and J. B. Neilson, Stock and Share Brokers, Exchange Street East, Liverpool.
" John Pollock,"Agent, 24, Water Street." Liverpool, September 15th, 1838."
As an instance of the great attention paid to the earlier Atlantic steamers, the following account of this notable vessel, condensed from the "Liverpool Mercury" of October 12th, 1838, will be of interest

" Transatlantic Steamship Company.
" The arrangement for establishing an intercourse by steam navigation between the British Isles and the United States of America being finally completed, and an union of interests in Liverpool being now satisfactorily arranged, the Directors of the Transatlantic Steamship Company have to announce that with the view of giving immediate effect to the operations, they have purchased the powerful and splendid steamship, the Liverpool, of 464 horse-power, by Messrs. George Forrester and Co., and 1,150 tons burthen, built by Messrs. Humble and Milcrest for Sir John Tobin, and intended for Transatlantic intercourse.
" The Directors have also to state that for the purpose of securing an efficient and permanent establishment between Liverpool and New York, two vessels are now building of 450 horse-power each, and 1,250 tons burthen each, by Messrs. Fawcett, Preston and Co., and Messrs. W. and J. Wilson, and will, it is expected, be available in the course of next year.
" Shares in the first instance will be issued to the amount of but one half the capital above-mentioned.
" In issuing the remaining half, priority of subscription will be given to the then existing proprietors. Instalments to be called for at intervals of not less than three months, and not exceeding £10 per share.
" On allotment of shares a deposit of £6 per share to

be lodged to the credit of Trustees with any of the Company's Bankers who will give necessary receipt for the same.

On 12th October 1838, the Liverpool Mercury gave this detailed account of the *Liverpool*:

" As this vessel is not only the largest steamer hitherto built at this port, but the first that has been fitted up a priori, expressly for Transatlantic conveyance, much interest and curiosity have been excited by the appearance of so noble a specimen of the united skill of the naval architect and the engine-builder ; and so numerous have been the visitors who have inspected her as the works approach towards completion, that some account of her dimensions and equipments may be acceptable to those of our readers who take an interest in the success already developed, and the high promise presented by the application of steam to the purposes of ocean navigation.

'The Liverpool, *it is generally known, was built last year for Sir John Tobin by Messrs. Humble and Milcrest, and was purchased some months ago by the Liverpool Transatlantic Steam Company, an association branching out of the Dublin Steam Company, to whose enterprise and exertions for years Liverpool, as a port for steam vessels, is mainly indebted for its growing prosperity. Her length is 235 feet from stem to taffrail her beam 35 feet (exclusive of the breadth of her paddleboxes)*

; the depth of hold is 21 feet ; and she admeasures 1,150 feet.

" She is considerably longer (we believe 25 feet) than the first-rate man-of-war, and had the mechanical genius in his aspirations imagined and depicted, some thirty years ago, such a floating Leviathan, bearing in its wonderful, and we may add, sublimely powerful means of rapid transit for thousands of miles, even against the adverse winds and the current of the ocean, she would have been set down as a rambling enthusiast, over whose safe keeping his friends should exert a watchful eye.

" Such, however, are the rapid strides of modern science, and such the enterprise and .liberality with which it is cherished and encouraged, that without wishing to disparage the high merits of the Liverpool *or* British Queen *as modern steamships, we venture to predict that in thirty years more vessels will, in the progress of improvement, be produced as much surpassing these in size and power, as they surpass them that have immediately preceded them. The* Liverpool, *it is expected, will carry (independently of 450 tons of coals) about 700 tons of goods.*

" She is what is termed ' shipbuilt,' there being no indentures or dimples in her sides for the reception of paddle-wheels, so that were these removed, she would appear like an ordinary sailing ship, and as such, might be safely navigated

" The fineness of her bottom, her length, and excellence of her engines, are all favourable , to this supposition, and the solution of the problem will in a few days put an end to further vague speculation. Steam being the principal, or almost sole motive power in contemplation, the rigging of the Liverpool *is very light.*

" She has three masts, a foremast like that of a ship, with a top and yards, taut, but light both in spars and rigging, and a mainmast and small mizenmast, each with a plain topmast and cross-trees like a schooner, also very light, and of moderate height, so that the foremast will spread as much sail as both.

" The paddle-boxes are of great size and height ; the figurehead and cut-water look well ; and her stern, which is decorated with carved work, emblematic of England and America, is extremely neat and appropriate.

Some of the standing rigging and chimney-stays are, we learn, partly composed of wire, and are thus stronger than common cordage of a greater thickness, while they present less resistance to the atmosphere.

" The diameter of the paddle-wheels is 29 feet.

" The engines, built by Messrs. Forrester and Co. Vauxhall Foundry, are well worthy of inspection, both in regard to their compactness and beauty in construction, the extraordinary strength, and their superior finish. They are 468 horse-power. The cylinders are each 75 inches diameter, and the stroke of the piston rod is 7 feet. The propelling force of these machines, (enough to drive the thousands of movements in ten or a dozen of our largest cotton-mills), will be prodigious.

" The iron shaft or spindle that turns the paddlewheels is equal in girth to a man's body, and but fairly proportioned to the revolutionary force which the cranks will communicate.

"There are two distinct boilers, and two funnels, placed at some distance from each other, and ranging with the masts. The fire-rooms are spacious ; the coals are supplied from lateral bunkers, made of plate iron ; and " The 'main or after cabin' is a splendid apartment of 58 feet in length, and 28 feet 9 inches in width at one end, slightly narrowing to 22 feet 4 inches at the stern; it is 8 feet in height to the beams, and 8 feet between them

" The state-rooms are exceedingly handsome and commodious.

There are in this cabin sixteen in number, each with two berths or beds, with the exception of two, which are each fitted, for the peculiar accommodation of a party, with three beds. They are well lighted from the roofs and sides by patent lights, those in the sides serving also, on being opened, as ventilators.

" The colouring of these rooms is a warm, delicate pink, with gorgeous damask silk hangings to correspond, of French white, with crimson satin stripes. At the broadest or mid ship end of this main cabin is the ladies' retiring or private room, where several beds are also elegantly fitted up, and every convenience for the comfort and adornment of ' the fair ' is provided

" There are tanks in abundance, in addition to which water will be daily and hourly distilled by an apparatus fixed for the purpose, and will undergo filtration, so as to be equal in purity *and coolness to that of the ' crystal well ' of the hermit. It may be added that in the main cabin, including the ladies' state-rooms, and the sofas, no fewer than fifty beds are provided.*

" The 'fore cabin' is 45 feet in length, by from 29 feet 4 inches to 23 feet 10 inches in width, and has eight dormitories or state-rooms on each side. This room is fitted in a style somewhat different to the other, but scarcely less beautiful or costly. The walls are empanelled in rosewood and other woods, with rich style, and separated by circular-topped pilasters."

The *Liverpool's* first journey began on the 20th October, 1838 when she set out for New York. She made her way past Ireland but on 30th October she had to put back to Queenstown (then called the Cove of Cork, and now Cobh) re-sailing on 6th November, and reaching New York on 23rd November. She made several voyages, averaging seventeen days out, and fifteen home but couldn't make any money. She was then sold to the Peninsular and Oriental Company, who changed her name to the *Great Liverpool*. On 24th February 1846, she was wrecked off Cape Finisterre following a fire. Two lives were lost.

```
Tons or tonnes?  There are a number of
references in this book to the weight of
vessels in "tons". Younger readers may
think that this should be tonnes.  This is
not the case - tons are tons or 1,015.87
kilograms.  In the age covered by this
book, the metric system had not been
invented, at least not as far as Britain
was concerned, and we used imperial weights
and measures such as tons, feet, furlongs,
quarts, pecks, drams, 1/64th of an inch,
pennyweights, firkins, roods and many more
long lost measures. How on earth did we
manage to produce precision engineering
using such measures? Well, actually, we
```

managed very well indeed and products were manufactured to very exacting tolerances. This was illustrated at the 1851 Great Exhibition when Whitworths, the famed manufacturer of high precision armaments and engineering tools, displayed a machine that could measure a length to a tolerance of 1/millionth of an inch!

● ● ●

Chapter 11

The Age of the Trans-Atlantic steamer begins

Despite what some people expected, the *Great Western* and the *Sirius* had made it safely to New York and there was tremendous excitement as the news spread over North America.

A few days later, the Royal Mail sailing packet, *Tyrian*, reached Halifax with news of the their safe arrival and the same day she set sail for Falmouth. On board was Joseph Howe, the Halifax newspaper man and transatlantic steam proponent, who was making his first trip abroad.

On the way, the *Tyrian* became becalmed and by chance alongside steamed the *Sirius* on her return journey. Because the *Tyrian* could be becalmed for some time, the decision was made to transfer the mail to the *Sirius* to take on to Falmouth. Whatever the weather, the steamer could get through. Joseph Howe understood the significance of what was happening right away and later wrote *"Now that the experiment has been fairly tried, there can be little doubt that ere long the Atlantic will be aswarm with these sea monsters, and that a complete revolution will be wrought in the navigation of the ocean, as has already been witnessed on the rivers and inland seas"*. Howe's vision was that Atlantic mail steamers would call at Halifax on their way to New York and would bring immigrants to develop Nova Scotia as had happened in the United States of America and in some parts of Canada. Life in Nova Scotia could be transformed.

Howe met up with Samuel Cunard at his hotel and they discussed the possibility of sending mail steamers across the Atlantic to Halifax. Howe had already been in touch with the owners of the *Great Western* and the *British Queen* who were supportive of his mail to Halifax idea. The British Government had recently changed to using private ships to carry mail to Ireland and the continent and had paid them a subsidy to do this. In 1838 a subsidy was granted to some mail shippers who used steamships. To ensure that ample ships were available to the Government if a new war should break out, which of course it would, the Government required that all steam vessels receiving a mail subsidy would be leased to the Admiralty as troop carriers when required. In 1837 the whole packet service had been turned over to the Admiralty and someone was appointed Comptroller of Steam Machinery and Packet Service to handle the conversion of the packet lines to steam. That someone was Sir Edward Parry, Samuel Cunard's old friend from Halifax. Up until this time, the Admiralty had been content to entrust the mails to America to military sailing brigs to make the dangerous Atlantic crossing. It has been suggested that these ships became known as "coffin brigs", "coffin ships" being the name that some vessels, which were way past their best and were potentially dangerous, were called, although this term seems to have been more generally used at a later stage. However it seems unlikely that the British Government would entrust mails, which would include important Government communications, to vessels which were considered dangerous and it could well be that the brigs received their name due to their coffin shape. The crossings were slow usually taking between thirty and seventy days and the British government had seen how slow communications helped Britain lose the American colonies. In addition trade between Britain and North America was now substantial and merchants were demanding a better service.

The Admiralty would have noted the successful journeys being made by the steamer *Great Western* in 1838 but Parry was reluctant to get rid of the sailing packets to cross the Atlantic until he was totally sure that a regular and safe steam service could be provided. It would, after all, be very embarrassing for him if he replaced the sailing brigs with ships that provided a worse service.

Sam, however, thought that steam travel across the Atlantic had already been proved practical and decided to move things along. He planned to raise the money to build three or four large passenger steamers that would carry the mail between Britain and Halifax with feeder steamers taking the mail on to the United States. Making Halifax the terminal would help turn the town, Sam's birthplace, into a major international port. He would go to Parry with this proposal which he was sure would be accepted.

First he searched for some funding for the enterprise but this proved to be much more difficult than he had imagined. He contacted the money men in Halifax and then Boston, but they all turned him down. Times were hard, and like many people in Britain and North America, they were not convinced that transfer to steam navigation across the Atlantic was a good idea. There were already many sailing packets successfully crossing the Atlantic. Why change to something that they still considered unproven and which may only be a passing fad or a novelty? And it was considered highly dangerous. Their views are understandable. Crossing the Atlantic on a sailing ship was already dangerous enough. Ships were often lost due to collision with other vessels or rocks, and it was not unknown for ships to set out and never be heard of again. Adding to the risk by having an engine that could explode at any time, as they sometimes did, and by carrying hundreds of tons of coal thus creating a fire risk, was seen as at best foolhardy and at worst, suicidal. He returned to Halifax empty-handed, but he wasn't too worried as he thought there would be plenty of time to put a proposal together. Unfortunately, he was wrong

On 8th November, an advertisement appeared in The Times in London *"Steam vessels required for conveying her Majesty mails and dispatches between England and Halifax Nova Scotia and also between England Halifax and New York"*. The service was to start the following April, with ships running once a month. The port of departure could be either Bristol, Falmouth, Liverpool or Southampton and all tenders had to be submitted to the Admiralty before December 15th. By the time this information reached Sam, it was already past the deadline. Nevertheless, he immediately arranged to go to London. In Sam's world, the fact that he had no funding and that he had missed the deadline was only a minor complication. He was determined to get that mail contract.

Chapter 12

"I want that mail contract"

When Sam arrived in London, he went to see Edward Parry where he learned that two companies had already submitted tenders. The Great Western Company had proposed a monthly service starting in about a year and a half whilst the St George Steam Packet Company offered to start at once, but only using small, coastal steamers. However, neither company wanted to risk their ships on winter sailings. Despite having no funding, Sam offered an all year round twice a month service to Halifax, although the royalty had only asked for a once a month service, with feeder services to Boston and Quebec. Sam asked for £55,000 a year for this mail service, which would start on 1st of May 1840. Parry suggested that the proposal might be acceptable so Sam started to look around for a good shipbuilder. His contacts at the East India Company recommended the Glasgow firm of Wood and Napier, the head of the firm being Robert Napier, the best marine engineer in Britain.

Cunard wrote to him saying *"I want a plain and comfortable boat not the least unnecessary expenses on show"*. He couldn't go over the top in the ship's designs; after all he didn't have the funding at this stage and of course he wanted to make some money out of the exercise. After an exchange of letters, he went to Glasgow to meet Napier and Wood.

Cunard negotiated a price of £30,000 each for three 800 ton ocean going paddle steamers. Sam reported back to Parry, who thought 800 tons was too small and asked for the ships to be increased in size to 960 tons. Sam agreed the new size with Robert Napier, at a cost of £32,000 each, and on 18th March 1839 the contract was signed. In doing so, Cunard introduced a revolution in shipbuilding – the construction of sister ships. Napier was already a well respected Marine engineer and designer and having this contract to build ships for the British mail service would be a further feather in his cap, a big feather. He promised to make the ships "very good and strong". If he failed, it would be very bad for his reputation, and costly. But Napier was not too concerned; as far as he was concerned, he was going to build the best paddle steamers so far. Sam now had to find some funding. Signing a contract for three ocean going ships without first establishing that funding could be provided was really risky. But that was Samuel Cunard.

    `Advice to prospective entrepreneurs: Don't do this!`

Cunard went back to Glasgow to take advantage of Napier's offer to help find funding. He was introduced to James Donaldson, a Glasgow cotton broker and to George Burns, who had recently been offered the mail contract but had turned it down. Glasgow-born Burns operated a fleet of sailing coasters to Liverpool and, later, steamers to Belfast. When it became time to upgrade the Liverpool run to steamships, he formed the City of Glasgow Steam Packet Company, along with David MacIver, who was based in Liverpool. McIver was born in Scotland and had spent his early years in the office of the American Consul in Greenock. Sam had several meetings with Napier, Burns and MacIver. Napier and Burns were very positive about the mail steamer project but MacIver was not sure. However Sam's powers of persuasion won through in the end and the funding was raised. A company was formed, which raised £270,000. Cunard put in £55,000, Donaldson £16,000, Napier £6,000, David MacIver £5,500 and his brother, Charles, £4,500. The company was called the British and North America Royal Mail Steam Packet Company. It would soon just be known as the Cunard Line or Cunard's. Whilst in Glasgow, Samuel Cunard received a letter from Boston merchants, asking him to persuade the Admiralty to agree to extending the mail run to Boston instead of terminating at Halifax. This was a difficult time for Sam. He saw the service terminating at Halifax as a way of turning the town into a major port; good for the town, where he was born, and good for the family business, S. Cunard & Co. The other shareholders supported the change and in the end Sam had to agree that it would be the best plan. Boston was a thriving expanding town, with a much larger populated hinterland, and could supply more passengers and cargo than Halifax. It was clearly the right business decision but Sam made it with a heavy heart.

The company presented a new proposal to the Admiralty. They would put up four ships for the mail run each of around 1,200 tons with cabin space for 115 passengers and would steam from Liverpool on the 4th and 19th of each month, terminating at Boston but with stops at Halifax each way. Liverpool was the obvious choice for the Eastern terminal. It was closest to Glasgow where the vessels would be built, David MacIver was based there, it was central to Britain, and it was already an expanding port near to manufacturing industries.

The Admiralty accepted the proposal and agreed a new subsidy of £60,000 per year. The contract, for a period of seven years, was signed on 4th May 1839. In July, Sam sailed for New York on the *Great Western*, leaving David and Charles MacIver, to set up construction of the Liverpool terminal. On the way he must have thought many times of the four new super-paddle steamers under construction on the

Clyde. Once again he'd overcome all the obstacles to win through, this time for a major international contract.

Sam now had to organise things in North America. He acquired a site in Boston on Noddle's Island and began organising construction of dock facilities. In Halifax he would be able to use one of Cunard's three wharves, which was of the right size. To get the mail to Quebec, it would go overland by existing stagecoach service to Pictou where it would link with a new steamer feeder service. The *Unicorn* steamer was under construction in Glasgow for this feeder service.

Meanwhile Robert Napier organised the building of the four mail ships to be named *Britannia, Acadia, Caledonia and Columbia*. They would all be wooden-hulled side paddlers with engines built by Napiers but with construction of the hulls sub-contracted to various shipbuilders. The *Britannia* would be built by Robert Duncan, the *Acadia* by John Wood, the *Caledonia* by C. Wood and the *Columbia* by Robert Steele. All of the steamers would be built to the same specification but with some minor differences because of the different hull builders. They each had two decks, one funnel, two huge paddle wheels, a square stern and a clipper bow. Gross tonnage of each was around 1200 tons and they were around 200 ft. with a beam of 34 ft., 56 ft. over the paddles which were 28 ft in diameter. The Napier engines, one per ship, were side-lever with a 6 feet diameter cylinder and a stroke of nearly 7 feet. They produced a nominal power output of around 425 h.p. and gave the vessels an estimated top speed of 9 knots. The engines, together with their 12 furnaces and 4 boilers, took up around a third of the ship's length.

Robert Napier was one of the most skilled and respected marine engineers in Britain. Born in Dumbarton, in 1791, he started as a blacksmith and toolmaker and later went to work for his cousin David Napier, whose company was involved in providing engines for early steamboats. In 1824 Napier built his first pair of marine engines which were fitted to the paddle steamer *Leven*, built by James Laing, of Dumbarton. Success as a marine engineer came rapidly and in 1842 he began the business of iron shipbuilding at Govan.

> **Memo. to Merseyside residents. Napier appointed, as chief draughtsman, William Denny, who became some years later, with his brother, Peter, founder of the famous shipbuilding firm Denny Bros of Dumbarton, builder of the much missed Mersey cruise-ferry Royal Iris III, the legendary fish and chip boat.**

Each vessel was fitted out to accommodate 115 passengers, all first-class, and 82 crew. The upper deck carried the officer's quarters, the bakery, the galley and the cow house, and the rest of the deck was open with areas for storing the sailing gear but with a lot of space left for passengers to wander, when the weather was fine. The Britannia was barque-rigged, fore and aft rigged on the mizzenmast and square-rigged on the mainmast and foremast.

The 8 feet by 6 feet cabins, which were a little on the basic side, could accommodate two persons with two bunks, a settee, two water jugs and two chamber pots. There was only very limited lighting to reduce the risk of fire. The standard was not up to that of the quality sailing packets but these vessels would be able to provide something that the packets could not provide - regularity of service - and this would be something that passengers would value.

Scotia the Brave

Chapter 13

The Cunard Line gets up steam

A large crowd turned up on the Clyde to see the launch of the *Britannia* but there was still a lot to do before she could set out on her maiden voyage across the Atlantic. She still had to be fitted out, have her engines fitted at Napier's and then undergo sea trials. It soon became clear to Samuel Cunard that the vessel would not be ready for the contract start date of 1st May. The other vessels, the *Acadia,* the *Caledonia* and the *Columbia* were still on the stocks, months behind schedule. This was potentially very serious. The Cunard line was faced with contract penalties of £1,000 for every departure that was delayed for 12 hours or more. This was a lot of money and would be a crippling cost to the company in its first year of trading. To make matters worse, Cunard realised that providing a twice a month service in winter, with only four ships, was far too optimistic. It seems that Sam had been a bit too enthusiastic on this occasion and had not fully thought things through. He contacted Parry to discuss the problem. The Admiralty agreed to the winter service taking place only once a month but the penalty for delayed sailings would have to remain. Cunard discussed this serious problem with his partners and they came up with a simple solution. Cunard had the little steamer *Unicorn* on standby in Glasgow ready to cross the Atlantic where she was planned to be used as a mail transfer ship between Pictou and Quebec. This vessel could be used until the *Britannia* was ready. This was quite a dramatic and risky decision to make. The *Unicorn* was only half the size of the new mail steamers and had only been designed to operate around coastal waters. However she would have to make at least one crossing of the Atlantic so why not let her carry the Royal Mail and some passengers as well. Still a bit of a risk though, this was something she hadn't really been designed for. Undaunted, Captain Douglas and his forty crew set out from Glasgow for Liverpool where the vessel made her way into Clarence Dock ready to be loaded with cargo and provisions for her long journey across the Atlantic. On 15th of May she left the dock to wait on the river for the mail and her 26 passengers, including Cunard's nephew Ned, to be delivered to her the next day. The passengers must have been almost over-whelmed by feelings of excitement and trepidation as they set off but the journey across the Irish Sea was not too bad and those on board probably relaxed as they looked forward to the rest of the crossing. But it was as if fate and the Atlantic Ocean had conspired to make life as difficult as possible for the *Unicorn* and for those on board. They encountered gale after gale and, at one point, were said to have been subjected to hurricane force winds. But the gallant little *Unicorn*, with the guidance of Captain Douglas, shrugged off everything that was thrown at her and behaved impeccably throughout the journey. On June 1st she reached Halifax where she received an enormous welcome and the vessel's commander, Captain Douglas, was toasted by the passengers and the citizens of the town led by the jubilant civic officials. The *Unicorn* stayed in Halifax for twelve hours during which over 3,000 people took the opportunity to inspect the ship and then she set off for Boston carrying a number of members of the Cunard and Duffus families. She arrived on 5th June and received another massive welcome, bands were playing, church bells rang, people lined the river banks, and a large flotilla sailed out to greet her. The United States ship-of-the-line *Columbus* hoisted the Red Ensign and her band played American and English national tunes. Her Captain and Officers were given a huge civic reception with Ned Cunard being the guest of honour. The poet Longfellow is said to have been the guest speaker. The *Unicorn* brought with her files of London newspapers from 15th May and Liverpool papers from 16th May and the Boston newspapers were soon filling their editions with copious reports of what was happening in the world. It was old news but, in transatlantic terms, this was still pretty good. Bostonians thought that they were now becoming one of the United State's premier cities and, not only that, they were leaving New York as an also ran in world affairs. The next stop for the *Unicorn* was Quebec which she reached on 29th June. It was as if every citizen, alerted by telegraph, had heard about her and was on hand to welcome her. The *Unicorn* was the ship of the hour throughout North America. She was the first vessel of the transatlantic Cunard Line and everyone knew that there was more, and better, to come. The British and North American Royal Mail Steam Packet Company, which would almost immediately be known to everyone as the Cunard Line, was now in business; the other transatlantic shippers had better watch out!

In England, the *Britannia* was being prepared in Liverpool for her maiden voyage. The Cunard Line partners wanted to make sure that this voyage and all future voyages were successful and safe. Steamers were still considered dangerous by many people so safety was considered a very important factor in ship procedures, particularly in the engine room. Accidents involving steam engines were still happening and many people remembered reading about the dreadful Hull explosion in 1837. In this incident the Union steam packet was preparing to leave the jetty at around 6.00 p.m. after loading passengers for her trip to Gainsborough. Suddenly there was a massive explosion when the boiler burst which caused the vessel to immediately sink. The air was filled with flying pieces of wood, bodies and bales of goods. Friends and relatives of those on board, who were congregated on the jetty to wave the passengers off, suffered terrible injuries as pieces of the boiler scythed through them. A porter on the vessel was thrown on to the roof of a three storey building and a truss of woollen goods, weighing around 200 lbs. was thrown completely over the roof of a dockside building into the next street. The number of people on board the Union was not recorded making it difficult to confirm the number killed but it was at least twenty and possibly up to seventy. It was thought at the time that the ship's engine was not of sufficient power for the vessel's size and that too much pressure had been put on the boiler but a later opinion was that it had not been kept filled with enough water. Twelve months later, the *Victoria*, another steamer from Hull, collided with a brig on the Thames which caused the boiler to explode and resulted in the deaths of nine men. It was against this background that Cunard planned his new mail ships. Crossing the Atlantic was dangerous enough without adding to the danger with steam. He realised that if safety standards were not high, his whole transatlantic venture could be put at risk; just one bad accident could put paid to the whole project. Safety and reliability, not speed, were to be important selling features. Key staff were to be fully trained in the jobs they were to do especially those in the engine room and it was an important requirement that sufficient lookouts should be on duty, especially when ice was expected. The plan was that, unlike the other shipping lines, the Cunard Line would get a reputation for safety.

Of course, a successful journey across the Atlantic requires the passengers to follow the rules as well as the crew. The following Rules and Regulations were posted on board the mail steamers so that everyone knew what was expected of them. A good maxim for any seafarer is "*A disciplined ship is a safe and happy ship"*. This applies just as much today as it did during the 19th century and before.

RULES AND REGULATIONS.

It being obvious that, on a Passage of some days' duration, the comfort of a numerous body of PASSENGERS must very much depend upon the manner in which they themselves assist in promoting it, a cheerful acquiescence is expected in the following Regulations and Suggestions, which, if in any instance at variance with the opinions, habits, or inclinations of the few, are framed with a regard to the comfort of the whole.

1.--In case of dissatisfaction with any of the Servants, it is requested that the Head Steward may be informed, and, if the grievance be not immediately redressed, that the Captain be appealed to, and, if of a serious nature, that it be represented in writing, in order that it may be brought before the Agents at the conclusion of the Voyage.

2--The Stewards and Boys are engaged on the express understanding that at Table they attend in becoming Apparel.

3.--The State-rooms to be swept, and Carpets taken out and shaken, every Morning after Breakfast. To be washed once a-week, if the weather is dry.

4.--The Saloon and Ladies' Cabins to be swept every Morning before Breakfast, beginning at 5 o'clock.

5.--Bedding to be turned over as soon as Passengers quit their Cabins. Slops to be emptied and Basins cleaned at the same time. Beds to be made once a day only, except in cases of illness, etc., and within one hour after Breakfast.

6.--Bed Linen to be changed on the Eighth day. Boots and Shoes to be cleaned and put back into the State rooms every Morning at 8 o'clock.

7.--Two Towels to be hung up for each Passenger, and to be changed every other day, or as often as required.

8.--Passengers are requested not to open their Scuttles when there is a chance of their Bedding being wetted. The Head Steward to see that the Scuttles are open when the weather will permit.

9.--The Stewardess only is to enter the Ladies' Cabin and State-rooms, and to make the Beds at the time before stated.

10.--The Wine and Spirit Bar will be opened to Passengers at 6A.M., and closed at II P.M.

11.--Breakfast to be on the Table at Half-past 8. and Cloths removed by Half-past 9.

12.--Luncheon to be on the Table from 12 to 1 o'clock.

13.--The before-dinner Bell to be rung at Half-past 3—Dinner to be on the Table at 4--The Cloths to be removed the instant it is over.

14.--Tea to be on the Table at Half-past 7.

15.--Supper, if required and ordered, to be before 10 o'clock.

16.--Lights to be put out in the Saloons at Half-past 11, and in the State-rooms at 12.

17.--As the labour of the Servants must be very great, and the space required for a larger number absolutely preventing an increase, the Passengers are requested to spare them as much as possible between the Meal Hours, and particularly preceding Dinner.

18.--No Passenger is allowed to change his State-room or Berth without the knowledge of the Purser: and it is understood that the Passage Tickets are to be given up to him before the termination of the Voyage.

LIVERPOOL, JULY 4, 1840.

Chapter 14

The *Britannia* casts off

The Britannia performed well on her sea trials and it wasn't long before she made her way into Liverpool's Coburg Dock to take over from th*e Unicorn* and start her maiden voyage. She must have been a very impressive sight with her bronze figurehead of Britannia under her bowsprit. Sam's Atlantic mail project was well reported in Britain and many people would have turned out to see the new ship. One of her famous passengers, not on her maiden voyage, was Charles Dickens who commented on seeing her for the first time *"And there she is! All eyes are turned to where she lies, dimly discernible through their gathering fog of the early winter afternoon; every finger is pointed in the same direction; and murmurs interest and admiration – 'How beautiful she looks!' 'How trim she is!' are heard on every side"* His views of the ship's interior and the journey itself, we shall see later.

On 3rd July 1840 the *Britannia,* with her 93 crew members, 225 tons of cargo and the passengers heavy luggage, left Coburg Dock on the high tide, her Britannia figurehead leading the way as she made her into the River Mersey where she would be anchored overnight. The next day her 60 passengers and the Royal Mail were delivered to her by small steamers. The passenger list included Sam and his daughter, Ann. At 6.00 p.m. Captain Woodruff ordered the crew to raise anchor and the Britannia set off for North America with the passengers on deck waving to the thousands of people who watched her chugging down the Mersey, her clipper bow and brightly painted paddle boxes helping to offset her otherwise functional looking appearance. She wasn't the first to make the steam mail run, of course, the little *Unicorn* had that honour, but the *Britannia* is the Cunard Atlantic pioneer that would be most remembered.

20   RMS Britannia leaving Liverpool
(Cunard)

Twelve and a half days later, the *Britannia* reached Halifax, arriving early in the morning, and berthed at Cunard's Wharf. The whole town was caught napping. They knew when her expected departure date was but they didn't expect her to make such good time. A cannon shot awakened the sleeping town and the prepared welcoming reception was hurriedly put into action with the officials and most of the townspeople rushing down to the wharf to see the new steamer. But by then the *Britannia* was already being coaled and prepared for the final stage of her journey, to Boston, and the planned full civic reception had to be shelved. Later that morning she set off for Boston leaving the townspeople and civic officials on the quayside feeling quite let down.

The *Britannia* reached Boston at 10 o'clock the next night, Saturday, and the town had more time to arrange a welcome and what a welcome it was. It was as if everyone in the town wanted to be part of the celebration and the following Tuesday was proclaimed "Cunard Festival Day" and was marked by a parade and a dinner for 2,300 people, presided over by the Governor of Massachusetts. Samuel Cunard really was the man of the hour and was apparently invited to over 1,800 dinners during the first 24 hours of his arrival in Boston. The arrival of the *Britannia* was such big news that some of the New England newspapers likened the event to the arrival of the Pilgrim Fathers or even the visit by Columbus. But the big prize was for Boston, which was now the eastern terminus for a twice a month transatlantic steamer service. The city really was now on the map. The *Britannia* left Boston on 3rd August and reached Halifax the next day where it stayed just long enough to collect passengers and mail for Britain after which she set off for Liverpool. Sam stayed behind to await the arrival of the *Acadia*, the line's second mail steamer. Whilst waiting he was invited to a public reception in the town where he received a scroll signed by several thousand people. Nevertheless the whole town was disappointed that the *Britannia* had stayed for two weeks in Boston but only hours in Halifax. Being a stopover for steamers is very different to being a terminal and, as time went on, it became clear that the expected big improvement in the town's fortunes was unlikely to happen. The elegant new Halifax hotel, built to accommodate steamer passengers, stood empty with most visitors having gone on to Boston. But many people in Halifax took a pragmatic view of the situation. Having a steamer stopover regularly at the port was still a big achievement, Boston being the only other port in North America to have that facility and it was all down to one man, Samuel Cunard, Nova Scotia's number-one citizen.

But what about New York, the United States fastest growing city? Visits to America were being made by other steamers - the *British Queen*, her sister ship, the *President*, the steamer *Liverpool*, and the *Great Western* but none of them operated to a set schedule. In March 1841, disaster struck when the *President* left New York with 106 passengers and crew and was never seen again. Her London owners withdrew from the transatlantic shipping service and sold the *British Queen*. The steamer *Liverpool* managed seven successful return passages but could not make any money for her owners and she was also sold. This just left the *Great Western* as the only transatlantic steamer visiting the port and even then without a regular service and not at all during the winter. New York was being left way behind as Boston took the Atlantic steamer prize. Were the New Yorkers worried? Well, mostly they weren't too bothered or at least they claimed not to be. They didn't have regular steamers but what they did have were their fine packet sailing ships, quality built and seen, even today, as the best vessels of their type in the world at that time. Classically styled, both inside and out, these were the ships that most New Yorkers and in fact most Americans wanted to travel in. They may take longer to cross the Atlantic but at least you could travel in style and not have to make the journey in a dirty, smelly, cramped steamer. There was also the not insignificant fact that the sailing ships were built in the United States and were run by established American shipping lines such as Black Ball, Dramatic, Black Cross, Style and Swallowtail. The Americans liked to sail under their own flag.

Also in America, perhaps even more so than in Britain, there were still concerns about the safety of steamers and accidents involving them were well reported in the press. One such accident was the tragedy that befell the *Pulaski* when en route from Charleston to Baltimore in June 1838. The vessel was about thirty miles off the coast of North Carolina when one of the boilers exploded with such force that the vessel was split in two. 132 of those on board perished. Many Americans thought that long distance steaming was just not worth the risk and wanted to carry on crossing the Atlantic on their sailing packets and later their sleek clippers which the United States would continue to build for many years. One of the last to be built was the *Great Republic,* a beautiful 3,400 ton and 305 feet long vessel launched in 1854 which, like so many great ships in the 19th century, would end her days as a coal hulk.

But the American shipping lines did not just carry wealthy British and American passengers across the Atlantic. They also carried emigrants, from Britain, Ireland and some continental countries desperate to start a new life in North America. These emigrants were able to cross the Atlantic on one of the packet ships for a fraction of the cost of travelling on a steamer, normally for only around 10% of the cost. But there was an extra price to pay. The cargo holds of the emigrant packet ships were converted to carry passengers and as many as possible were crammed on board, usually between five and seven hundred but some journeys are said to have had a thousand passengers. Up to the mid 1840s they even had to bring their own food and these were normally very poor people who would have struggled to find the cost of the ticket let alone anything else. The journey east to west, against the prevailing wind, would often have been horrendous and could take about forty days, sometimes much more, with the emigrants often having to spend days, or even weeks, battened down below decks. In 1837, the *Diamond* is said to have taken 100 days to make the crossing with seventeen passengers dying from starvation en route. Disease, especially from cholera, was another problem and would spread amongst the tightly packed passengers like wildfire during the long sea crossing. But the danger was not just during the crossing. Many people died below decks even before the ship set sail as the captain waited for favourable winds. In 1834, three or four hundred ships were held up for up to six weeks in Liverpool waiting for the right time to set off. All this was a big risk for the emigrants but if they made it to North America safely they would have the chance of a much better life than the one they were leaving behind. And of course they were not the only ones who would benefit from the high level of emigration from Europe; the New York ship owners, and the city, would do very nicely out of it. New York may have been off the regular Atlantic steamer route but there were still lots of sailing ships bringing in thousands of immigrants for the developing city.

So, for many, things were going well. Boston had become a transatlantic steamer terminal, and the people were happy; New York had its sailing packets and clippers, and the people were happy, and Halifax had a steamer service and the people were fairly happy but they would have been happier if they had become a steamer terminal as they had expected. But who was the real winner? Undoubtedly that was Liverpool, because most of the ships sailing between North America and England would make their way in and out of the River Mersey. Liverpool was not just happy, it was ecstatic with the town booming at an unprecedented rate from the vast trade and the wealth pouring in. All in all, it was looking good for the main North American east coast towns and for Liverpool, and everything was right with the world, at least for the time being.

By the end of January 1841 all four of the Cunard transatlantic steamers were in operation. and gradually becoming more and more popular. Unlike the sailing ships, the steamers could provide a regular service and were usually faster west to east and definitely faster east to west. But Halifax was not doing so well out of the new service. The town's dream of being the main port on the eastern seaboard for transatlantic travel remained just that - a dream. Being a stopover point for the steamers helped the town's development to some extent but it did not bring many visitors and any cargo arriving had to be re-shipped. Many visitors heading for Canada found it best to continue on the steamers to Boston and then travel north on the railroad. The smart new hotel built to handle all of the expected visitors still stood empty. Samuel Cunard, intentionally or unintentionally, had promised the people of Halifax so much but in the end he had not delivered and some people started to turn against him. The people of Halifax had assumed that their position as the closest port to Britain, combined with an ice-free harbour, would mean automatic first place in the transatlantic steam race but really it could never have happened, the town was just too remote from most of the North American population and internal communications were very limited. It could only ever have been a dream - but it wasn't all over yet.

Meanwhile, the New Yorkers were becoming unhappy and, led by the New York newspapers, were sniping at the Bostonians and Cunard. The city of Boston was doing very well and was expanding at a fast rate, building on the success of the Cunard steamers and the sailing ship trade from around the world. New York was being left behind with only one transatlantic steamer, the *Great Western*, visiting the city following the loss of the *President* in 1840 and the removal of the *British Queen* and the *Liverpool* soon after. But at least they had the well-used packet ships with some fine clippers soon to be added to the fleet, and the booming immigrant trade was mostly using New York based vessels. New York was doing very well but, as time went on, New Yorkers started to feel second rate. People relied on vessels crossing the Atlantic to keep them up to date with what was happening in the world and, with the new steamer service, the people of Halifax and Boston received the latest news well before the people of New York did. This was something New Yorkers became increasingly unhappy about.

Meanwhile the *Britannia,* and the other mail steamers, carried on their work and transported many important and well known people across the Atlantic. One such person was Charles Dickens who travelled on the *Britannia* in January 1842 and who gave a detailed definitive account of the journey in his book *"American Notes"* - and what a moaner he turned out to be! He and his wife visited the vessel in Liverpool's Coburg Dock on the day before departure and he took a dislike to the *Scotia* as soon as he went below. He passed through the saloon which he likened to a gigantic hearse with windows and then he reached the cabin for him and his wife - and this was where it really started. He sneered at its name, a state-room, and made it clear he thought that this cabin was not something suitable for a person of his standing. It was very small, even the doorway was small, it only had one small sofa and hardly any room for luggage. But soon he met a stewardess whose jovial nature cheered him up immensely and when he went back on deck he was much happier. He watched the activity on deck as the meat and fruit was loaded into the ice-house, the cow was brought on board and the crew were busying themselves coiling ropes - a pleasant and interesting scene on that cold frosty January morning.

21   Cabin on board Britannia
(Cunard)

With many other passengers, Dickens spent the night at Radley's Adelphi Hotel in Liverpool and the next morning he and everyone else became increasingly excited as one o'clock approached, the time they were to be taken by small packet steamer to join the *Britannia* on the river. As the packed little steamer left the river bank and headed out most passengers were in awe at the sight of this fine vessel with her funnel gently smoking and waiting patiently to take them 3,000 miles across the Atlantic Ocean. There was great commotion on the deck of the *Britannia* as the passengers, together with their luggage, are loaded and despatched to their cabins, a scene described by Dickens as an "*extraordinary and bewildering tumult*". But then suddenly it is all over and the little packet steamer heads back to shore. Unfortunately this is where Mr. Dickens becomes angry again as he and everyone else has to wait over two hours on a cold foggy river for the mail boat to arrive. Eventually the mail is loaded and it is time to go, the captain appears on the paddle box with his speaking trumpet, the officers take their stations and then everyone feels the vessel throb as steam is released into the cylinder and the giant paddle wheels begin to turn - Atlantic Ocean, here we come.

That evening, after dining, Dickens stayed with his new acquaintances and had a few brandies. At midnight he made his way below and commented in his book on the dreadful atmosphere of "strange smells" he found there. He found his wife lying on the sofa, not happy at all with the journey, and her maid was lying on the floor, similarly unhappy.

The next two days were marked by fine weather; Dickens was coping with journey - not sick but not too well either. On the third day the vessel met a strong head wind and heavy seas and Dickens must have been sorry he had ever decided to make the journey. *"Not seasick in the ordinary acceptation of the term",* he explains, but *"excessively seasick"*. The ship took a very heavy beating from the waves and the wind with a lot of lightning, hail and rain thrown in for good measure. It was a tribute to the shipbuilder that the only damage suffered was to the crockery. Everything seemed to be going wrong on the journey - the cabins were leaking water, the baker and pastry cook were ill and, someone all the passengers depended on, the ship's cook, was found drunk! Dickens wasn't happy at all with the journey and often had to spend time in his cabin or the saloons recovering. It didn't stop him finding more things to complain about though including the mouldy fruit desserts, the cold when the fire didn't burn properly and things moving about as the ship rolled.

Dickens was glad to get off the vessel when she reached Boston and, on his travels, he delighted in telling anyone, who would listen, of the terrible journey he had experienced. He had no intention of trying an Atlantic steamer again and returned home on the Swallow Tail sailing packet ship *George Washington*.

Dickens may not have thought much of the Cunard steamers but many other people liked them. The four steamers - the *Britannia*, the *Acadia*, the *Columbia* and the *Caledonia*, may have been cramped, noisy and dirty but they were doing exactly what they had been designed to do - providing a regular fast all year service across the Atlantic and, so far, they were safe ships.

But an accident in 1843 could have changed everything. The *Columbia,* en route to Halifax from Boston, ran aground in thick fog on a rock near the treacherous Seal Island. No one was injured and the 85 passengers were taken onshore with the help of the lighthouse keeper who had heard the *Columbia's* distress guns. He made them comfortable in the island's few buildings with articles taken from the *Columbia* until Sam arrived on his ship, *Margaret*, to rescue them. The *Columbia* was salvaged as much as possible before she broke up in a storm and became a total loss. The *Margaret* later took over her transatlantic mail run to Liverpool. Despite the seriousness of the incident, it proved to be a good advertisement for the Cunard steamers and enhanced Cunard's developing reputation for safety. No one had been killed or injured and no cargo had been lost, the outcome could have been very different if it had been another vessel. The *Columbia* was replaced by the *Hibernia*, a slightly bigger and faster vessel, 219 feet long by 36 feet beam and 1,422 tons gross, and her sister ship, the *Cambria,* soon appeared on station. She proved to be faster still, averaging 9.6 knots, and would become known as the "flying *Cambria*."

The following year, the importance of the steamers to the people of Boston was well-illustrated when the *Britannia* became well and truly trapped in an unusually wide expanse of two feet thick ice in Boston Harbour which increased to seven feet thick around Cunard dock. The merchants and civic officials got together and funded a team of fifty men who, with help from a lot of volunteers, hacked out a seven mile channel from Cunard docks to the edge of the ice sheet. Two days later the *Britannia* was able to leave her dock and make her way down the channel to safety. Many jubilant Bostonians went out on to the ice for the first mile, some in sleighs and some in small sailing craft fitted with iron runners, like skates, to escort her and cheer her on her way.

There was a little gloating in New York about the plight of the *Britannia* and the Herald took the opportunity to snipe at Cunard for not sailing to New York which usually had an ice free harbour.

But, other than occasional sniping, the people of New York do not seem to have done much to encourage Cunard to sail to their city and just waited to see what would happen next in transatlantic steaming. This is a surprising policy in view of the fact that the Hudson, at the time, would have been awash with river and coastal steamers. The Americans knew how to build small and medium size steamers and they were experts in hull design so it is surprising that, up to that time, the city had not made its own contribution to a regular transatlantic steaming service or indeed even show any great interest in providing such a service. The problem was that they were just too wedded to the idea of their sailing ships crossing the Atlantic Ocean, fine vessels though they were. And they would become even better; around the mid-1840s the Americans starting producing their clipper ships - fast, sleek vessels with lots of sail area which were way beyond other sailing ships produced elsewhere. Donald McKay, said by many to be one the finest U.S. shipbuilders of his day, produced his first clipper in 1846 and it was a world-beater in sailing ships. The Americans were really proud of these clippers ships, and rightly so. However, as it turned out, their do-nothing policy with regard to transatlantic steamers proved to be the right one for New York - at least at first.

Commercial trade between Britain and the U.S. was increasing at such a rapid rate that the Admiralty had to consider extending and improving the mail service. In 1846 a new contract, worth £173,340 per annum, was agreed. Cunard would build four more steamers and provide a once a week service calling, alternately, at Boston and New York. The service would be once a fortnight in the winter and weekly for the rest of the year. The amount of mail now crossing the Atlantic was phenomenal with the *Caledonia* delivering 30,000 letters to Boston on one voyage in April 1846.

The Great Western company had made an unsuccessful bid for the mail to New York contract. The company only had two ships, the wooden-hulled paddler *Great Western*, and the revolutionary new iron steamer, the *Great Britain*, which had a screw propeller. Unfortunately for the Great Western Company the future would not be good. The *Great Britain* ran off course and ran aground onto the Irish coast. She was floated some months later, but the owners decided to withdraw from transatlantic steaming.

Cunard's new New York service was scheduled to start on first of January 1848 with the new wooden hulled steamers *America, Niagara Europa* and *Canada*, each ranging from 1800 to 1900 tons and 600 to 700 h.p. The vessels could each carry up to 800 persons, 140 of them first class. This brought the fleet up to 9 ships and they were now the only steamers running a transatlantic service. Two years later, two more even bigger ships were added, the *Asia* and the *Africa* each of 2,200 tons and 750 h.p. Then followed the *Arabia,* the biggest so far at 2,400 tons and 285 long. This was thought to be the limit for wooden transatlantic paddlers; any bigger and they could be seriously damaged in North Atlantic gales.

After a lot of hard work and sharp business decisions, Samuel Cunard had now achieved what he had wanted since those early days as a young man in Nova Scotia; he really was now king of the North Atlantic.

Chapter 15

Isambard Kingdom Brunel - man of iron

Samuel Cunard was reluctant to try anything that not been proven and so seemed almost wedded to wooden hulls and paddle wheels. Isambard Kingdom Brunel was the opposite, he wanted to be ahead of the game and was not afraid to try something new.

The first voyage of the *Great Western* showed what a success steam navigation could be in crossing the Atlantic. He immediately set about planning another similar vessel. Initially he designed it as a wooden hulled ship, like the *Great Western*, but then his thoughts turned to iron. By chance, in October 1838, a little iron hulled steamer, the *Rainbow,* entered Bristol harbour to load for Antwerp. Captain Claxton and the shipbuilder, Patterson, joined the *Rainbow* on her trip to monitor her performance. Their findings were conveyed to Brunel and the directors of the Great Western Steamship Company who quickly decided that the new ship would be built of iron. The final design of the now named *Great Britain* was for a large vessel of 3,270 tons gross, 322 long and 51 feet wide over the paddle boxes and the keel was laid down in July 1839.

The engines needed to drive the paddles of such a big ship would themselves have to be big and would require costly special tooling to be built or purchased and manufacture of the engines would prove very difficult.

While the engineers were trying to overcome the engine problems, fate took a hand again when another revolutionary ship came on the scene. She was the *Archimedes*, a three-masted schooner driven by a newly invented form of screw propeller and was the first significant sea-going vessel to be driven by this method of propulsion. Brunel was initially impressed by the vessel and the directors agreed to hire her for six months for testing. The decision was then made to provide the *Great Britain* with screw propellers, thus writing off a lot of the money wasted on the paddle engines.

Driving such a big vessel by a screw propeller had never been attempted before and needed the limit of Brunel's great expertise. He decided that the six-bladed screw should be 15 ft. 6 in. in diameter and he had to devise a practical way of converting the slow revving output of steam engines at the time to the faster rate needed at the screw. He did this by an arrangement of chains and pulleys which upped the speed output by a power of three. Perhaps surprisingly, this system worked but it could be problematic. The immensely powerful engines consisted of four inclined cylinders, 7ft. 4in. in diameter and with a stroke of 6 ft. To provide the engines with sufficient steam, a double-engine boiler, 34 ft. in length was constructed, this being divided into six compartments each with a furnace fore and aft. The vessel would consume 65 tons of coal per day and generate 25 lbs pressure, high pressure for the time and double that of the *Britannia*.

On 19th July 1843, the *Great Britain* was launched by the Prince Regent and the whole town of Bristol went wild as the ship was floated out. This was the town's biggest ever occasion and no-one wanted to miss it.

In the following January, she set out for the Thames for her final fitting out which took much longer than expected. Eventually she made her way to Liverpool, from where she set out for New York on 26th August on her maiden voyage. This was successful but her second trip was marred by the failure of her propeller on the return trip and she had to use her sails for the remainder of the journey.

The propeller problem rectified, she left Liverpool on 22nd September for her next voyage to New York with 180 passengers. But this would not be a successful trip. During the first night, the vessel ended up miles from where she should have been and ran aground on Rathmullin Point in Dundrum Bay, County Down. The vessel's commander, Captain Hosken was initially castigated for allowing the ship to go off course and run aground but it later emerged that he had been supplied with a new chart which was incorrect although Brunel suspected that the iron hull of the vessel might have affected its compass. Whatever the reason, Captain Hosken was still a long way from where he should have been!

The passengers were taken off the ship the next morning and attempts were made to refloat her. These were not successful and it looked as if the vessel would have to stay in that exposed position for the winter and would almost certainly not survive. Brunel visited the scene and decided that she could be saved and drew up a plan to protect her from the winter gales. The local Irish people struck gold when they were engaged to cut vast amounts of wood and transport it to the shore to create a poultice to cover the ship's hull and keep it safe. Their standard of living changed almost overnight.

In August 1844, the *Great Britain* was refloated and, despite the problem of water needing to be continually pumped out, she was successfully towed to Liverpool, only just though, as soon as she was berthed in Liverpool and the pumps were turned off, she promptly sank.

She might have only just made it back to Liverpool but the fact that the iron clad *Great Britain* had survived the winter at all in the harsh environment of Dundrum Bay amazed shipbuilders and ship owners; a wooden hulled vessel would have been destroyed, protective poultice or no protective poultice. However they could never have imagined how long her iron hull would actually last.

The *Great Britain* was put back into sailing condition and in October 1845 made a successful crossing to Boston. But the cost of repairing the vessel was crippling for the Great Western Steamship Company and it was wound up. Their two vessels, the *Great Western* and the *Great Britain* were disposed of. The *Great Western* was sold to the Royal Mail Steam Packet Company where she gave exemplary service operating between Southampton and the West Indies for ten years. The *Great Britain*, however, would get the opportunity to travel even further afield. She was bought by Gibbs, Bright and Company, based in Liverpool and Bristol and, after having new engines and new rigging fitted, was put to work carrying emigrants to Australia with her first voyage, to Melbourne, taking place in 1852 when she carried 630 passengers. Over the next 23 years she made 32 successful voyages to Australia and proved to be a popular and reliable vessel. She also served her country when she transported troops during the Crimea War and the Indian Mutiny. In 1882 she was sold to A. Biggs, Sons and Company and made two long journeys to San Francisco carrying wool and coal without major incident but, on her third voyage, to Panama, she was badly damaged in a storm when rounding Cape Horn. She managed to make the Falkland Islands where she was sold and became a wool and coal storage hulk. An attempt to preserve the ship was made in 1933 but the idea was soon abandoned because the cost was too high and she was towed to a quiet spot in Sparrow Cove where she was left to die.

But the *Great Britain* did not want to die, and she wasn't prepared to go down without a fight. Day after day, year after year she fought off relentless attacks from pounding waves, stormy winds and salt laden rain. Somehow she managed to hang on but all the time she was gradually getting weaker and couldn't hold on forever. For more than thirty years she languished alone in Sparrow Cove seemingly forgotten by the world and facing the end all alone.

But in Britain the old lady hadn't been forgotten and, in the early part of 1970, salvation came in the form of a team of expert ship salvagers who arrived with a huge pontoon and a determination to get her back home. The salvagers checked every inch of the vessel and found that the hull was still largely intact, she had managed to hold on just long enough. They got to work plugging any holes and, on 13th April 1970, the *Great Britain* was refloated and placed on the pontoon. This was only the beginning though; she now had to face a gruelling and highly risky 8,000 miles journey across treacherous Atlantic seas to see home again. So much could have gone wrong on that journey and the *Great Britain* would have been lost forever but she made it and, when she reached the lower reaches of the River Avon, she was removed from the pontoon and sailed under tow to see Bristol for the first time in 126 years. Thousands lined the river banks to see her, just as it was when she first set out for London in 1844, and there were especially iconic scenes as she passed under Brunel's Clifton Suspension Bridge which had only been partially completed on her first journey.

The *Great Britain* has now been extensively restored and is open to public viewing in Bristol's Great Western Dockyard - where she was born all those years ago.

22 The Great Britain restored
(Courtesy Matt Buck)

Chapter 16

The Atlantic Paddlers - Competition!

By the end of 1841 all four of the Cunard Mail Steamers were in service and were soon joined by two more. All of them provided a regular all year round service but only called at Halifax and Boston. Samuel Cunard was proud of his mail steamers, they were not always profitable but overall he was making money and the name "Cunard" was beginning to really mean something in transatlantic travel. He was pleased with the way things were going.

But not everyone was happy with the developing Atlantic steam service. The American Government was not happy, not happy at all.

The Americans considered their sailing packets to be the finest vessels in the world and, the reality is, they were. The country had vast forests of oak and pitch pine, both ideal for shipbuilding, and the early vessels sailing out of New York were beautiful ships, some of three decks and up to 1,800 tons. Quality of build and design was second to none and many Americans preferred to travel on these vessels rather than a noisy, dirty paddler. In the spring and summer they were as fast or almost as fast as steamers, at least west to east, but in winter the journey in either direction could be slower, usually somewhere between 60 and 90 days. Many Americans thought that the transatlantic steamers had no real future and were just a passing fad, so why worry about them.

The general consensus in Government circles however was very different. The United States was now an independent country and should not be relying on British steamers to provide a year round mail service to Europe, or a mail service at all. Also what particularly galled some people in Government, and the country, was the fact that the United States had been responsible for some very early steam boat developments and many already operated on inland waters and coastal services. What made things even worse was the fact that the first steamer to steam at least a small part of the way across the Atlantic, the *Savannah*, was an American designed and built vessel and that was over twenty years previously, since when there had been nothing on the American Atlantic steam navigation front. Despite this, the American sailing packets still retained their dominance in passenger and goods traffic on the North Atlantic. Everyone liked to watch the mail steamers travel along the River Mersey in and out of Liverpool but most of the vessels travelling to and from America were still American sailing ships. This was good for the United States but not good enough for the American government. Dominance of the steam mail trade by a British company, especially one headed by Samuel Cunard, whose ancestor, Robert, did not support them during the revolution was just not acceptable, something had to be done.

A Mr. Forbes, together with his partners, decided to do take action and, in 1845, had the *Massachusetts,* a 161 feet long wooden sailing ship, of 70 tons with a 170 h.p. steam engine, constructed in the yard of Samuel Hall of Boston. The engine had two cylinders of 26 inch diameter with a three feet stroke powered by two boilers. Her steam engine provided auxiliary power only and her paddle wheels could be raised out of the water when not required. A smart looking ship, she could carry 35 first class passengers.

AUXILIARY SCREW-STEAMER "MASSACHUSETTS."

23 The Massachusetts
(Unknown PD US - 1923)

She managed two voyages between New York and Liverpool before being purchased by the United States War Department for use as a troop ship in the war with Mexico. Good sailing ship though she was, the *Massachusetts* had little effect on the Cunard steamer monopoly.

The United States Government realised it couldn't just sit back and do nothing. It didn't like the idea of trade subsidies but an exception had to be made. Cunard and Britain were being allowed to run the whole show and it was time for the people of the United States to have a piece of the action.

The United States Post Office invited tenders from American companies to provide a steam mail service to Europe. The Ocean Steam Navigation Company was successful and was awarded a five year tender to carry mail between New York and Bremen with a stop off at Southampton. The Americans were not confident about competing directly with Cunard with a service to the key port of Liverpool. The Bremen service began in 1847 with two paddle steamers, the *Washington* and the *Hermann*, built by Westerfeld & McKay of New York with machinery built by Stillman, Allen & Co, and chartered from the South Western Steam Packet Company. The 1,700 ton *Washington* was 280 feet long, 30 feet wide and had paddle wheels 35 feet in diameter, the *Hermann* being a little bigger. In June 1847 the *Washington* set off from New York with 127 passengers and the first U.S. mail cargo on the same day that the *Britannia* set off from Boston. New Yorkers thought their two new vessels were more than a match for anything Cunard could offer and the *Washington* was sure to leave the *Britannia* trailing in her wake. But they were very much mistaken, the *Washington* arrived two days behind the *Britannia,* despite fine weather on the way. Not only that, she didn't make a good impression on those who saw her when she arrived in Southampton. People were surprised by the appearance of this big, ungainly, vessel. The London Times was moved to describing her as "*an elongated three-decker about as ugly a specimen of steamship building as bad as ever been seen at Southampton*". Yet when the *Washington's* sister ship, the *Hermann*, arrived in Cowes in April the following year, the London Standard reporter thought she was *"a fine looking ship"*.

Despite the sniping from the London Times, the return journey for the *Washington* proved to be popular with 170 passengers on board and her holds were brim full with 80 tons of cargo from Britain, 80 tons from France and 100 tons from Bremen. The evening before she sailed, there was a dinner at the Dolphin Hotel in Southampton attended by many dignitaries including a number of British based representatives of the United States government. At the dinner there was universal support for the suggestion that there was no jealousy or bad feeling between the two countries because the United States was taking over its own transatlantic mail service. This was all nonsense of course, there was considerable rivalry between the two countries over the service but everyone wanted to enjoy the event so they didn't let anything ruin it. Neither did the comment that the *Express,* a new American steamer, which had already been trialled and which would be the fastest in the world, would soon be in service delivering mail from the U.S.

But after that, everything started to go pear-shaped. The *Washington* and the *Hermann* did not prove to be successful transatlantic steamers and the poor old *Express* was never heard of again. The Americans would have been stung by British newspapers often taking the opportunity to comment on the fact that two vessels, which they expected to lead the way, were in practice much slower than the Cunarders. In fact the poor performance of these two vessels surprised many people on both sides of the Atlantic. The Americans at the time were masters of hull building for transatlantic ships and had made considerable progress in building steamers for river and coastal traffic. People expected better than these two poorly designed and built specimens. The two vessels maintained a U.S mail service but it was clear they could never compete with the Cunarders and, after a couple of years, both vessels were withdrawn from service.

It became increasingly clear to the United States government that they were nowhere near to competing with Cunard on the transatlantic steam service. Moreover the American's (almost) monopoly of transatlantic sailing ships was being put under more and more pressure by steamers from, not just Britain, but also France and Germany.

Then it got worse.

News came through that Cunard was going to receive a greater subsidy from the British Post Office and was going to start a service to New York in 1848. The service would run fortnightly in winter and weekly for the rest of the year, alternating between Boston and New York. Cunard's ordered four new wooden hulled paddlers for the service, the *America,* the *Niagara,* the *Europa* and the *Canada,* each around 1,850 tons and with 600 to 700 h.p. engines.

The new service got off to a flying start on 1st January 1848 and the town of Halifax was a big beneficiary. Each week one steamer would arrive from England and one would visit going in the opposite direction from Boston or New York. In addition, new Cunard steamers would arrive each week from the Caribbean bringing passengers for transfer to Atlantic services and Halifax had become an important telegraph terminal. What Cunard had promised some years before, and had not produced, was now happening - Halifax was becoming the main marine communications centre on the eastern seaboard. For the time being at least, things were going well for Halifax.

At first New Yorkers were delighted to be a transatlantic steamer terminal. They would not be behind the times anymore and each alternate voyage would bring them the mail and the international news before Boston, so at least fortnightly, New York would have boasting rights over Boston. Although they had been reluctant to admit it since the Boston service started, a steamer service to New York was what they really wanted. But, it came at a price; the expression *"be careful what you wish for"* quickly became very appropriate. The Cunard steamers showed themselves to be safe and reliable - qualities which the sailing ships just couldn't match. They were also punctual; if the ship was scheduled to sail at 1.00 p.m. that is the time it would normally sail, a sailing ship could not hope to manoeuvre itself into a sailing position to depart at a set time. Samuel Cunard was providing a quality of service for long distance sea travel that was unrivalled anywhere in the world at that time. There were still many sailing vessels operating out of New York, of course, many of which brought the immigrants who normally could not afford to travel on a steamer. The Cunard service may have only taken a small percentage of the transatlantic trade but it was increasing all the time. And what it did take was significant, it tended to carry the important people and the prime cargo. The operators of the packet ships and the new clippers started to lose custom and their valuable customers; the United States really felt it was losing face.

The U.S. government realised that it was now way behind and would have to up the ante substantially or give in. But members of the government were not prepared to give in and came up with a plan. They wanted to defeat Cunard but realised that to do so they needed to put up a lot of money and they needed the services of one of their big guns, of which, in the U.S. sailing ship merchant marine, they had many. In an all or nothing move the Post Office offered a massive subsidy of $385,000 per year to a company that could beat Cunard. Eventually the big gun they chose to run the operation was Edward Knight Collins, who had lost out when the original contract was awarded. This time he offered a plan to build five paddle steamers, each bigger and better than the Cunarders. Probably the American Post Office realised it should have awarded the original contract to E.K. and not bothered with second-raters. They were not going to make the same mistake this time. After all, in transatlantic shipping, E.K. had form. He was born in 1802 in Truro, Massachusetts and went to sea when he became a teenager. Soon afterwards, he joined the family business which ran a successful shipping merchants in New York with sailing packets operating between New York, the West Indies and Mexico. E.K. proved to be a big asset to the firm and it became even more successful. After the death of his father, he took over management of a New York - New Orleans packet line and expanded into transatlantic shipping with trade of cotton to Liverpool. He liked to build bigger and better equipped ships and in 1836 he established his "Dramatic Line", so named because his ships had theatrical names such as *Shakespeare* and *Garrick,* and he soon became a leader in transatlantic shipping.

E. K. took over his new role as U.S. steam mail supremo with gusto and famously declared that "*he was going to run the Cunarders off the Atlantic*". This was music to the ears of many people, in shipping, in New York and in the U.S. Government.

Not everyone was so enthusiastic though. Many people were still wary of the Atlantic steamers and were very ready to wax lyrical about the beautiful American clippers and sailing packets that filled most of the Atlantic shipping routes. They did the job better than a few noisy, dirty paddle steamers. Why change something that wasn't broken? Why invest in a project like that?

But there were others who took a much more enlightened view and were jubilant about E.K.'s plan to deal with the Cunarders. What an opportunity the United States had! If Cunard was taken out of the equation, the U.S. could become dominant on the Atlantic, not only in sailing ships, but in steam navigation as well. What a prize that would be! It would open the door to the U.S. developing trade routes all over the world. Britain prided herself on being the custodian and controller of the high seas but the U.S. now had a chance to relegate her to the second division. The Americans were ready and willing to take over the role as masters of the seas.

E.K. Collins realised that that the new ships would have to be good to beat the Cunarders and would be very expensive to build. He got busy organising funds for the venture. This took some time as those with funds available were not always the ones who wanted to invest in steam or wanted to risk a lot of money. Eventually, he raised the necessary funds which included funds he raised himself by divesting some of his own shipping interests and the New York & Liverpool United States Mail Shipping Company (the Collins Line) was formed. E.K. set up a plan to build five wooden hulled paddle steamers for the service and hired George Steers to design them. But it was soon realised that five steamers could not be operated profitably and the scheme was scaled down to just four vessels, operating a slightly reduced service. The final proposal was for 4 three-decked vessels each of around 2.860 tons, 282 feet in length and 45 feet beam, bigger than the Cunarders and the biggest vessels ever built after Brunel's *Great Western*. The vessels, which would be named *Atlantic, Arctic, Baltic* and *Pacific,* would be built by W. H. Brown of New York and their hulls would be constructed of oak frames with pitch pine planking and diagonal iron straps. But building them wasn't going to be easy. They were designed to be faster than the Cunarders, in fact this was written into the contract between the U.S. Post Office and the Collins Line. To have a chance of doing this, they needed to be fitted with huge engines and these would turn out to be the biggest pieces of machinery so far built in the United States. Even to make the engines needed special tooling to be manufactured or imported. The engines were designed by Faron and had cylinders of 95 inches and a 9 foot stroke and were bigger than those in the Cunarders. Steam was provided by 4 boilers each served by 8 furnaces and producing 17 p.s.i. pressure.

24 The S.S. Atlantic's huge engine
(Thurston)

Eventually the ships were completed and the *Atlantic* was the first to take to the water to tremendous acclaim from the crowds lining the river banks. Some of the ship purists, though, were not impressed at all by the ship's chunky and workmanlike appearance especially if an American clipper was gracefully gliding by. And they really didn't like the vertical bow shape, very much ahead of its time, when even the Cunarders still had clipper bows with a figurehead. E.K. would have happily ignored them because he knew what the *Atlantic* and her sister ships were like inside. They were like no other shipping line's vessels anywhere on earth with their carved furniture, velvet sofas, thick carpets, paintings, sumptuous stained-glass cabin windows adorned with representations of New York and Boston, mirrors - the list goes on and on. They also had some startling innovations including steam heating, electrical signals from the bridge to the engine room and to call for servants and - luxury of luxuries - a bath room, with a system for pumping up water from the Atlantic to provide a salt bath. They were even equipped with barber shops (well it was a long journey!). These vessels were not just better than the Cunarders - they were in a different league. And so they should be; they each cost around $700, 000 (£160,000), an enormous sum.

25   Collin's Baltic
(Currier lithograph - Courtesy U.S. Library of Congress)

This was just what the Americans wanted - advanced, luxurious steamers that were designed and built in the United States. Everything was perfect. Even fears about steamer safety started to fade.

Now could the ships be faster across the Atlantic?

Chapter 17

Cunard puts up a fight

As the mid 19th century approached, the Cunard Line would have to face up to some real competition in the Atlantic steamer trade. They had had it easy for their first ten years of operation but new kids were now on the block - the Collins super-paddlers.

The Collins *Atlantic* was the first and set out for Liverpool on 27th April 1849, reaching her destination in a very fast time. At Liverpool, a few problems had to be attended to but she then sped back across the Atlantic and broke the Cunard east to west record, a big achievement. The writing was now on the wall for Cunard. As had been promised, the Collins ships were better than the Cunarders. They had been designed for speed and that's exactly what they gave with the *Atlantic* reaching 12.3 knots in 1850, the *Pacific* 13 knots in 1851 and the *Arctic* 13.2 knots in 1852. These vessels provided just what Atlantic travellers wanted and had so far been denied - speed, comfort and style, all in one ship. All four Collins vessels were better than the Cunarders in every way and passengers, especially Americans, flocked to them.

The British Government watched what was happening with increasing concern - Britain was being left behind. In 1850 the British Post Office agreed a new twelve year mail contract with Cunard but included was a condition that Cunard ships carry more tonnage and, importantly, they had to compete with the Collins ships. However, even while the Collins ships were under construction, Samuel Cunard realised that they were bound to be better than his pedestrian mail steamers and he ordered two ships from Robert Steele to meet the challenge on the new York service - the *Africa* and the *Asia*. They were both oak hulled paddle steamers of around 2,226 tons gross, 266 feet long and 40 feet beam with engines of similar size to those on the Collins vessels but with a little more nominal horse power. Fine ships though they were, they still couldn't compete with Collins on speed or refinement. Even the steam heating on board the *Asia* couldn't save the day!

Sam wasn't prepared to be beaten and commissioned a new vessel from Robert Steele, the *Arabia,* as long as the Collins ships at 285 feet but less in the beam. Her large engines had 17% more nominal power. This made her a very fast ship, achieving 15 knots in calm seas, but handling was poor in bad weather when her bow tended to dive under head waves. She also demonstrated the problem of bigger engines reaching the point where the wooden hulls couldn't cope with the stresses, however well the vessel was built.

Cunard were now finding it difficult to compete with Collins and fewer and fewer passengers were using their mail steamers during much of the year. The popularity of the Collins steamers with the travelling public continued to increase. In just 11 months in 1852 they carried 2,420 passengers from New York to Liverpool with only 1,780 being carried by Cunard. People wanted speed and the Collins steamers had got the crossing down to 9½ days. However Cunard did provide a winter service which Collins declined to risk so overall the Cunard Line was making money although not a fortune. But at least the company was making money while the Collins Line, even with its greater passenger number was not. E.K. Collins, and his co-investors, had found out early on that transatlantic steam navigation is not easy. Making one steam passage was not normally difficult, a number of small steamers had done it but a regular service, using large steamers, is a very different matter and there is a steep learning curve. A problem the line had right away was the need to make faster crossings than Cunard with the result that their vessels used vast amounts of coal - a big expense. This was compounded by the inexperience of their firemen. Being a firemen is much more than just opening the furnace door occasionally and shovelling in coal. It needs more expertise than that to prevent coal and steam being wasted. That's exactly what happened on some of the early Collins voyages resulting in the vessels running out of coal and having to continue under sails only. But the quest for speed caused even bigger problems. On each journey, the only speed on open water for a Collins ship, was "fast" and their big engines took a terrible pounding crossing the Atlantic day after day. Also, as with Cunard's *Arabia,* the wooden hulls were compromised by the power of the engines. The vessels required intervention after every journey and expensive repairs were often necessary.

Things had not gone as well as E. K. had expected and his backers were asking where their returns were. Something dramatic had to happen to keep the Collins Line going and E.K. calculated that the only answer was for the U.S. Post Office to increase the annual subsidy - and it would have to be increased substantially, from $358,000 to $858,000. E.K. lobbied Congressmen; some were supportive but not all. Some were concerned about Government money being effectively used to help New York whilst other big cities like Boston and Philadelphia were getting nothing.

E.K. and his partners prepared their petition to Congress to try and get the new subsidy. A lot of thought went into it. They realised that they would have to make a very good case and everything they could think of went into the petition.

They soon decided that the best thing to put in their petition was an appeal to national sentiment, backed up by a some general anti-British comments. This was a good plan and it would help unite those in Government who may not otherwise be supportive of the steamers.

To get off to a good start they highlighted the view of the U.S. Postmaster General that the Collins Line had established *"the superiority of American skill and enterprise in the construction of the [their] steamers"*. It is true that they were the best paddle steamers so far built anywhere and, as Collins pointed out, *"had supremacy in steam navigation of the Atlantic"*.

But the cost of building steamers to match and even exceed the standard of the British steamers had been enormous, as was the cost of running them. Not all vessels were insured at the time, but Collin's were and the annual cost, because of the quality of the vessels, took over half of the Government subsidy. The petition noted however that the U.S. Government still did very nicely out of the arrangement with the U.S. Post Office earning $1.1 million in the year to June 1851, money that would otherwise have gone to the British steamers.

Collins could not financially continue with the current set up and asked for more time to repay a Government loan plus an increase in the annual subsidy to $858,000. Now that the facts were out of the way, Collins changed tack to ensure that the petition would appeal to the heart.

Collins said that the group was not in it to make profits (of course not!); they wanted to prevent supremacy of the seas (the Atlantic) falling into the hands of a rival power (i.e. Britain). If the Collins Line should fail, Britain would benefit from the increase in trade that Collins had developed. There also seems to have been a desire amongst many Americans at the time to be able to face up to Britain militarily. Collins noted that the Royal Navy had around 600 ships, including steamers which was more powerful than all other European navies combined. There was a feeling that if the United States did not do something, Britain would continue to have mastery of the seas.

Collins thought that the attitude of many in Britain was disingenuous with the British still thinking that "Britannia ruled the waves" while ignoring the volume and speed of the American clipper and packet ships crossing the Atlantic and the fact that the Collin's steamers were better than anything Britain had ever produced. It was suggested that Americans had been taunted for a long time by Britain for inferiority in everything and enough was enough..

Collins complained that Britain wasn't playing fair. Ship owners, including Cunard, were alleged to have reduced freight and passenger rates when American steamers were in port thus taking trade away from Collins. Also some British newspapers were said to write untrue and damaging stories about Collins vessels whilst others were said to write stories with the opposite view, suggesting that Collins vessels were even better than they were as a way of stimulating British action to deal with the threat. E.K. did quite well bringing together two opposing arguments to make the same point! However some of what he said was true. The London Daily News referred to the British "*passion for racing - horse, donkey etc. - but the country was now faced with a race of terrible magnitude - the Collin Line".* Many were concerned that if England were to lose, it would be a bad omen for her being able to maintain pre-eminence on the seas; the implications for trade and for Britain's military power would be enormous. This was a danger highlighted in many newspapers and people became very worried.

But for the United States, through the Collins Line, to compete with Britain would not be an easy task and E.K., in his petition to Congress, highlighted the inequalities between the two countries when it came to transatlantic steam travel. It wasn't a level playing field and it just wasn't fair - wasn't fair to the Collins Line and the United States, that is. For instance, a problem for the Collins Line was the fact that Britain had vast supplies of coal and iron ore and waterways to deliver them, something that the United States could not compete with at that time. Also Britain's labour costs, for building and operating steamships were much lower than in the U.S. Well, that wasn't Britain's fault, Mr Collins. The fact is, life isn't fair; it isn't fair now and it wasn't then. In any case the U.S. had vast quantities of wood available for shipbuilding which Britain didn't have.

```
Just making a point here. E. K. Collins was
right to put anything in the petition to
help get the increased funding, as long as
it's true or it is a reasonable opinion or,
come to that, just an opinion!
```

E.K. Collins and his partners had put together a really good petition to try and get the increase in funding. It was a little imaginative at times but the aim was to get to more money, not to produce a thesis on social and economic theory. They deserved to succeed, and they did - they got the money. But it came with an important proviso in that the U.S. Post Office could reduce or cancel the subsidy at any time on giving six months notice.

E.K. told his partners that they been successful and they all heaved a sigh of relief; they hadn't made any money so far but now their investment looked safe - at least for the time being.

Chapter 18

The Collins Line begins to founder

Cunard's contract specified that vessels would be made available to the government if the country went to war. In 1854, Britain was sending troops to the Crimea and a number of Cunard vessels were made available to the government, including the *Niagara*, the *Cambria*, the *Arabia* and the *Europa*. The reduced fleet made it difficult for the Cunard line to keep up a regular New York and Boston service and the Collins Line ships were ready and willing totake up the slack.

It was all going well for the Collins Line, passenger numbers were up, the government subsidy was helping to meet costs and now there were fewer Cunard vessels on the North Atlantic. And, on top of all that, the line was enjoying a good safety record .... until, one day in 1854, tragedy struck.

On 20th September, the Collins steamer *Arctic* set out from Liverpool for New York with 250 passengers and 135 crew. She was considered to be the best of the four Collins steamers and had become known as the "Clipper of the Seas". A fast ship, she made good progress across the Atlantic and on 27th September was about 60 miles from Cape Race at the south eastern tip of Newfoundland. This is a notoriously dangerous area and, true to form, it was foggy although visibility was generally adequate. However there were banks of dense fog which would sometimes envelop the *Arctic*. In one of these fog banks, unknown to those on board, was the small French iron clad screw steamer *Vesta*. Both vessels were travelling at speed and the *Vesta* slammed into the starboard side of the *Arctic*, neither vessel having time to take avoiding action. Both vessels came to a shuddering halt and were then backed away from each other to check what damage had been caused. At first it was thought that the *Vesta* had come off much worse in the collision. Her bow had suffered substantial damage and she was going nose down into the water. Those on board the *Vesta,* who had felt the impact much more than those on board the *Arctic,* were convinced that the vessel was about to sink and panic ensued. The captain immediately began evacuation procedures. Two lifeboats were launched but one turned over when entering the water. Some of those on board, thinking they had very little time, jumped into the water and headed for the *Arctic*.

Meanwhile, on board the *Arctic,* the commander, Captain Luce, saw, through breaks in the fog, what was happening on board the *Vesta* and ordered the two front quarter boats to be launched to provide assistance. The starboard boat with the Chief Officer and six crewmen on board got away but the launch of the port boat was cancelled when it was found that damage to the *Arctic* had been much worse than first thought. She had been holed twice below the water line, with one gash being five feet wide, and water was pouring in. Captain Luce ordered some crewmen to inspect the damage and to try and stem the leaks but they soon reported back that it was impossible. The captain immediately decided that the only chance for the vessel and those on board was to head for land as quickly as possible. No help was expected from the other vessel which had disappeared into the fog and, in any case, it was assumed that she had sunk or would soon do so.

Captain Luce ordered full ahead and, just as they were moving off, there were cries to stop the ship when a lifeboat from the *Vesta* was spotted in the ship's path. The Chief Engineer refused to stop the engines fearing that it would further compromise the ship's safety. The *Arctic* ran over the lifeboat and all of those on board perished apart from one Frenchman who was able to grab hold of a rope thrown over the bow by an *Arctic* crewman. He was safely pulled on board.

Then the *Arctic's* rescue boat appeared but again the vessel couldn't stop and it was waved away. What Captain Luce didn't know, and what the crew of the rescue boat, may have been able to tell him, was that the *Vesta* was not sinking. Her forward watertight compartment was holding and keeping the Atlantic at bay. But, like the *Arctic,* she was making her way to land as quickly as possible and was not available or was not willing to help. What happened to the crew of the rescue boat is not recorded.

As the *Arctic* powered through the waves, every effort was made to keep the water out. The steam pumps were brought into use and the four manual pumps were set up on deck with teams of crew members and passengers working themselves to the point of exhaustion.

For four long hours the Vesta struggled to make land but, as time went on, those on board started to lose hope, even the experienced Captain.

Captain Luce had been a seaman since the age of sixteen and had had his own command before he was twenty one. He had been in command of the *Arctic* since the beginning. An experienced captain, he had commanded the sailing packets the *Argus* and the *Constellation* carrying emigrants to the New World. These could be difficult trips and required stern discipline on board. However, on this occasion, he found it increasingly difficult to control the crew as it became more and more apparent that they were not going to make it. In fact the word "mutiny" is appropriate as most of the crew became interested in only one thing - ignoring the captain and saving themselves. The Chief Engineer, together with some of his engineers and firemen, got away at an early stage after seizing one of the deck boats at gunpoint.

However some of the firemen were heroes when they stayed at their post trying to keep the engines going despite being up to their waists in water. But eventually the incoming water extinguished the furnaces and the *Arctic* only had her sails to try and get her to land. She almost made it, managing to get to within about fifteen miles but that was it, it was time to abandon the vessel. Captain Luce ordered "head for the boats" hoping to get some of the women and children away. The lifeboats had been prepared and were hanging from their davits and some passengers, exhausted by their work on the pumps, had already boarded them.

The situation on the ship now became chaotic with order breaking down completely. The undisciplined crew members stormed the lifeboats demanding the places the passengers had and many crew members jumped into the already overloaded boats as they were being launched causing them to tip into the water. One boat, containing, Mary, the wife of E. K. Collins, his daughter and one of his sons, together with some female passengers, was heading for a successful launch until one of the straps broke casting most of those on board into the water. Two persons managed to save themselves but the Collins family members were lost.

While some of the crew were trying to save themselves in the boats, the remaining passengers and the senior officers got busy building rafts using whatever materials could be found but conditions on deck were now very bad. Weather conditions had changed since the collision. It was still foggy but the wind had built up and a heavy swell was washing waves over the deck which was now quite low in the water. Some people were washed overboard. Nevertheless, a large raft was successfully constructed and put to sea with 76 persons, 72 men and 4 women, on board but, by 8 o'clock next morning, all were washed off or died except for one man, Peter McCabe, who was eventually picked up by the *Huron*. McCabe was a 24 year old Dublin born waiter who had lived in Liverpool for a number of years. This was his second trip on board the *Arctic*.

   Captain Luce, in the true traditions of the sea, went down with his ship while standing on the paddle box above the paddle wheel and clutching Willie, his nine year old sick son. However destiny decided that it wasn't his time to die and he and his son came back to the surface as the paddle box broke away from the hull. But the captain's gift of life came with a terrible price. As the paddle box rose to the surface it hit his young son on the head, causing serious injuries. Captain Luce climbed on board the floating paddle box and pulled Willie on board but the child died soon afterwards. He was joined by eleven other people on the paddle box. One person left for another raft as there was little room on the paddle box and those on board were standing up to their knees in water. By the following evening, only Captain Luce and two other men were left alive on the paddle box but they managed to hold on and were rescued the next day.

   The sixth, and last, boat to leave contained 31 survivors, and was under the command of Third Officer Francis Dorian who had remained on the *Arctic* until commanded to leave. They were picked up by the *Huron*.

   A second boat, commanded by Second Officer Mr. Balhan, managed to make land. In total the two boats were said to have rescued 31 crew members and 14 passengers.

There were around 250 passengers on board the *Arctic* and around 135 crew. If all of the crew had behaved in a disciplined and controlled manner it is possible that up to 180 people could have got away in the lifeboats. It wasn't a requirement at the time to provide a lifeboat place for everyone on board. There are differing accounts of how many people perished in the disaster but it is probably between 320 and 340.

A Collins Line transatlantic paddle liner, combined with fog, was always an accident waiting to happen and, on this day it did, with tragic consequences. The *Arctic* was said to have been travelling at top speed, around 13 knots, when the collision occurred but the *Vesta* was running under sail with the wind behind her and was also going very fast. So perhaps blame can be shared. In any case, Captain Luce was following Collins Line standing orders - full speed on the open ocean. There were however allegations that, in the conditions, the Captain should have been more careful. He should have slowed down when entering a fog bank, posted more lookouts and ensured that the warning horn was sounded regularly.

Despite this Captain Luce was treated as a hero and was feted wherever he went. Not so the crew members who were castigated for putting themselves first and leaving the passengers to drown. Most of those who were rescued were crew members. There was particular concern about the fact that there were over 100 women and children on board the *Arctic* but not one was saved. Obviously conditions on board the *Arctic* must have been horrendous and those who criticised the crewmen were not there at the time. Also the "Birkenhead Drill" of "women and children first" had not yet been established but this incident and the experience of H.M.S.

Birkenhead would soon change attitudes in times of crisis on the sea.

Birkenhead Drill. In 1852 the Royal Navy steamer H.M.S. Birkenhead hit rocks near Cape Town when carrying 634 on board, mainly troops, to fight in the frontier wars in South Africa. The ship was badly damaged and the order to abandon ship was given. The women and children were loaded into a cutter whilst the soldiers who had so far survived were assembled on deck and ordered by Captain Seaton *"The cutter with the women and children will be swamped, I implore you not to do this thing and I ask you to stand fast".* **Despite the clear danger, the men, some only recently enlisted into the army, stood fast. All of the women and children survived but most of the soldiers were drowned or became prey to the prowling great white sharks. Just 183, including the women and children were saved, plus a few horses which managed to make shore after being cut loose and pushed over the side.**

Rudyard Kipling immortalised the heroic soldiers when he wrote:

> *'To stand and be still*
> *to the Birken'ead Drill*
> *is a damn tough bullet to chew'.*

On the wall of St Mary's Church in Bury St Edmunds is a memorial to the men of the Suffolk Regiment who were lost in the disaster.

The loss of the *Arctic* caused terrible angst throughout the United States. There were up to 150 first class passengers on board who were lost and included some very important and well-known people including Mrs Collins brother, leading lawyers and businessmen.

This narrative in the New York Times, published soon after the full details of the disaster came to light, gives an illustration of the strength of feeling experienced by many people.

"The city was filled with mourning for the loss of so many valuable lives, and all classes of the community felt for the calamities of others as though they had been their own. We do not remember an occasion when sympathy so universal and unaffected has been bestowed upon the sufferers by a terrible catastrophe".

Some well-known British passengers were also lost.

After the tragedy, Captain Luce vowed never to go to sea again and he became an inspector for the Great Western Marine Insurance Company, a position he held until his death in 1879 aged 74.

At a stroke, the gloss had come off the Collins Line, the pride of the U.S. merchant marine. It's excellent safety record was in tatters and American cross-Atlantic travellers started to question whether they wanted to sail on Collins ships. But most however decided to stay with the brand. They were. after all, American built and American run, they were luxurious and they were fast - and being fast was important. Travellers were pragmatic about the risks of crossing the Atlantic and indeed there were real risks with any form of sea travel at the time, with ships being lost at an alarming rate. In fact, just ten months before the *Arctic* was lost, the *City of Glasgow,* an Inman Line paddle steamer launched in 1850, disappeared with 480 on board, largely steerage passengers, whilst en route from Liverpool to Philadelphia. The *City of Glasgow* was the first of the Inman Line screw steamers. Launched in 1850 this strong three-decked iron-hulled ship was built on the Clyde by Tod and McGregor and was one of the best ships of her day. She could carry 52 cabin, 85 second class and 400 steerage passengers and was well equipped with a surgeon, ladies-only staterooms, a well-stocked library, a bathroom and a crew of about 70. Safety was paramount and the vessel had five watertight bulkheads, six large lifeboats each fitted with copper tanks to keep them buoyant and a system of fire pumps in case fire should break out on board. Even a ship so well built and with safety a key feature could still just vanish on the Atlantic. This illustrates the danger that cross Atlantic travellers faced each time they set out.

Seven months later the *City of Philadelphia* was wrecked on her maiden voyage but this time those on board survived.

This illustrates the dangers you had to face if you wanted to cross to North America or to Europe at that time. In his book "*The Atlantic Ferry*" Arthur John Maginnis lists 14 transatlantic steamers that were involved in incidents between 1841 and 1861 which resulted in loss of life. These incidents claimed over 2,300 lives.

But, although steamers were gradually taking over on the Atlantic run, there were many more sailing vessels still making the crossing and they had their fair share of problems. One such, was the tragedy that befell the *Ocean Monarch*. In September 1848 this 1,300 ton packet boat set out from Liverpool on the morning tide. She was filled with mainly emigrant passengers heading for Boston to start a new life. After she had cleared the River Mersey the captain set her on a course fairly close to the North Wales coast but far enough away to ensure that she was clear of any rocks that may not have been marked on his charts. Taking this course had some advantages. It was the shortest route and delayed having to cope with any rough water in the Irish Sea until it was necessary. There was however another big advantage. As well as the navigation charts, vessels also usually carried drawings of key coastal navigation features which the captain could refer to when necessary to confirm his position. Only with strong coastal features being visible could a ship's captain at the time be really sure where he was. As the *Ocean Monarch* rounded the North Wales coast, two features came into view which really confirmed the ship's position, the Great Orme and the Little Orme encompassing the town of Llandudno. The time was around noon and many of the passengers would have been on deck watching the spectacle as the vessel sailed past the resort town. Passengers who came from Merseyside may have seen the sight before as pleasure steamers regularly made day trips to North Wales from Liverpool and they may have already visited Llandudno. At least, that is, if they could have afforded it. The passengers would have been mainly very poor people who had invested all they had in to this chance of a new life in the United States. It is likely that many had not seen the Great Orme or Little Orme before, in fact, many may not even have heard of them or indeed of the town of Llandudno. The passengers would have been tremendously excited at the thought of the Atlantic crossing and their new life ahead and the view from the deck must have added to that sense of excitement. But for some it would be the last bit of Britain that they would ever see. No-one is really sure how it started but a fire broke out on board. The cause was thought to have been due to emigrant passengers possibly smoking their pipes near flammable material or starting a fire at the base of one of the ventilators thinking it was a chimney. However it started, it rapidly spread throughout the ship which was soon blazing from stem to stern. Some of those on board clambered on to the bowsprit to try and escape the inferno but, one by one, they lost their grip and fell into the water and eventually the wooden spar failed completely flinging many people into the water. Captain Murdock described the scene on board *"The fire produced the utmost confusion amongst the passengers; all appeared infatuation and despair; yells and screams of the most horrifying description were given; all control over them was lost; my voice could not be heard, nor my orders obeyed".* Passengers were leaping into the water but the crew did their best for them, throwing wooden spars and loose materials into the water to give them something to cling to. The *Ocean Monarch* had left Liverpool with 399 passengers and crew and almost half lost their lives in the incident. In fact, the loss of life would have much greater if there had not been a number of vessels not far away who would provide assistance including the Brazilian steam frigate *Affonso* which was on a trial trip and carried a number of foreign V.I.P.s. Her captain launched boats to pick up survivors and also managed to moor alongside the *Ocean Monarch,* at great risk, and get a rope across which allowed many people to cross to safety. A lot of bravery was displayed on the day particularly by the crew of the *Ocean Monarch* and by those on board the *Affonso*. However there were reports in local newspapers that the *Cambria* mail ship passed by and failed to provide any assistance. This seems very unlikely so may be an unfair accusation. It was usual for vessels to go the aid of other vessels in distress although it was certainly not always the case. If a ship's captain felt that intervention would put his own vessel at risk for whatever reason, he may well decide it was best to keep going. Also, with very limited methods of communication between ships at the time, there would have been occasions when a ship's captain did not realise that a vessel he passed had a serious problem. It has to be said though that, in this case, the sight of a vessel ablaze from end to end with people in the water and other ships rushing to help, would seem to be a good indication that something was seriously wrong!

This was the reality of crossing the Atlantic at the time; it was dangerous, vessels were lost with alarming regularity. Imagine the outcry there would be today if aircraft crossing the Atlantic were being lost at such a rate! And imagine how many people would not consider even making the crossing because it was too dangerous. But 19th century people had perhaps a different approach to life. They were tough and were prepared to face up to whatever life would throw at them.

But transatlantic travellers were not soft and, to reduce the risk, many travellers felt that getting across the ocean as quickly as possible was the best policy. This may or may not have been a sensible course of action but, if they could afford it, many preferred a fast Collins ship to those of the other lines.

So the Collins Line continued but it became difficult for them to maintain a regular service with one less of their super ships to call on.

By a cruel twist of fate, just 12 days after the loss of the *Arctic,* the name of the founder of the Collins Line, featured in another shipping tragedy. The steamer *E. K. Collins*, owned by a Captain Ward, left Detroit for Cleveland but was lost near Malden after bursting into flames. Twenty three of those on board were lost. The fire was said to have been caused by steerage passengers emptying their pipes on to the ship's woodwork. The steam engine on this recently built vessel played no part in the tragedy.

Chapter 19

The *Great Eastern*

No book on paddle liners would be complete without mention of Brunel's Great Laviathan, the *Great Eastern.* How could you best describe this iconic vessel? I would describe her as *almost* one of the greatest vessels ever built and *almost* one of the most useless, perhaps an odd description but it will all become clear.

Samuel Cunard had a very different character to Isambard Kingdom Brunel. Cunard was a sharp, go-ahead entrepreneur, always looking for new opportunities, but when it came to ships he was more conservative and preferred things that he had confidence in. Brunel, on the other hand, was a real go-ahead engineer with a fervent mind who liked to push the boundaries, to come up with something new, and even to try and turn the impossible into reality. Sometimes things went according to plan, but sometimes they didn't.

As the middle of the 19th century approached, British eyes were increasingly looking not just to the west, where the United States was providing unrivalled trade opportunities, but also to the Far East, where the East India Company's monopoly had finally been removed and the doors to India, Pakistan and China were open to all. It began in 1813 when the monopoly was partially repealed but trade with China was still controlled until 1833 when all restrictions were removed. Liverpool merchants were jubilant as the Far East had been in the hands of London merchants for too long, now it was their turn but it started fairly slowly. In 1814 the first Liverpool ship to trade directly with India, the *Kingsmill,* set off from the

Mersey and eventually many more followed. The Brocklebank Line, operating out of Birkenhead's East Float, became a key player and commissioned a number of new ships at their Whitehaven yard for the new trade routes.

But there was a new land that had now come into the frame - Australia. The first convict settlements were established there around 1786 and during the first half of the 19th century they were joined by a number of emigrants who had plans to make a fortune out of sheep or cattle farming. But first they had to get there and they faced a dreadful journey. Vessels would have to travel around the horn of Africa and the voyage would last five months or more. Conditions on board were often horrendous and perhaps not much different to those being endured by the prisoners under transportation. Deaths on board were not uncommon. The trade mainly operated from London, which had all the contacts, with Liverpool's burgeoning port playing catch-up but the volume of trade was still at a much lower level than that across the Atlantic.

That all changed in 1851 when gold was discovered in Australia and, in the same year, the Great Exhibition brought home to many people the agricultural opportunities that the vast land could provide. Many people realised that fortunes were there to be made and trade routes between Britain, especially Liverpool, and Australia really took off. Shipyards in the United States and Nova Scotia, which could build the fast clipper ships, were inundated with orders and the vessels were put on to the Australian run as soon as they arrived in England. Many people wanted to try their luck in Australia and in 1852 alone, 102,000 emigrants arrived in Victoria. But, even on the sailing clippers, it was still a long and difficult journey.

Steam had been used on the Far East and Australian trade for some time with the first, sail assisted, steamer being the Clyde-built *Australia* which set out from Plymouth on 5th June 1852 under the command of Captain Hoseason. A number of coal bunkering ships had to be sent out in advance to refuel the vessel. On 20th August, after quite a difficult journey, she reached Western Australia and, a couple of weeks later, she made it to Melbourne. Despite the difficulties, she proved that a steamer could do it and a number of other steamers followed including Brunel's fine paddler the *Great Britain* when she had been repaired following her Dundrum Bay mishap. But the big problem persisted, coal had to be sent in advance on bunker ships and stored at re-coaling points, an impractical and expensive procedure. In any case the clipper ships, if they were well skippered and the winds were favourable, could often do the whole journey faster than the steamers which had to detour to visit the coaling points on the way.

Following relaxation of the East India Company monopoly and the interest produced by the Great Exhibition, the Eastern Steam Navigation Company was formed in 1851with great plans to provide a steamer mail service to Australia and the Far East. But the company was unsuccessful, the British Government gave the mail contract to P & O.

During the previous years, Brunel had been living in Devon while he worked on the South Devon Railway and he took the opportunity to find some time for himself. But during these quiet periods his mind wasn't resting and he filled his notebooks with ideas, one of which was a proposal for a ship that could carry its own coal for a journey to Calcutta or Columbo where feeder ships would be on hand to carry passengers and cargo to Australia, or even directly to Australia. He was not just thinking of a vessel that could carry its own coal for the outward journey but the return journey as well. Such a vessel would have to be enormous and almost certainly beyond the thinking of anyone else at the time. But of course this was Brunel, the man who was prepared to think things that other people couldn't even imagine. But his plans didn't always work out; would his sketch for a large steamer ever become reality?

Brunel went to the owners of the Eastern Steam Navigation Company with his proposal and, after much discussion, they took on board the idea and Brunel was appointed engineer to oversee the project. That was the easy part organised - now the vessel had to be funded, designed and built, a much bigger operation and a very rocky road lay ahead. The company didn't have enough capital to fund the project and not all owners were totally in favour. By early 1854 the problems and been sorted with the company being re-capitalised and Brunel and others replacing the dissenting shareholders.

Brunel sat down with the proposed shipbuilder, J. Scott Russell, and together they finalised the design for the *Great Eastern*. To do what she was required to do would mean that the ship would have to be massive and when she was completed her gross tonnage would be 18,915 tons. In relation to today's huge cruise liners and freighters, this may seem like a small vessel but, at that time, a vessel with a gross tonnage of around 3,000 tons was considered big. The *Great Eastern* would be six times bigger, an enormous leap and beyond the comprehension of most people. This left Scott Russell with a big problem - how do you quote for something so big and so new without any history to go on. Brunel thought the cost may be £500,000 but Scott Russell quoted only £377,200 for the complete vessel including hull, engines and boilers. This would be nowhere near enough and during the construction of the vessel there would be allegations of financial impropriety against Scott Russell and many accusations of bad faith; but that is another story.

The final specification for the *Great Eastern* was for a vessel that was unlike anything seen before or since. The ship would be 692 feet long, 83 feet broad (118 feet over the paddle boxes) and her thick iron hull would have an inner and an outer skin, 2 feet 10 inches apart with transverse plates providing watertight compartments. The iron plates for the hull skins would be 3/4 inch thick. There would be little in the way of a keel with the bottom being largely flat and made from 1 inch thick iron panels. In total the hull required around 30,000 iron plates each weighing an average of 600 lbs. Accommodation for passengers was luxurious and she would be fitted out to carry 800 first class, 2,000 second class and 1,200 third class. The passengers would have access to 10 saloons with the main saloon being 100 feet long by 86 feet wide. The berths would be comfortable, 14 feet long by 7 to 8 feet wide.

26   Construction of the Great Eastern's hull
(Courtesy U.S. Naval History Center)

The vessel would be propelled by both a screw propeller and paddle wheels. Brunel's *Great Britain* had been powered by a screw propeller but obtaining sufficient horse-power to move a vessel of this size was not considered an option. Additionally there was an issue with the screw on the *Great Britain* which was connected to the engine's crankcase by a chain drive. This arrangement did work but it was problematic and Brunel wanted the propeller shaft on the *Great Eastern* to be connected directly to the engine's crankcase. The shaft when eventually built would be 160 feet long and would weigh 60 tons. This would require a large screw, the actual version being 24 feet in diameter. One of the requirements of the *Great Eastern* was that she should be able to enter the Hooghly, a tributary of the Ganges and, to enable her to do this, the vessel had been designed with a shallow draught of around 23 feet. This would have resulted in the screw being partly out of the water as the ship would have used a lot of her coal supplies by that time and would be riding high. A single screw, perhaps five feet out of the water, would have had difficulty moving the ship forward; therefore the addition of paddle wheels was considered essential. In fact, without the paddles wheels, it could have been virtually impossible to manoeuvre the huge bulk of the *Great Eastern* whether in the Hooghly or anywhere else so the paddle wheels turned out to be a really good idea.

To move this huge vessel required the services of two huge powerhouses and their specifications are mind-numbing. The engine for the paddle wheels was an oscillating type and was made by Russell. It had four cylinders each 74 inches diameter and a stroke of 14 feet. The engine was powered by four 17 feet long boilers each served by ten furnaces and each weighing 50 tons and carrying 40 tons of water. The enormous paddle wheels were 56 feet in diameter and had thirty 13 feet long by 3 feet wide floats. The engine was designed to turn the 185 ton wheels at around 11.r.p.m.

The horizontal engine for the screw was made by James Watt and was at the time the largest marine steam engine ever built. It had to be because it was required to turn the 160 foot drive shaft, weighing 60 tons, and a screw propeller weighing 36 tons at 40 to 50 r.p.m. The direct connection to the screw, without any gearing up, meant that the engine had to be powerful enough to maintain a high rate of r.p.m. at all times. Power to do this was provided by four 84 inch diameter engines with a stroke of four feet and steam was provided by six 18.5 feet boilers. The ship had five funnels. Handling this monster was not going to be an easy feat, even with newly-developed steam assistance, and the rudder was controlled by four wheels each needing two crewmen. In difficult conditions a further four wheels could be added each requiring two more crewmen.

The ship had so much power in the engines that perhaps little use would be required of the large volume of sail (6,500 square feet) available to the seven masts, the larger ones being iron tubes and the smaller ones being made of wood. Two of the masts would be square rigged and the others rigged fore and aft.

To carry out the long journey envisaged would require huge amounts of coal to be carried and this drawing by Webb shows the vessel's huge coal stores:

LONGITUDINAL SECTION.

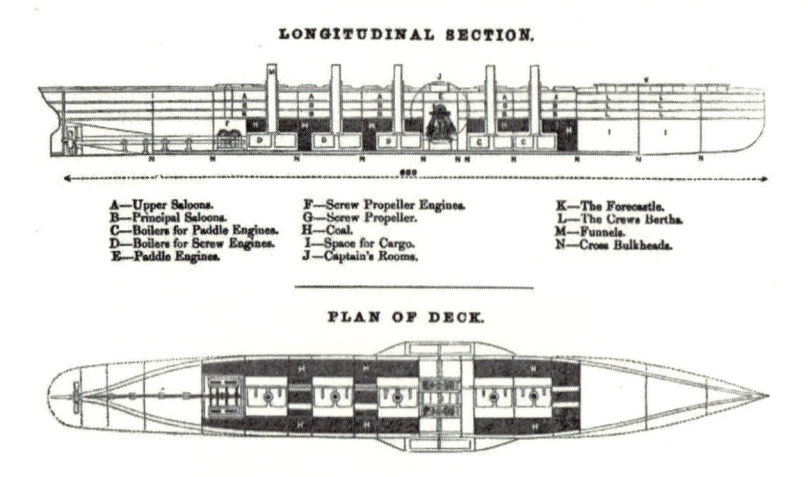

A—Upper Saloons.
B—Principal Saloons.
C—Boilers for Paddle Engines.
D—Boilers for Screw Engines.
E—Paddle Engines.
F—Screw Propeller Engines.
G—Screw Propeller.
H—Coal.
I—Space for Cargo.
J—Captain's Rooms.
K—The Forecastle.
L—The Crews Berths.
M—Funnels.
N—Cross Bulkheads.

PLAN OF DECK.

27 Plan of the Great Eastern
(Webb)

The vessel's safety standards were considered high. Apart from the twelve watertight compartments and the inner skin, she carried twenty large lifeboats and two large steamers for transferring passengers. Brunel thought that waves would not reach the deck so he had the lifeboats permanently fitted to their davits on the outside of the ship. In principle this seemed a good idea, it would help keep the decks uncluttered and would save time evacuating passengers in case of emergency.

The vessel was to be built on the Thames, but finding a location was not easy. The river frontage of the Scott Russell Yard was inadequate, but next to it was another yard, which was empty and belonged to David Napier, the Clyde shipbuilders. In 1853 the Eastern Steam Navigation Company leased the yard and, with the Scott Russell Yard, it would provide enough space. The Napier yard would build the vessel and the Scott Russell yard would produce the manufactured components which would be transferred to the Napier yard by a specially constructed railway.

The initial proposal to construct a dry dock or to launch the ship off an end-on slipway was not considered practical by Brunel, who decided that the vessel should be launched sideways-on down an inclined plane. But this created a major problem; the banks of the Thames at this point consisted of a layer of mud, thirty feet thick, on a bed of gravel, totally unsuitable for carrying the weight of such a massive ship. Today no doubt the answer to such a problem would be to give in and go elsewhere. Not the Victorians though, who were always ready to find a way to overcome problems, in this case by driving 1,400 piles into the banks of the river to provide a firm base for the construction. How to carry out the launch was now the problem. The company directors rejected the idea of a launch using rollers, because of the cost. So this left the small problem of how to move an inert mass of 12,000 tonnes a distance of 200 feet to low water level on the Thames. This would prove to be the greatest challenge of Brunel's career but he came up with a plan. The ship would be supported in two cradles, each 120 feet wide. Beneath the cradles, inclined ways of the same width would be extended 240 feet down to the river. The hydraulic launching gear Brunel had designed was ruled out by the company board so he had to design a mechanical system instead to get the vessel into the water.

Towards the end of 1857 the *Great Eastern* was completed and the launch was set the 3rd of November. The vessel had been under construction for two years and her progress had been reported widely in the national press. Everyone in the country seem to know about it and thousands turned up to see the big event and perhaps catch a glimpse of the great engineer.

At around 12.30 Brunel took up his position on the high control platform and gave the order to remove the wedges holding the support cradles in place. When this had been done Brunel signalled that it was time to launch the ship. The steam winches on the moored barges took the strain on the chains and a wave of a white flag gave the signal to heave on the chains to launch the *Great Eastern*. The excited crowd surged forward to watch the ship glide into the water and then - nothing. The *Great Eastern* didn't move an inch. Brunel called in two hydraulic rams, which caused the bow support cradle to suddenly move three feet. This caused great terror to those on the barges and amongst the launch crew as they worried what this great vessel towering above them might do. An Irish labourer died in the general breakdown in discipline and the launch had to be postponed.

28 Brunel
(CC-BY i PD-US)

On 19th of November, a new attempt was made. The launching winches were moved into the yard and two more hydraulic rams were installed which succeeded in moving the vessel a little but it was a very slow process. By 28th of November the *Great Eastern* had been moved just 14 feet and by 30 November at total of 33½ feet. Further attempts were made as the end of 1857 approached but progress remained slow.

Eventually Brunel decided that the best plan would be a big attempt on Sunday, 31 January when a very high tide was forecast. All efforts would have to be put into getting the ship into the water this time. If it failed, the next attempt would have to be delayed until the next spring tide.

Fortunately this time it was successful, and the biggest vessel so far seen on the Thames took to the water. But all of this had been a terrible price. The effort and strain of building the ship had ruined Brunel's health, and also ruined the company. In May Brunel travelled to Vichy and later to Switzerland, in an attempt in an effort to regain his health. He returned in September to find the *Great Eastern* still lying at Deptford and still waiting to be fitted out. The company could not raise the funds to complete the vessel. Later that year a new company, the Great Ship Company was formed which acquired the vessel and eventually undertook the fitting out.

After some recovery, Brunel's health problems caught up with him. On the 5th September 1859 he boarded the *Great Eastern* for the last time. Whilst on board he suffered a stroke which left him paralysed. He later rallied and was able to give instructions regarding the ship right up until 9th September, when his last letter was dated and signed.

Meanwhile, the *Great Eastern*, set out on her sea trials to Weymouth where the efficiency of the engines could be monitored. As the vessel made her way along the south coast she was worked up to 13 knots with her screw engines making 32 r.p.m. and her paddles turning at 8 r.p.m. The privileged passengers and reporters that had been invited on board were enthralled by the sedate and purposeful way the monster ploughed through the choppy sea. After a hearty lunch the guests vacated the saloon and went up on deck to watch as the ship steamed past Hastings.

Then tragedy struck. A huge explosion in the paddle room filled the area with scalding steam, blew off one of the funnels and destroyed the saloon which the guests had only recently left. The crew and passengers on the bridge had to run for shelter as the area was enveloped in scalding white steam and was showered with pieces of glass, window frames and wood fragments. The Captain's young daughter was just entering the saloon when the explosion struck and had a miraculous escape when the iron bulkhead protected her from the blast. It was clear that the men in the stoke-holes had borne the brunt of the explosion and some crewmen immediately made their way below decks to help them, despite the danger. Twelve firemen had been hurt with five of them being horribly burned by the scalding steam although a couple could still walk. One firemen made it out of the boiler room but then jumped into the water where he was caught by a paddle wheel. The five who initially survived, despite appalling burns, were treated by three doctors who happened to be on board but the only treatment they could give was to douse the firemen in plenty of oil and then cover them with dressings. They all faced a lingering death with no amount of water able to quench their raging thirst.

Despite the enormous damage and the loss of two boilers, the vessel was able to continue as normal to Weymouth. It is certain that other ships of the time would have foundered in such circumstances.

John Scott Russell laid the blame for the tragedy squarely on Brunel stating that the design for a feed-pipe casing around the funnels to cool the saloons and to economise on heat was forced upon him and that he was totally against it, Scott Russell seemingly forgetting the time, at the beginning of the project, when he, allegedly, tried to claim full credit for the design of the ship with Brunel playing no great part. Anyway the knives were all out now for Brunel and it was made worse by the claim that the Collins Line had tried a similar system but it had been abandoned it as serving no useful purpose and was considered dangerous.

By now Brunel was in no position to defend himself. As he lay on his bed, partly paralysed after his stroke and becoming increasingly frail, he waited for news of his ship expecting it all to be good. Eventually it was decided that he had to be told of the tragedy. It was too much for his body to bear and his spirit was finally broken. He died on 15th September 1859 and, as so often happens, members of the press who had derided him so much in life now began preparing their glowing obituaries. His colleague, Daniel Gooch, who had remained a true friend, wrote this in his diary:

'By his death the greatest of England's engineers was lost, the man with the greatest originality of thought and power of execution, bold in his plans but right. The commercial world thought him extravagant; but although he was so, great things are not done by those who sit down and count the cost of every thought and act.'

After repairs at Weymouth, the *Great Eastern* made her way to Holyhead but it was considered too late in the year for her to make her maiden voyage to New York so she was taken back to Southampton Water to over-winter. But, even before her maiden voyage, fate had one more cruel blow to inflict. When being taken ashore in a gig, Captain Harrison was drowned when a squall blew up and the vessel capsized.

The *Great Eastern's* maiden voyage to New York was scheduled for 16th June but the heavy weather caused a delay until the following morning. At 7.00 a.m. the order was given to unshackle the mooring chains, which took 45 minutes, and then her sails were set to point her in the right direction. When everything was ready the order "Easy ahead with screw" was given and the monster smoothly headed up the Solent, despite the prevailing raw and gusty weather. She had on board 38 passengers, eight guests and over ten times as many crew. The vessel was under the command of Vine Hall who had taken over after the death of Captain Harrison. This was the first transatlantic trip for Captain Hall but he was a very experienced mariner having been involved in many passages for the East India Trade.

Most of the passengers found the trip fairly agreeable with lots of food and drink available and regular concerts by the ship's band. The ride was noticeably smooth with little vibration but the vessel did roll a little too much for some people. She had been expected to complete the run in nine days but a 300 mile detour to avoid ice added around one a half days to her journey. She managed a top speed of 14.5 knots and consumed 2,877 tons of coal during the journey.

29 The Great Eastern Dining Room
(Courtesy and Copyright of the National Library of Ireland)

When the *Great Eastern* reached Sandy Hook, she was met with a massive reception with dozens of steamers, all decorated with flags, and crowded with passengers waving handkerchiefs and cheering. The ship's band stood on the paddle boxes and played "Rule Britannia" and "God save the Queen". The journey had gone well with no major problems; could it be the beginning of a great new future for the *Great Eastern*?

On her return she was chartered by the British Government to take troops to Quebec and this was where she came into her own, her vast bulk being able to hold 2,100 troops, 470 women and children, 200 horses and a few paying passengers. In fact, in time of crisis the vessel was expected to be able to carry up to 10,000 troops.

She made a further trip to New York from Milford Haven but, with a lot less passengers than crew, it was not a profitable exercise.

Her next scheduled voyage was from the main transatlantic port of Liverpool; if the *Great Eastern* was going to make a profit on regular transatlantic crossings, it would have to be from here. On 7th September 1861, she set out to New York under the command of Captain James Walker. She was by far the biggest vessel to dock in the port, in fact at the time she was the biggest vessel to dock anywhere. Crowds lined the dock walls to see her depart on what may kindly be described as a memorable voyage. Everything about the *Great Eastern* was big - her tonnage, her paddle wheels, her screw propellers, her high hopes, in fact she was somewhat over the top in every way. Her first Atlantic voyage from Liverpool would prove to be no exception.

Three days out she encountered a heavy gale which stripped her paddle wheels and then smashed her rudder leaving her wallowing helplessly in mountainous seas for three days, her lack of a substantial keel doing her no favours at all. Some of her boats were swept away by the waves. Brunel had designed the lifeboats to be permanently fixed on the outside of the ship because he thought the ship was so big that the waves would never reach them. Unfortunately it was another of those occasions when Brunel didn't get it quite right. This storm came with enormous waves and easily reached the lifeboats. Everything on board that could move was smashed, including all of the crockery, and one of the ship's cows, along with two swans, were propelled through the skylight into the saloon. It was usual to carry various types of fowl in coops on the deck and the swans were presumably intended as a special meal for the first class passengers. Another example of standards of the day! In the mayhem the crew became uncontrollable and some broke into the storerooms where the alcohol was kept which made them even more uncontrollable. Some of the passengers were enrolled as guards to try and keep a bit of order on board, a white handkerchief tied around their arms being all that was necessary to give them some authority. The passengers did their best to keep calm and wait for the conditions to abate but it wasn't easy, especially as some had been injured by flying debris. The ladies, however, came up with a good plan, they found a place in the saloon where they coped with the ship's continual pitching and swaying by knitting and singing hymns. The captain of a passing brig, the *Magnet*, a small vessel seemingly able to cope with the heavy seas with no trouble at all, saw the plight of the big ship and sailed his vessel around the *Great Eastern* for a whole day until the weather moderated. A passenger authorised Captain Walker to hail the vessel with an offer of £100 per day to maintain station plus an offer to even buy the brig but no reply came back and it is not certain if the brig's captain heard the offer. However it is reported that the captain of the brig tried to claim £200 a couple of years later, only after hearing of the offer from a passenger, but it was a bit too late. The experience for those on board the *Great Eastern* was so bad that all thought they would never survive and few wanted to travel on her again. After the crew managed to complete a temporary repair to the rudder with some chains, she was able to return to Queenstown just using her screw propellers.

During the early part of 1862 the *Great Eastern* made two voyages to New York, setting off from Milford Haven and returning to Liverpool. The return journeys carried many more passengers and were profitable, thus displaying the importance of the Port of Liverpool in transatlantic trade.

On her third voyage in the later part of the 1862 summer, her bad luck returned. After a reasonably uneventful journey from Liverpool, she was slowing down at the entrance to Long Island to pick up a pilot when she hit a submerged reef which was not marked on the charts. She was able to continue into the harbour with most of her passengers probably not knowing about the incident until they read it in the papers. However the damage was massive with an 85 feet long by 4 feet wide gash in her bottom. Any other vessel would have been destroyed by such an event but the *Great Eastern* was saved by her inner skin; Brunel was certainly on the right track with that idea.

Scotia the Brave

30 The Great Eastern docked in Dublin
Note the lifeboats in their permanent external positions
(Courtesy and copyright of the National Library of Ireland)

The *Great Eastern* managed to make a few successful trips to New York the following year but, although she carried a lot of passengers and a huge amount of freight, the company struggled to meet the high running costs and to recover the high cost of repairs following her earlier mishaps and, unlike Cunard, they did not have a mail subsidy to rely on. Eventually it became too much for the company to bear and the vessel was sold to some of the bondholders for a knock down price of £25,000 who promptly made a financial killing. They immediately chartered her to the Telegraph Construction Company who re-fitted her and she took to the water as the C.S. *Great Eastern,* the *Cable Ship Great Eastern.* After all her problems, the Great Leviathan had now found her position in life and would soon make her mark on the world.

In July 1865 she set out to lay the first ever transatlantic cable but on 2nd August a fault developed in the cable and, as it was being hauled up from 12,000 feet, it snapped. All efforts to drag the cable up failed and the *Great Eastern* had to head back home.

But the *Great Eastern* had shown that she was ideally suited to cable laying and in June 1866 she left her mooring at Sheerness with thousands of miles of new cable on board. On 26th July, to wild acclaim, she steamed into Heart's Content Bay in Newfoundland with the cable intact. For the first time Europe and North America were joined and important messages could be sent the same day instead of taking ten days or more. But it became even better. The *Great Eastern* had been fitted with new grappling equipment and she went off in search of the broken cable from the previous year's attempt. On 2nd September she managed to grab the cable and returned triumphantly to Heart's Content Bay with the second telegraph link. The *Great Eastern* was in her element now and over the next ten years she would lay thousands of miles of submarine cable across the Atlantic and in the Far East. But it couldn't go on forever and around 1878 her cable-laying days came to an end. She was re-fitted for passenger service but was never a commercial success and a decision had to be made about her future. Despite the fact that she was still in good condition with her deck having been recently replaced, no-one wanted her.

This left the problem of what to do with the old girl. She was so huge, she couldn't just be abandoned in a creek somewhere and forgotten about, and many ports didn't want her taking up space and spoiling the view, something that they would no doubt take a different view on if she was available today.

Eventually, in 1886, she was moved to the River Mersey where she became a floating concert hall and showboat, and provided illuminated advertising for Lewis's, the Liverpool department store.

31 The Floating Advertisement
(Courtesy and copyright of the National Library of Ireland)

Brunel could never have imagined that his potentially fine vessel, his "great babe", would end up as a huge floating advertising hoarding with trapeze artists flying between the rigging. It could all have been so different. If she had turned out as he had hoped and, as he and worried ship owners had expected, the *Great Eastern* would have been the greatest ship in the world, in fact no other vessel would have come close. She would have set a new standard in long distance sea travel. The reality is, though, that she was pretty much doomed from the beginning. She was just not right - too big, too clever and the wrong ship for the time. Even when she was being built, the Suez Canal was being planned and the need for a ship able to carry her own coal for a trip all the way round the Cape of Good Hope to Australia and the Far East would diminish. The *Great Eastern* couldn't even have made it through the first cut of the canal as she was too big. Unfortunately the *Great Eastern* was just a step too far.

She visited a couple of other ports in her new advertising role but, in November 1888, she was sold to a firm of ship breakers for £16,000 and returned to the Mersey where, at New Ferry and after a lot of time and effort, she was broken up. The famed engineer, Daniel Gooch, who did so much to make steam projects work and who had been appointed Chief Engineer at the Great Ship Company, is reported to have lamented "*Poor old girl. You deserved a better fate*" - a very fitting eulogy.

But even as she languished on the Wirral shore like a beached whale, awaiting the wreckers, she still held on to her "fifteen minutes of fame". She may have been thirty years old but she was still the biggest vessel that had ever, so far, sailed the sea and would remain so until eclipsed by the *Oceanic*, in length, in 1899 and by the *Lusitania*, in tonnage, in 1907.

It doesn't end there though. She may be gone but the *Great Eastern* still holds on to one record, and will continue to do so - she will always be the ship that had the biggest paddle wheels!

```
It has been claimed that massive ships
were in use in China during the 15th
century Ming Dynasty.  These vessels were
not quite as long as the Great Eastern
but were much wider, perhaps twice as wide
or more. Admiral Zheng He is said to have
had a fleet of these huge wooden vessels
which, if they had been built, could have
had a greater gross tonnage than the Great
Eastern. The story is that they had been
```

built so big to carry masses of troops, horses and goods and their final displaced weight would have been enormous. It is difficult to imagine how such a huge wooden vessel could have been built in the 15th century and what sail configuration could be devised to propel and control such a wide, ungainly vessel. Personally, I don't believe a word of it.

Liverpool has more than just far off memories of the *Great Eastern*. When the vessel was being broken up, Liverpool Football Club was looking for a flagpole and they acquired the ship's topmast, which is said to still stand today at the ground's Kop End.

32 The Great Eastern on the banks of the River Mersey awaiting breaking
(Courtesy State of Victoria Library/Green)

Chapter 20

New situations

The loss of the *Arctic* seriously reduced competition from the Collins Line but they were still there and still had better ships than Cunard had on the Atlantic run. Samuel Cunard realised that it was no use producing more vessels of the same type that might end up still inferior to those of Collins. It was time to move up a level and produce something really special. The success of the iron hulled Great Western had proved to Sam that this was the future and, in any case, if you wanted a really large vessel, you had to move to iron, a large wooden hull would not be strong enough to stand the stresses of a stormy Atlantic journey.

Sam discussed the possibilities with Robert Napier and they came up with a design for the *Persia,* a 3,300 gross tonnage vessel, 376 feet long and a beam of 45 feet. Since the launch of the *Britannia,* Cunard had added 26 vessels to their fleet, mostly for coastal British or their Mediterranean service but the *Persia* would have something special - an iron hull. Iron-hulled ships were not new, in fact by this time around 100 had been built in Britain but it was a first for Cunard and the *Persia* would turn out to be superlative in every way and the second largest vessel in the world, after the *Great Eastern.* To the consternation of many, inside and outside of the Cunard Line, she would be driven by paddles wheels and not a more modern screw propeller. Power would come from one massive two-cylinder 100 inch diameter steam engine with a ten feet stroke producing around 917 tons of nominal horse power. To provide the steam were 8 tubular boilers each served by 5 furnaces and working at a pressure of 20 p.s.i.

There were also two small donkey engines for pumping water and waste heat around the system. To fit everything in took an engine room 115 feet long by 45 feet wide.

Fittings and accommodation on board were luxurious and she was designed to carry 250 first class and 50 second class passengers with, as with the other Cunard paddlers on the prestige mail service, no space on board for steerage passengers. To be able to provide for the needs of the passengers required a vast stock of equipment including 1,200 blankets, 1,600 sheets and 4,600 towels. The main 60 feet long by 20 feet wide main saloon was beautifully appointed with red velvet upholstery and curtains, maple panelling and elegantly framed mirrors and paintings on the walls. The skylight was filled with stained glass with a prominent feature being a representation of a Persian man and woman in native costume. Above the saloon was a uninterrupted promenade deck for passengers, at 370 feet long it was virtually the length of the ship. Cargo space was also provided, up to 1,200 tons, but a paddle steamer crossing the Atlantic also had to find space for the vast quantity of coal that would be consumed en route, 1,400 tons. To look after the ship and its passengers required a large complement of crew which totalled 170 including a doctor, 8 cooks and 2 woodworkers. To do the key work below decks, which the passengers seldom saw or probably seldom thought about, were 8 engineers and 54 firemen who would toil in their dark, dirty cave every day the ship was at sea.

RMS Persia under construction
(Courtesy SMU University Libraries)

The *Persia* wasn't just designed to do a job, she was also planned to look smart and, compared with the other transatlantic steamers, she did, right down to her figurehead of a Persian maiden and her ornate paddle boxes with an inset design of a lion bordered by two palm trees.

This stupendous vessel was launched on the Clyde on 25th July 1855 with thousands watching from the river banks. After fitting out, she set out on her trial trip from Greenock to Liverpool, a distance of 203 miles, which she competed at an average speed of 16 knots. For a large paddle steamer, this was fast.

Once again she was the centre of attention as she made her way up the Mersey, many of those watching no doubt remembering the sight of Cunard's first specially built steamer for the Atlantic run, the *Britannia* steaming along the river and noting how this vessel was double the size. Then the day approached for the *Persia's* maiden voyage to New York.

Three days before the Persia set off, the Collins steamer *Pacific* started her journey from Liverpool to the same destination with 25 first class passengers, 20 second class, all mainly American, a crew of 141, thousands of items of mail and $2 million dollars worth of cargo. The *Persia's* captain would no doubt have watched the *Pacific* chugging down the Mersey and may have thought that, despite the *Pacific's* three days start, as he had a brand new ship, he could well be in New York harbour first to welcome the tardy *Pacific*. He probably realised that that was just wishful thinking. It was well known that the Collins ships would do all they could to beat the Cunarders, sailing at top speed was the order of the day even if it meant taking risks. The instruction to Cunard's captains was the opposite - just get their safely.

But whatever the captain of the *Persia* had been thinking, he could not have imagined what fate had in store.

The day for the *Persia's* maiden voyage arrived, 26th January 1856. At 10.30 a.m. the passengers left the landing stage by small steamer to join the *Persia* moored in the river. At 11.50 the mail was delivered to her and the steamer immediately set off on her long journey soon running into squally weather but eventually finding her way into the Atlantic Ocean without too much difficulty.

This account in the Illustrated London News, published not long after her departure, gives some impression of the wonder of the new vessel.

This leviathan vessel, the largest steam-ship afloat in the world - far exceeding in length, strength, tonnage, and steam-power the Great Britain *or the* Himalaya; *and exceeding also by no less than 1200 tons the internal capacity of the largest of the present splendid Cunard liners - left Liverpool on the 26th ult., commanded by Captain Judkins, the respected Commodore of the Canard Company's mail-packets, on her first voyage across the Atlantic.*

Stupendous as the Persia is, the lines of beauty have been so well worked out in the preparation of her model that her appearance is singularly graceful and lightsome. Yet this mighty fabric, so beautiful as a whole, is made up of innumerable pieces of ponderous metal, welded, jointed, arid riveted into each other with exceeding deftness. The framing of the ship is very heavy. The space between each frame is only 10 inches, and the powerful frames, or ribs, are themselves 10 inches deep, with double angle irons at the outer and inner edges. The bow is constructed in a manner at once peculiar and affording the greatest possible strength to this important part of the ship. The framing is so placed to the stern that the effect is that, in the case of collision with other ships, or with rocks, or icebergs, the strain would fall upon the very strongest material within the structure, and the Persia would have a good chance of safety and successful resistance while ordinary vessels would be in great peril. She is not clinker-built, as some ships have been constructed of late. The plates or outer planking of the ship, so to speak, are laid alternately, so that one adds strength to the other, and they form a whole of wonderful compactness and solidity. The keel-plates are 11-16ths of an inch in thickness; at the bottom of the ship the plates are 15-16ths of an inch in thickness; from this section to the load water-line they are ¾ths of an inch; and above this they are 11-16ths of an inch in thickness. The plates round the gunwale are 7ths of an inch in thickness.

The Persia has seven water-tight compartments. The goods are stowed in two of these divisions - each about 90 feet long by 16 in breadth, and 20 feet in height. These goods stores, or rather tanks, are placed in the centre line of the ship, with the coal-cellars, or bunkers, on each side of them. At the same time the vessel is so constructed as to have in reality a double bottom under these goods chambers, so that if the outer were beat in or injured the inner would, in all likelihood, protect the cargo dry and intact. The chambers are perfectly water tight; and in the event of accident to the hull these tanks would of themselves float the ship. This liner has two engines, and eight large tubular boilers and two funnels; and we need only speak of her machinery in general, as being first clam. The firing apace for the boilers is placed in the fore and aft line, instead of across the ship, as is usually the case with smaller vessels.

She has separate sleeping accommodation for 260 passengers, disposed along what may be called the main deck, lying immediately above the goods and coal stores. These cabins have each 8 feet 6 inches of head-room; and, coupled with the excellent system of ventilation introduced into all the Cunard liners, we need scarcely say that they will be alike pleasant, airy, and healthful. Exclusively of the wholesome accommodation for the officers and engineers, there are in the forward part of the ship about 120 berths for the sailing crew, firemen, and stokers. The total number of persons employed in working the ship, from the captain downwards, is 150. Above the main deck there is a deck-house covered in, the roof of which affords a promenade from stem to stern. It contains the main dining saloon, about 60 feet in length, by 20 feet in width, and 8 feet in height. It is copiously lighted from the sides by plates of glass placed in the alternate panels. In front is that important adjunct, the pantry, which has about 300 square feet of area; and before the funnel is the kitchen, of equal size, with its cooking-ranges, exceeding most and equalling any of the culinary establishments of the most extensive and noted hotels in the kingdom. But we have not space to enter further into detail than to say that on this deck and below it are also to be found the bakery, the butcher's shambles, the carpenter's workshop, the lamp-house, the doctor's shop, the icehouse, the bath rooms, &c.

Her coal cellars are constructed to receive 1400 tons of coal - an ample supply to carry her on her voyage across the Atlantic as fast as she can burn them. She has also accommodation for about 1300 tons measurement of goods.

The Persia has been constructed entirely by Messrs. Robert Napier and Sons, of Glasgow, and in the trip from Greenock to Liverpool her performance gave the greatest satisfaction. With from 20 lb. to 21 lb. of pressure upon the square inch, she easily made 18½ statute miles an hour, while the paddles gave 17¾ to 18 revolutions in the minute. She accomplished the distance from the Clock Lighthouse to the Bell Buoy, a distance of 175 knots, or 203 miles, in 10 hours and 43 minutes, making an average speed of 16 knots, or 19 miles an hour.

Crossing the Atlantic at this time was still a risky operation. Vessels were lost with alarming regularity. There were Atlantic storms to contend with, risks of collisions with other vessels, particularly in coastal waters, dangers from hitting rocks as the ships neared the coastline and the danger from the main thing which crews of ships on the Atlantic northern route had to keep a special watch for – icebergs.

Unfortunately, despite the Cunard Line's safety ethos, it is now clear that the crew were not paying enough attention. Half way across the Atlantic the *Persia* encountered an ice field and the vessel ploughed straight into an iceberg or, more specifically, ploughed through an iceberg. The vessel's bow suffered damage, ruining the figurehead, and, as the ice-berg broke into pieces, the debris was drawn into the paddle wheels causing a lot of damage, particularly to the starboard wheel. The *Persia* came to a shuddering halt and those on board must have wondered what would become of them and their ship. But they needn't have worried, the *Persia* was built of iron and had been well put together at the shipyard of Robert Napier, Britain's top shipbuilder and marine engineer. Her bow had been strengthened with diagonal iron bracing and her watertight compartments did their job. She was also helped by her clipper bow design which absorbed much of the impact before the main part of the hull was compromised. The main thing, though, was that everyone on board was safe and Cunard's record of having never lost a passenger was still holding good. After a delay for essential repairs to the paddle wheels, which took thirty hours, she was able to continue her journey with a 150 mile detour to go around the ice field.

After a journey of 14 days, 4 hours, the *Persia* approached New York harbour. At this point many thoughts must have been going through the mind of Captain Judkins. He had nearly lost his brand new ship and would shortly be parading his damaged vessel before the captain and crew of the Pacific who would surely by now have reached port. Certainly not a good moment in his illustrious career.

However when the *Persia* finally made her way into New York harbour, the *Pacific* was nowhere to be seen. She had never made it to her destination. In fact neither the vessel, nor her passengers or crew were ever seen again. A search boat was rapidly chartered by E. K. Collins and sent to look for her but no trace could be found and it was assumed that she had probably suffered disaster when crossing the same ice field that had caught out the *Persia*. This was a terrible blow for the Collins line. After the loss of the *Arctic* in 1854, this meant two major losses within two years, one from collision with another vessel and one from a probable collision with an iceberg. Yet here was the *Persia,* Cunard's luxury brand new iron hulled ship, seemingly able to smash into an iceberg but still get her passengers safely to their destination. People liked travelling on the Collins steamers, and Americans really wanted to support the flag, but there were limits. Travelling by Cunard stood out as a much safer way of crossing the North Atlantic. The Collins Line started to lose trade.

But Collins had something up their sleeve, their fine new ship, the *Adriatic*, was under construction and she was thought capable of giving Cunard a run for their money. They just had to get her into service.

So much was going wrong for the Collins Line that the owners must have thought that things couldn't get any worse. Unfortunately they were wrong; they could and they did. Many people had not been happy about the U.S. Government granting subsidies to the mail steamers. The subsidies only seemed to benefit New York, and merchants in Boston, Philadelphia and other eastern seaboard cities started to complain loudly to Congress as did the owners of the sailing packets who felt that they were being left out. The U.S. government had to take note of their views and decided to give Collins the required six months notice that their subsidy would be substantially reduced. The company was already struggling to make a profit against the Cunard competition, even with the subsidy, so things were now looking financially ruinous. Then, their one chance, their new ship, the *Adriatic*, which was on the stocks and which might just have saved them at the eleventh hour, was delayed in construction. The *Adriatic* was by far the best vessel of the Collins Line - luxurious, classy and, at 355 feet long and 50 feet broad and 3,670 gross tons, she was much bigger than her siblings. She was constructed by Steers of New York and her huge engines, supplied by Novelty Ironworks, had two 100 inch cylinders with a stroke of 12 feet capable of turning her 40 feet diameter paddle wheels at 17 r.p.m. She was expected to be fast, and she was. Eventually she was completed and brought into service with her maiden voyage for Collins ending in Liverpool in December 1857 after a very fast crossing. But it was all too late for E.K. Collins. His company could not recover from all of its problems and it folded in early 1858 after which E.K. gave up on his Atlantic steamer dreams and started to pursue other interests. The *Adriatic* was laid up until the following year when she was bought by the North Atlantic Steamship Company. She was put into service on a Galway - Newfoundland run but this was not very successful and the service was discontinued. It was getting increasingly difficult for the smaller steamship companies to compete with the likes of Cunard and Inman who had enough vessels to run regular services. With no use for the *Adriatic*, her owners sent her to the Mersey where she was laid up in Birkenhead docks and put up for sale. But sadly there wasn't a queue of people wanting to buy her. This was a great tragedy for the *Adriatic*, the last of the great wooden hulled paddler liners built for the Atlantic crossing and, in the eyes of many, the finest vessel of her type ever built. In fact, she was certainly one of the best vessels built in the United States during the whole of the 19th century. But she came on the scene at just the wrong time. Britain was now in control of the Atlantic ferry service and new ships being built for the crossing were modern, iron-hulled vessels, mostly with screw propellers. The days of the big wooden paddlers were rapidly coming to an end. It had taken the

United States a long time to make the grade in transatlantic paddle steaming and, just when it did, everything went wrong with steamers being lost or becoming out of date. It would be many years before America would have any further influence on the Atlantic steamer trade. Eventually someone bought the *Adriatic,* but not to use her as a paddle liner; this little used vessel had to suffer the ignominy of being sent to West Africa where she would end her days as a storage hulk, a fate that would await many great ships at the time.

Samuel Cunard wanted safety at sea and would have taken no comfort from the loss of two ships of his main competitor, along with hundreds of lives, but the fact remains that the loss of the *Arctic* and the *Pacific* took the Collins Line out of the equation and left Cunard as the premier shipping line for travel between Britain and the United States, a position the company would hold for many years.

Meanwhile Cunard's new vessel, the *Scotia,* was on the drawing board. She was planned as a sister ship to the *Persia* and, like her, she was envisaged as another luxury vessel able to take on the best of that Collins could offer. But, with the demise of that shipping line, there was no need for a rush to get the vessel built and the opportunity was taken to revise her design. Cunard were not totally happy with the *Persia;* fine ship though she was, they thought her hull was a little weak in the bilges and, with her large coal stocks, she rode low in the water at the beginning of her journey which limited her speed. Time was not now of the essence and Cunard took the opportunity to put into practice all that they had learned about ship design over the years and to build a vessel that was bigger, better, faster, safer and more luxurious than anything that had gone before, apart from the ill-fated *Great Eastern.*

The iron-hulled, 4,000 ton *Scotia* was launched on 21st June 1861 and she did everything that was expected of her, soon taking over transatlantic speed records and proving a big hit with her passengers.

But the *Scotia* would be the last of the Cunard paddlers. Paddle steamers for river and coastal use and for ferry boats were still popular because of their manoeuvrability but for use on the high seas everyone else was moving to screw driven vessels which were much cheaper to operate and, as technology had improved, their speed could match that of even the fastest paddlers. Samuel Cunard did not want to give up the paddle steamer for the important transatlantic mail run until it could be proved that screw propulsion was reliable and efficient. That position had now been reached and all future Cunard vessels would be screw driven.

With the demise of the Collins Line, Cunard once again became head of the premier transatlantic shipping table. It was also doing well on the transatlantic emigrant trade with its non-mail steamers, *Andes, Alps, Etna* and *Jura* all of which could carry steerage class passengers as well as second class and cabin. To provide room for the steerage passengers, all of these vessels had screw propellers. The launch of these emigrant steamers was music to the ears of his friend, Joseph Howe, who had urged Samuel Cunard to set up an emigrant service hoping that it would bring people to Nova Scotia. Meanwhile Cunard's Mediterranean service was also doing well with its six mail steamers.

But nothing stays the same and, for the Cunard Line, it would be no different. Sam retired in 1863 at the age of seventy six, following a heart attack, and visited Halifax where he spent some time at his old house in Brunswick Street, a house he built for Susan almost fifty years before.

The American Civil War was in process at the time and many Nova Scotians were increasingly worried about an invasion from the south. The three Atlantic provinces, New Brunswick, Nova Scotia and Newfoundland, were in talks about creating a combined strong colony while the provinces of Canada had proposed incorporating them into Canada. Some Nova Scotians were concerned about becoming a *"servile dependency of Canada"* but nevertheless the plan went ahead and Nova Scotia became part of the Dominion of Canada. That was in 1867, the year that the last Cunard liner would enter the port of Halifax for almost fifty years. Sam would not know any of this. In 1864 he returned to England on board the *Scotia*. His health was failing and he must have known that this would have been his last journey to his home town of Halifax. The following April he had another heart attack but then seemed to recover. Five days later however, on 28th April 1865, he died with his two sons beside him.

This was a difficult time for the Cunard Line. Sam's guiding hand was no longer on the tiller and his son, Edward who took his place, did not have his father's qualities or business acumen. In 1869, Edward too died from a heart attack.

In 1867, the existing mail contract expired. Cunard tendered for a new one but now there was a lot of competition and Sam wasn't available with his persuasive negotiating powers to help the process. Cunard won the contract but at only half the price of the last one.

Passenger traffic across the North Atlantic was increasing all the time and more and more vessels arrived on the scene from other shipping lines to compete for the business - and most of them were better than Cunard's conservative and old fashioned ships.

The Inman Line put up strong competition with its "City" line of steamers which often proved to be the fastest on the Atlantic and then the White Star vessels appeared which were state of the art in luxury with some eventually being fitted with electric lighting and one even reported to have been fitted with a self-levelling floor in the saloon. But what these super new ships did not have was Cunard's standards of safety. The *City of Boston* went down with 200 passengers, the *Austria* caught fire and 470 perished and, in 1873, the White Star *Atlantic* went down with 545 people. Up to then, the Cunard Line had never lost a passenger and, for many, this was time to move back to the safety of the Cunard Line.

Despite its ups and downs, the Cunard Line remained a force to be reckoned with and by 1877 it was operating 46 vessels including 19 on the Atlantic mail and passenger services, 12 on the Mediterranean and Havre services and 8 between Liverpool, Glasgow and Belfast. But it had to do something to fend off the competition. In 1879 a joint stock company, The Cunard Steamship Company Limited, was formed to take over from the partnership and to raise capital for some new vessels that would match or exceed the standard of its competitors. In 1881 the luxurious *Servia* appeared, Cunard's first steel vessel and its first to have electric lighting throughout, and two years later, it built the even more luxurious *Aurania*.

By the mid 1880s the Cunarders were in the lead again with the fastest Atlantic crossings. The world's premier passenger shipping line was back at the top and its name would become a byword for luxury sea travel for generations to come. Once again, Sam, although now deceased, would be king of the Atlantic.

Chapter 22

End of an era

33 The Scotia
(Courtesy Liverpool University)

The Cunard partners had many discussions about the design for their new steamer, the *Scotia*. They talked about the hull, the engines, the vessel's size - all the usual things but, as with the *Persia,* the topic that brought about disagreement and heated discussion was - paddle wheels or a screw propeller. Samuel Cunard was again adamant that the new ship should have paddle wheels and he stood his ground despite the preference for a screw propeller by the other partners. George Burns was strongly against fitting the new ship with paddle wheels and faced up to Samuel Cunard demanding that the ship should have a screw propeller. But, as with the *Persia,* Sam stood his ground. What Burns really thought of Sam has not been recorded, and perhaps it is best that it hasn't, but, by now he'd had enough and decided to retire from the company, leaving his son, John, to look after his interests. Burns got away from it all and bought the Wemyss Estate in Renfrewshire which overlooked the Clyde Estuary. He was 65 years old at this time but retirement gave him a new lease of life and new opportunities. He became very involved in local community and religious affairs and retained a great interest in scientific matters. He lived at Wemyss House, collecting a Baronetcy on the way, until his death in 1890, aged 95 years.

Meanwhile the remaining partners had to carry on with plans to build the *Scotia*, even though most of them really did not want the vessel to have paddle wheels. But Sam had spoken, the *Scotia* must have paddle wheels and that was all there was to it.

At that time, and even now, it is difficult to imagine why Sam didn't want to move to driving the *Scotia* by a screw propeller. No-one else was building paddlers for the Atlantic crossing and the Inman Line, a developing competitor, had used screws since the company's formation ten years before. Even the Cunard Line was using screw propeller ships on its Atlantic emigrant trade. But there were some special factors that are thought to have influenced Sam on this occasion, not least the fact that the *Scotia* was required for the Atlantic mail service and the Admiralty was still not fully convinced about propeller driven steamships. The other Cunard Atlantic mail steamers were all paddlers and they were reliable and did the job. Why risk ending up with a new screw driven ship that might perform like the dreadful *Great Eastern? Stick with what you know* Sam thought. But there was a big price to pay for this. The *Scotia* would use twice as much coal as a screw-driven steamer of the same size and the extra coal stocks, and the central paddle engines, would take up space that could have been used for extra passengers or cargo. In a way, running a paddle liner had turned into an expensive luxury and such a project today might not be signed off by the Finance Department. However these were different times and Sam was effectively in control of the company. He must have known in his heart though that this would be the last of the big paddlers and he wanted her to be the best, and to look the best. The new screw driven steamers tended to have a more functional appearance and Sam felt that the *Scotia*, with her gold figurehead and her black and gold paddle boxes, would give an elegance that reflected the design of the many beautiful sailing ships that had been carrying passengers across the Atlantic for many years, a view that would be shared by her passengers.

The contract for the *Scotia* was given to Robert Napier and he set about building the last of the big paddle ships and the last to have a side lever steam engine.

Originally envisaged as a sister ship to the *Persia,* the *Scotia* would turn out to be a somewhat different vessel. The loss of the Collins Line, Cunard's main competitor, gave time to review the design for the new ship and, following the incident with the *Persia* hitting an iceberg, additional safety features were brought in. When she finally took to the water, she would be a bigger vessel than the *Persia*. She had an extra deck and was 412 ft long with a beam of 48 ft and a gross tonnage of 3,871 tons. Like the *Persia,* she was iron-hulled and had iron bracing 14 inches deep and four inches wide. Her double-bottomed hull, which was made up of iron plates up to one inch thick, was divided into seven compartments with six transverse watertight bulkheads, and four watertight caisson compartments were also added to provide extra safety. The *Scotia* would be the strongest and safest vessel so far built. Power was provided by one twin cylinder 4,700 i.h.p. side lever engine which powered her enormous 40 ft diameter paddle wheels. The cylinders were 160 inches in diameter and had a twelve foot stroke. As with the *Persia,* steam would be generated by 8 boilers each served by 5 furnaces but the steam would be provided at higher pressure than the *Persia,* 25 p.s.i instead of 20 p.s.i. This uprated engine gave an increase in speed but did not provide the hoped for reduction in coal consumption, in fact she used more coal than any of the other paddlers.

She is reported as having 157 roomy cabins and could carry up to 300 passengers. For use in times of war, she was expected to carry up to 3,000 troops. She could also carry 1,400 tons of cargo plus 1,800 tons of coal.

Her launch took place on 25th June 1861 and thousands lined the River Clyde to see her. The Glasgow Herald gave this account of the day:

Yesterday afternoon, the steamship Scotia second iron paddlewheel liner built by the orders of the Messrs. Burns of this city for the Cunard or British and North American Royal Mail Steam Packet Company was launched from the building yard of Messrs. Robert Napier and sons at Govan. Although the weather was rather unfavourable, slight drizzling showers falling continually, yet an immense concourse of spectators assembled to witness the event. To Messrs.Napier whose eminence as marine architects and engineers we need not advert are the builders, both of the hull and the engines. The Scotia is intended to be a sister ship to the Persia, a vessel belonging to the same owners and built by the same architects and which we were able to characterise at the time of her launch six years ago as the largest steam building both in capacity of hull and steam power than in the world. Since that time the launch of the Great Eastern has taken the palm of precedency from our Clyde built vessels. Nevertheless, the

Scotia, which is somewhat larger than the Persia is the second vessel in point of magnitude and capacity that has his hitherto been constructed for mercantile service. The contrast between this magnificent ship and Henry Bell's Comet of 40 tons and 3 hp, which was the first vessel propelled by steam in the British waters; or between it and the Glasgow, the first steam vessel that ventured so far to sea as the island of Cambrai, or between it and the Rob Roy, the first steam vessel that ran from the Clyde to Belfast, is so vast as almost to exceed belief. Yet in all probability, there were persons at the launch of the Scotia yesterday, who had also witnessed the starting of the tiny comet in 1812 of the Glasgow in 1816, and of the Rob Roy in 1818. From the adaptation by the builders of every improvement and scientific auxiliary, the Scotia is expected to attain a very high degree of speed, and no doubt is felt that she will, in ordinary circumstances, perform the voyage between New York and Liverpool in nine days.

The preliminary arrangements were the extreme of simplicity, but also of effectiveness. After the launch of the Black Prince from the same yard in February last little anxiety as to the result was felt among the numerous visitors had assembled to witness the launch of the Scotia. There were no hydraulic rams applied to the prow of the vessel as there was to that of the war frigate, the success of the launch being trusted to the gravity of the vessel. There were however attached to her bow two chain cables, which stretched across the river and were fastened to anchors weighing 5 tonnes each, firmly fixed into the ground on the north side. Chain cables were of 2 1/2 inches in diameter and were each capable of resisting the strain of 120 tons. There was no checking gear on the south side of the river. The inclined plane or sliding plank along which the vessel was to glide into the water was constructed in the usual manner as were also the framing, the bilgeblocks and dogshore. On deck floated the Union Jack, Stars & Stripes and several pennants.

The yard, presented a very animated appearance, notwithstanding the disagreeable rain which was falling, and varying in its intensity every few minutes. For two hours before the launch visitors, among whom are many ladies – thronged to the building yard, and by the time fixed for the event it was almost completely filled. There were several steamers also on the River, crowded with spectators. The band of the 76th Regiment and the Govan band were on the ground and performed some excellent music.

Shortly after three o'clock the knots of workmen stationed at various parts of the vessel knocked away the bilge blocks, when the vessel sunk down upon her own weight resting on the two artificial heels or movable base, which slide along the surface of the fixed inclined plane or sliding plank. Between the movable base and the immovable inclined plane was the usual composition of tallow and black soap to facilitate a smoother descent into the water. There was only at this moment the little dog sure, with its one end fastened to the immovable plane and its other secured to the movable base, to hold back the enormous structure weighing as it did 2500 tons and prevent the vessel from rushing down into the water.

The ship was then named the Scotia by Miss Arbuthnot, the youthful daughter of G C Arbuthnot Esq. of Mavisbank, mid Lothian. For the performance of this interesting ceremony, a small covered stand had been erected at the stem of the vessel.

One moment's anxious expectation and the loud stroke of the hammer is heard, which removes the little dogshore near the stern. Instantaneously the vessel moves. The sound had scarcely reached the ears of spectators at the stern when the magnificent hull was in motion of her own accord, gliding smoothly and beautifully into the water amid the plaudits of the multitude. The two checking cables were not put to the strain and within a single minute from the sound of the stroke that removed the dogshore, the vessel was sitting safely and gracefully on the bottom on the bosom of the tide. The band struck up "I'm afloat", and the vessel was towed up to Lancefield Dock where her machinery will be put in.

As soon as the Scotia was firmly in the water, a large number of the ladies and gentlemen in Messrs Napier's yard retired to one of the large working sheds in connection with the yard, where a sumptuous champagne lunch had been provided. Mr John Naylor proposed "Success of the Scotia", which was responded to with cheers. He then proposed "Success of the Cunard line", which was also warmly responded to. The band of the 76th Regiment were present in the hall and played a selection of musical pieces in a very chaste manner.

A handsome stand was erected in front of the Clyde rope work belonging to Mr Black, of Kelvinhaugh, on the north side of the river. It was occupied by a select number of our influential and distinguished citizens. Viewed from this capital position - than which none could be better for witnessing the launch - the Scotia, as she left the stocks and glided gently into the river, presented a very pretty appearance and her noble and elegant proportions appeared to great advantage when she lay serenely on the bosom of the waters. The company having retired to a large room in connection with the rope work were its sumptuous repast had been provided.

This account from the Glasgow Herald raises a couple of interesting points.

First, note the eloquence and detail of the account, all from a copy originally composed by the reporter of a provincial newspaper. Would such a story be so well written today? Perhaps it would and perhaps it wouldn't but one thing is for certain - quality, in anything, always show through.

Secondly, who exactly was the "youthful daughter" of G. C. Arbuthnot and why was she chosen to launch the Scotia? She was, in fact, Emily, the 20 year old daughter of George and Caroline Arbuthnot. The Arbuthnots were very important people at the time with various business interests including trade with India and then the Caribbean. Their business operated out of Liverpool where George spent some of his time but he preferred to spend the summer at Mavisbank, their country mansion at the head of the Firth of Clyde. So why chose her to launch the vessel instead of Mr. Arbuthnot? Perhaps it was because Mr. Arbuthnot made the suggestion and no-one dared to contradict him. Or it may be that she was a very important person in her own right. Or it may because she had seven months earlier married John Burns, the son of George Burns, who was a co-owner of the Cunard Line. Or perhaps she was chosen by the organisers because she was seen as the local "stunner" and it was felt that her presence would add great weight to the proceedings. In the absence of any definitive information, let's stick with the last option!

When his father, George Burns, retired from the Cunard Line, John assumed his position and took a key part in taking the company forward as increasing transatlantic travel brought new opportunities as well as more competition. Ships and sailing were a big interest in his life. In 1890, John inherited the Baronetcy from his father and in 1897 he was granted a peerage and became Lord Inverclyde. He and Emily had many happy years together, raising two sons, George and James.

They were both involved with the Cunard Line but George took a greater interest in Cunard whilst James ran the Burn's Glasgow shipping operation. As John Burn's health problems started to have an increasing effect on his life he was not able to spend so much time in Liverpool and left George to take over the reins at Cunard. This gave John more time to spend at Wemyss Castle and on his yacht. In February 1901, John became very ill and on the evening of the 12th he died. Poor Emily was inconsolable and the following day she too died. A few days later the well-liked and respected Lord and Lady Inverclyde were buried together and their large funeral cortege was headed by 80 sailors.

After fitting out, the *Scotia* was scheduled for her first trial sailing. She carried Inspectors of Machinery and representatives of the Admiralty and the Board of Trade. Despite the breezy weather and a strong flood tide, the *Scotia* performed almost faultlessly managing 13.9 knots against the wind and tide and 16.7 knots on the home run. Since there were no major problems to deal with, the next day she was able to set out for Liverpool on her first full sea trial, making the passage in a little less than 12 1/2 hours, again with no major problems.

On arrival in the Mersey, the *Scotia* made her way to her berth in Canada Dock where she was opened to visitors who wanted the chance to go on board what was the finest ship in the world at the time. Hundreds of people queued for the opportunity to see inside the vessel, paying sixpence or a shilling, depending on the day. All monies raised were distributed amongst local charities.

The *Scotia's* maiden run to New York was set for 10th May 1862. Cunard's top ship needed a top man at the helm and Captain Judkins, Cunard's Commodore, was transferred from the Persia, his little mishap on the maiden run of the *Persia* seemingly forgotten. On her way she called at Queenstown briefly to collect the mail and some more passengers, not berthing but just loitering in the harbour until the mail and passengers were ferried to her and then it was time to face the Atlantic.

After an uneventful crossing the *Scotia* reached New York on the 21st May, missing out on the usual big welcome for a new prestige steamer because she arrived at 1.00 in the morning. Nevertheless many people visited the harbour to see her during the day. One of the big benefits of the fast steamers to Americans was being able to receive news of what was happening in the world, particularly Britain, much more quickly than when it was brought by the sailing ships. On this occasion, the New York Times reported that the *Scotia* brought news of rumours of British intervention in the U.S. Civil War, an interesting debate in Parliament and distress amongst the (British) working classes. Surprisingly one correspondent of the New York Times thought that on this occasion the *Scotia* had not brought any news of significant importance!

The *Scotia* was a bigger, more powerful ship than the *Persia*, and although she still had to carry a large stock of coal, she rode a little higher in the water. This helped her take the *Persia's* westbound speed record in July 1863 and the eastbound record the following December. Her average speed on both occasions was over 14 knots and this would remain unchallenged for another six years.

The *Scotia* was the last of the transatlantic paddle ships and no other paddlers of such size would be built anywhere. The improving technology of the screw liners had finally caught up with and surpassed the paddlers and there was no going back.

In 1869, the Inman Line's *City of Brussels*, a single screw steamer, broke her eastbound speed record but it was another three years before she lost her westbound record to the White Star's *Adriatic*.

She may have looked a bit old fashioned but the *Scotia* was a very popular vessel amongst the travelling public, as was the *Persia*. She was reliable, comfortable and, for the time, luxurious. She would remain the second largest vessel on the seas after the *Great Eastern* until Cunard's *Bothnia* and *Scythia* were completed in 1874. These vessels were each a little over 4,500 tons and carried 300 first and second class passengers and 100 steerage passengers.

The Scotia's Chief Engineer was Robert Weddell who had started out as fifth engineer on the *Britannia*. The following image shows an extract from his log book which covers one of the Scotia's many trips.

The *Scotia* stayed in service with Cunard for more than twelve years making at least 82 Atlantic crossings. She was a safe, reliable vessel, loved by her passengers, but she used twice as much coal as the new screw vessels and often did not make a profit on her journeys.

As the *Scotia* became older, she was usually laid up in Liverpool for the winter when passenger numbers fell. In October 1874 she was laid up in Liverpool's Canada Dock and Robert Weddell, her chief engineer who had started as fifth engineer on the *Britannia*, made this entry in the log book.

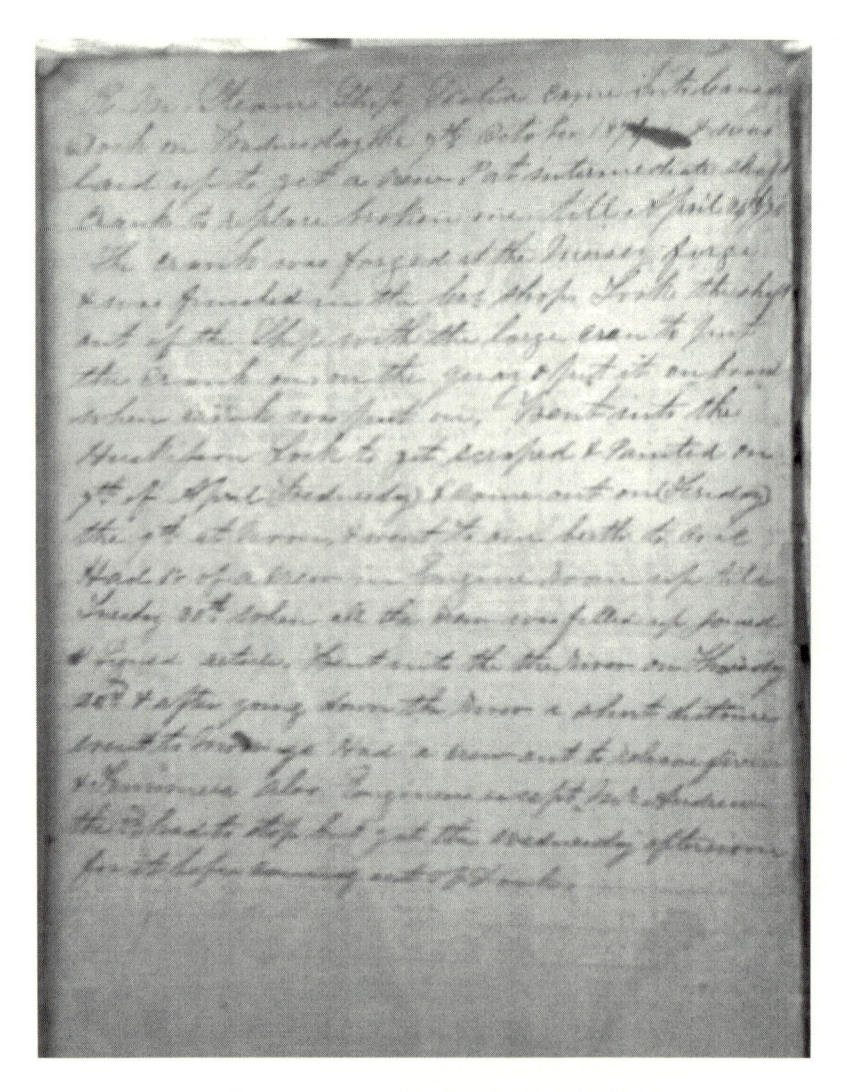

34   Laying up of the Scotia for the Winter
(Author's Image - copyright Gordon Fraser)

This is a transcript of the entry in the log book, with some words proving difficult to decipher despite the copperplate writing of Mr Weddel:

R. M. Steam Ship Scotia came into Canada Dock on Wednesday, the 7th October 1874. It was laid up to get a new port intermediate shaft crank to replace broken one till April 24th 1875. The crank was forged at the Mersey forge and was finished in the company's shop. Took the shaft out of the ship with the large crane to put the crank on the quay and put it on board when the crank was first run.

Went into the Huskisson Dock to get scraped and painted on 7th April (Wednesday) and came out on Friday 9th at noon and went to our berth to coal. Had 18 of a crew in Engine Room up till Tuesday 20th when all the crew was filled up, joined and signed articles. Went into the river on Thursday 22nd and after going down the river a short distance, went to moorings. Had a crew out to release xxx and trimmers. Also engineers except Mr Andrew the 3rd had to stop but got the Wednesday afternoon for it before coming out of dock.

● ● ●

Chapter 23

Life on board the *Scotia*

So what was it like to be a passenger on board the Scotia?

Well before we consider the passengers' journey, let's give some thought to those men the passengers probably seldom thought about - the firemen and stokers, and the helmsmen.

Imagine what it must have been like for the firemen and stokers toiling every day in the bowels of the ship. Imagine the heat from forty furnaces, the noise, the limited ventilation (which would be even less in stormy weather), the masses of coal dust and the pitching and rolling of the ship. Sounds bad? Well now imagine all that plus the fact that the furnaces had to be fed with up to 165 tons of coal each day. Even when the firemen and stokers were off shift, their berths were probably not that far away from the engines so it never really stopped until the vessel reached her destination. Construction of the early Atlantic paddlers went ahead despite the warning of Dr. Dionysius Lardner that transatlantic steamers were impossible because the firemen and stokers would have to work so hard that they would die of exhaustion. His warning may have overstated the danger but some of the engine room crew must have come close. They really are the unsung heroes of long distance steam navigation.

So let's hear it for the firemen and stokers.

So what was it like to be a passenger on board the *Scotia*?

Not yet, there were more unsung heroes on board the *Scotia* to consider. While the firemen and stokers were toiling down below, the helmsmen were often struggling on deck. The *Scotia* had four wheels for steering which needed perhaps four men to operate and in bad weather eight men were often needed, sometimes even more. It was a very difficult job especially when the sails were set and they could sometimes work against the paddle wheels. And imagine the situation when the ship was rolling badly and each paddle wheel in turn was rising out of the water. This would have caused the vessel to turn to port and then to starboard and the helmsmen would have had to continuously struggle to counteract this and try and keep the vessel on course. It was also very dangerous. If a sudden wave caught the large rudder, the impact would have been transferred to the wheel instantly without any warning and the helmsmen could easily be thrown off and injured. Perhaps a nice job when the weather was fine but, in a storm, it must have been horrendous and the passengers, safely down below and perhaps complaining about their seasickness probably gave no thought to the helmsmen, in their exposed position on deck, trying to control the ship.

So let's hear it for the helmsmen.

So what was it like to be a passenger on board the *Scotia*?

Well, if the weather was fine, it was probably pretty good. The passengers could wander up and down the long promenade deck, play deck quoits or just chat with the other important people on board. The men could retire to the bar which was open early in the morning until late and there were nice meals to look forward to, which unfortunately tended to deteriorate as time went on. If the ship encountered a bad storm though, there was for most a new procedure - stay in your cabin with your chamber pot close by and wish that you had stayed at home.

Of course the only way we can really know what is was like to be a passenger onboard the *Scotia* is to ask someone who actually made the journey and it is far too late for us to do that. We do however have the next best thing. During the 1860s, James Macaulay, editor of the weekly recreational magazine *The Leisure Hour*, made a return trip to New York on board the *Scotia* and, very helpfully, has provided us with a detailed account of his outward and return journey. The following chapter is his account of the return journey and is the only known definitive study of life as a passenger on board the *Scotia*.

Chapter 24

James Macaulay's trip on the Scotia

I went on board the Cunard steamer "Scotia," at Liverpool, on Saturday, the 13th of August, at 10 A.M., sighted the American shore at noon of Monday, the 2nd, and was at anchor in the Hudson river, off Jersey City, at 8 p.m. of the same day. We were detained seven or eight hours at Queenstown, Cove of Cork, waiting for the last mail from England via Holyhead; but setting against this the gain of time in going westward, about an hour a day, the voyage was nearly nine days and a half. The distance from Liverpool to New York is about 3,060 miles, more or less, according to the course taken. Old travellers talk lightly about "the "ferry", but to those who, like myself, cross the Atlantic for the first time, every detail of the voyage has its interest, and some practical points may be worth noting for the benefit of others.

During the summer months the number or passengers is so great that it is advisable to secure a berth a long time in advance. It is well, also, by a letter to the chief steward, to secure a good place at the table, which is retained throughout the voyage. The nearer to midships the better, both as to seats and sleeping berths, provided the latter are not too near the noise of the engine, or the still noisier "donkey engine," which is at work every four or five hours, heaving up the ashes from the furnaces. The outside cabins are the best for light and ventilation. It is rare in summer to have the comfort of a whole cabin, or state room, as it is called. The berths are in pairs, and have room for only one to dress at a time. The "Scotia" being a favourite ship, every berth was filled in its August passage, and the tables in the fore as well as the after saloon were crowded. Of the Cunard ships, which sail from Liverpool every Tuesday and Saturday throughout the year, some do not carry steerage passengers. The rates of cabin passage to New York by the Cunard ships are, first class £26, second class £18; return tickets 250 dollars, and 150 dollars, gold, according to the current rate of exchange. By steamers carrying steerage, the fare is 15, 17 and 21 guineas according to accommodation. This includes a plentiful and even luxurious table, but without liquors.

There is ample choice of good steamers to all the great American ports. To New York, the Inman, the Guion, the National and Allan lines have well-built and well-appointed vessels, with fares from 21 guineas down to 6 guineas for emigrants. There are also French and German lines. By sailing ships the fare is as low as £3.10s.

I was recommended to the "Scotia" as a paddle boat—in fact, the last of the paddle-wheelers of the great transatlantic lines. The motion is said to be less disagreeable than that of screw steamers. All the recently built ships have the screw, and the machinery of the others has been converted. Economy of fuel and of space caused the change, the paddle boats requiring half as much coal again as the screws. The "Scotia" lays in for every voyage 1,900 tons of coal, the daily consumption being about 150 tons. But, besides its paddlewheel machinery, this is, or was, the largest steamer on the Atlantic, 4,000 tons burden, and nearly 400 feet in length. It requires a rough sea to disturb the steady movement of a ship of this size. The only inconvenience in moderately rough weather is that the spray of the paddle-wheels is blown upon the deck, and keeps the after part of the ship in a dripping state.

There was even this discomfort in the outward voyages. The weather was superb except one day of fog, followed by a night of chopping sea, as we neared the great bank of Newfoundland. Each day was bright with sunshine, and each night clear and brilliant. A light north-easterly wind filled the sails, tempered the summer heat, and crested the blue waves with white foam. On several nights were beautiful displays of the aurora borealis, and on others the ship ploughed through water flashing with phosphorescent light. Whales "blowing" far off and shoals of porpoises gambolling near the ship, gave occasional enlivenment to the monotony of the sea. Not more than two or three ships were sighted throughout the voyage. The rare occurrence of vessels gives a striking illustration of the vastness of the ocean, even when the course is more direct than that taken by the "Scotia". At seasons when ice is not dreaded, the most northerly route is preferred, sometimes even sighting Cape Race, on purpose to diminish the risk of meeting vessels. The danger of collision, or in spring of encountering ice-bergs, makes fog the chief source of anxiety. During our foggy day the look-out was doubled, two of the officers being also at the bow, and the captain keeping his post near the compass on the bridge. From this his orders were conveyed by electric wires to the engine-room and the wheel-house. The speed was not slackened, the only precaution being the frequent sounding of the deep-toned fog-whistle. The remark was made that, in case of striking an iceberg, the only difference between going at half speed and full speed was, that in the former case the ship would go down in a minute, in the latter in half a minute! Nothing else could injure the "Scotia," and it was the business of other vessels to look out for themselves. Towards night the wind rose and cleared away the fog. Early next day the pilot-boat hove in sight. We were then about 200 miles from land. The first pilot that meets a ship being taken, the pilot-boats push far out to sea, and are often cruising about for ten or even fifteen days. They belong to associated pilots. Not long before, an adventurous boat was rewarded by putting a pilot on board each of three European steamers, above 300 miles from shore. The payment is by regulated rates, according to the tonnage of the ship, with an increase when the pilot goes on board out of sight of the farthest lighthouse or the coast.

In general routine, the arrangements of all steam-vessels on a voyage are much alike. Landsmen soon come to understand the mysteries of the watches and the ship bells. The correction of time by the observation taken at noon, the heaving the log, and the report of the course, were topics of daily curiosity. It was pleasant at night, after the bell struck, to hear the "all's well" ringing out clear, like a muezzin call. The order and discipline on the Cunard ships are as perfect as in the Navy itself.

We were two Sundays on board, on each of which divine service was held. It was pleasant to hear "the church-going bell," and to see the crew mustered in their Sunday best. The saloon was crowded as far as the seats allowed, and groups of passengers were within earshot at the doors and windows. The captain read prayers—the usual morning service, with the special forms for sea, and a petition interpolated in the Litany for the President and magistrates of the United States. A sermon was read, but it was only a rhetorical discourse, apparently one of old Blair's sermons. The captain of the "Scotia" always conducts the service himself, to avoid, it is said, the difficulty that might arise from the claims of ministers of divers sects or communions. The captain was well supported by the doctor of the ship, who acted as clerk and precentor.

Of Captain Judkins, commander of the "Scotia," and commodore of the Cunard fleet (since retired), many amusing anecdotes are told, which I withhold because I have heard some of them associated with other names. Thus it was the captain of another ship, and not of the "Scotia," who said in reply to an old lady who, off the Newfoundland banks, asked if it was always foggy there, "Don't know, ma'am; don't live here." It was just such an answer as the old Commodore might have given; a bluff John Bull of man, in appearance and in manner, and no doubt regarded as a typical English sailor by the thousands of Americans who have crossed with him. The other officers of the ship were also men of long-tried efficiency. The chief engineer, Waddell, for instance, had been above thirty years on the line. The purser, Fleming, and the boatswain, also a Scotchman, were veterans in the Cunard service, From men like these, who had crossed the Atlantic hundreds of times, I had many interesting recollections of voyages and of voyagers. The ship's company, officers and seamen, engineers and stokers, stewards and attendants, not forgetting the cooks, numbered fully two hundred, all told.

There were about 250 passengers. In the fore-saloon, which received the overflow of the larger state cabin, we had a curiously miscellaneous assembly at table. There was a group of ecclesiastical dignitaries, a Canadian Archbishop, a Mexican bishop, and several of the American bishops, returning from the Ecumenical Council at Rome. There were other clergymen, including the senior bishop of the Methodist Episcopal Church, Bishop Simpson, who had attended the Wesleyan Conference held last summer at Burslem. We had an English M.P., and the Chamberlain of New York, T. B. Sweeny,—Bismarck Sweeny, as he is called from his political influence. There were American officers who had fought through the Civil War, and American merchants from every part of the Union. An unusually large number of American families were returning home in consequence of the war on the Continent. With such a company there was opportunity for obtaining much useful and interesting information. I learned more about various regions of America in a week than long reading could have conveyed. It was not now that I first valued the society of travelled Americans. I had met them at home and abroad, in all conceivable circumstances. No devouter pilgrims visit the holy places of the East, or wander with truer enthusiasm through classic lands. In our own country, the American is always more than the intelligent foreigner. Some of them know more about our island than the majority of Englishmen. It is not only at Abbotsford or Stratford-on-Avon that you meet them. If you see a stranger ruminating on the island of Runnymede, or pencilling his name on Cowper's summer-house at Olney, or deciphering the inscription on the Covenanters' Tomb in the Greyfriars' churchyard at Edinburgh, he is likely to be an American. I know few greater treats than wandering with an intelligent New Englander through the old sites of Haunted London. A voyage even of only a week gives time for pleasant intercourse with such associates. The days passed all too quickly. I saw with regret the last of the glorious sunsets in the west, towards which we were steering, and look back with pleasant memory on the truly social and republican club that broke up in New York harbour, never all to meet again.

But an Atlantic voyage is not always such a pleasure sail. I came back in the "Scotia" in October, during tempestuous weather, when few of the passengers were in the mood for talk or recreation. There was no playing at rope quoits or shovel-board this time; and the plates of the diners, few and far between had to be secured to the tables by a double fence. The equinoctial gales were supposed to be over, but we had heavy head winds against us all the way, and at last came in for part of the weather which proved fatal to the "Cambria." A storm at sea is the time for deepening the sense of human helplessness, and for strengthening the feeling of dependence on Him who is mightier than the waves of the sea. Next to this trust I was helped to quietude by the coolness recorded of Captain Scoresby in his Life, which I found in the ship's library. During a storm in the Atlantic he occupied himself, with the coolness of an old sailor and a Christian philosopher, as he was, studying the size and force of the Atlantic waves. Mounted on the paddle-box, and holding on to the railings, during a violent north-west gale, he watched the waves, and the following is the general result of his observations :-

Highest altitude . . .	*43 feet*
Mean distance between each wave	*559 feet*
Width from crest to crest . .	*600 feet*
Interval of time between each wave	*16 seconds*
Velocity of each wave per hour .	*32 1/2 mile.*

"This" he says, "is the measurement of a rough Atlantic sea, not of the highest possible waves." He writes as if he regretted he had not the chance of observing a stormier sea! I was glad to get safely back again to terra firma on old England.

During the outward voyage it was strange to reflect that while we were tearing along at the rate of fifteen knots an hour, the latest telegrams from Europe were being flashed deep down under us with lightning speed. W had left just after the opening of the war. "To Berlin" was still the cry resounding on the Parisian boulevards. The first shots had been fired, and the Imperial Prince had received his "baptism of blood ' at Saarbruck. It looked as if the French armies were to cross the Rhine and invade Germany. The last papers

Scotia the Brave

received at Queenstown threw doubt on the easy triumph of the French, though the mitrailleuses were said to have "mown down the enemy like corn" in the first engagement. Throughout the week, blank of news, the prospects of the belligerents were keenly discussed. From some ship on its way to Europe we might have got tidings of what was going on in the old world, but no ship came near enough for signals. As we approached the American coast, the first sight of the pilot's boat, always welcome, was eagerly expected, in order to relieve the anxious curiosity about the war. Great was the excitement when the pilot, after a few moments' conversation upon the paddle-box with the captain, threw down a New York newspaper among the crowd on the deck. I happened to catch the paper, and was immediately required to mount a bench and read aloud. The large capital headings were first proclaimed, amidst cheers and counter-cheers from French or German sympathisers. The first great battles had been fought, but the result was still doubtful; at least the brief headings told nothing decisive. Then the details of the telegraphic despatches were read, till the reader was hoarse and gave up the paper to another speaker of more stentorian voice. What's the price of gold?" "What are Consols?" "How is Nancy?" A volley of such questions having been answered, the crowd broke up into knots of conversation and discussion. Sympathy seemed pretty equally divided. There were only two or three Frenchmen on board, and many Germans. The English were neutral, but the majority of the Americans and of the Irish cheered when the news appeared hopeful for the French success. It was altogether a curious scene, and prepared me for what I witnessed during my stay in America of conflicting voices and sympathies concerning the war.

Reprinted from the Leisure Hour 1863

Chapter 25

The *Scotia's* New Life

In 1875 questions were being raised about the *Scotia*. She was now looking increasingly old-fashioned and her original problems of high coal consumption and limited passenger carrying ability remained The decision was made to take her out of service and lay her up in Liverpool while a buyer was sought. And there she stayed, month after month - but no-one was interested, apart from Mr. Weddell who did his best to keep her in good condition. But who would want a tired old paddle steamer when the new screw steamers were better, just as fast and were bigger and cheaper to run? The *Scotia* was history and things were not looking good.

The years pass by and there is still little or no interest from buyers and a final journey to the breaker's yard looked to be the only way out for the vessel.

But, despite all the odds, the ship breakers never got their hands on her.

In 1879 she was bought by the Telegraph Construction and Maintenance Company and sent across the river to Laird Brothers of Birkenhead to be converted into a cable layer. Those who knew the *Scotia* would have found it difficult to believe that this sleek modern vessel coming out of the Laird's yard on to the Mersey was indeed the same vessel.

Scotia the Brave

Figure 35   C.S. Scotia
(Courtesy Liverpool University)

Her funnels and paddle wheels had all been removed and a new spar deck had been added. Her old side lever engine had been replaced with an up to date compound engine which would drive her two screw propellers, perhaps not as quickly as when she crossed the Atlantic, but she was now a working ship – and work she did. For the next twenty years the Scotia would cross the globe laying telegraph cables in the Middle and Far East, Europe, the Caribbean, Canada, U.S.A., South America and Africa. She replaced part of the transatlantic cable and even ventured as far as the antipodes to link Sydney with Wellington. Her importance to the world in the latter part of the 19th century should not be under-estimated. She would help enable a fast method of communication for countless millions of people all over the world.

Obviously working so hard all over the world resulted in the occasional mishap. In 1896, when sixty miles off Eddystone, an explosion in her cable paint store removed her bow but, being the well made Scotia, she stayed afloat and was soon repaired and back in business.

The *Scotia* relished her new life and all was going well until, one day in 1904, disaster struck.

Chapter 26

The final journey

After many years of hard work laying cables, the *Scotia* was becoming tired and, in 1902, she was sold to the Commercial Cable Company for use as a repair vessel in the Pacific Ocean based at Guam.

On 11th March 1904, whilst on route to Honolulu to deliver supplies, the vessel ran aground on Spanish Rock off Guam. Once again the quality of Napier's engineering and, in this case, also the quality of Laird Brother's engineering, kept the vessel in one piece and all of the crew were taken off safely.

But this time the *Scotia's* luck ran out. It wasn't possible to arrange early salvage of the vessel and, in a storm two weeks later, she suffered serious damage and sank.

It was now all over for the *Scotia*.

After a lifetime of excellent service during which she had carried thousands of passengers safely across the Atlantic and a second life of laying thousands of miles of telegraph cable, she was now a crumpled mess lying in 30 feet of water off Guam. Because of the wreck's shallow depth, it was possible to salvage some valuable items but, in doing so, substantial damage was caused to what remained of the vessel's hull.

However it wasn't quite the end for the *Scotia* and she had a brief third life. Because of her position and shallow depth, together with the clear waters, she became a popular site for divers although with movements on the sea bed it is doubtful if any recognisable pieces of the vessel now remain.

Although thousands of large vessels have put to sea over the years, comparatively few are now remembered. Often we remember them because of a military event, such as *H.M.S. Victory* and *H.M.S. Hood,* or because they have been preserved such as the *Cutty Sark,* or because they were huge, such as Brunel's *Great Eastern.* Some are remembered because of their transatlantic passenger voyages or their Blue Riband transatlantic speed records such as, the Cunard Queens, the *United States* and the *Normandie.* But who remembers, or has actually heard of, the *Scotia,* holder of the transatlantic speed record on more than one occasion? Unfortunately few people now know the story of the *Scotia* and, eventually, it could be as if she had never existed at all.

Well, maybe not!

For as long as there is an interest in classic literature, the name of the *Scotia* will live on.

In Jules Verne's book, *20,000 Leagues under the Sea*, the futuristic submarine, *Nautilus,* collided with the *Scotia* and her serrated snout punched a hole in the vessel's hull. The mighty *Scotia,* however, was certainly not prepared to be brought to grief by some wayward manmade monster from the deep and, after some repairs, she continued her journey safely to Liverpool.

All fiction, of course, it never really happened.

Or did it?

THE END

Chapter 27

Postscript

In this book reference has been made to James Macaulay, who edited the 19th century weekly publication "The Leisure Hour" and who gave us an eloquent account of his journey on board the *Scotia*.

As well as being a skilled writer and editor, he was blessed with other qualities in that, morally and ethically, he was way ahead of the thinking of most people during his time.

When at Edinburgh University in 1839 he entered a competition set by the Theological Faculty which offered a prize of twenty sovereigns to the student who could write the best essay on the subject of cruelty to animals. His 135 page essay, detailing the horrors of animal cruelty over the ages, won the prize comfortably. This was a topic he would return to much later in life.

During the early nineteenth century, as in the years before, this is a subject that few people, whether in government, the community or even, it has to said, the established churches, would have given much, if any, thought to. But there were some who did.

In a London coffee house, in 1822, a group of people, including the Rev. Arthur Broom and the M.P. for Galloway, Richard Martin, got together and formed the *Society for the Prevention of Cruelty to Animals*, an organisation supported by the anti-slavery campaigner, William Wilberforce. The society later received its *Royal* prefix when it met with the approval of Queen Victoria.

However, even before then, in 1809, a group of people, said to be market traders, got together in a coffee house in another great city and formed the *Society for the Suppression and Prevention of Wanton Cruelty to Brute Animals,* probably the world's first animal welfare organisation, which was later incorporated into the R.S.P.C.A. That great city was Liverpool, home of the Cunard Line and home port of the *Scotia;* a tenuous link perhaps but an interesting way to finish this story of the *Scotia*, the finest paddle liner that will ever set to sea.

Printed in Great Britain
by Amazon.co.uk, Ltd.,
Marston Gate.